KEEPING THE DREAM ALIVE

KEEPING THE DREAM ALIVE

An Insider's Account of a Tumultuous Decade in Scottish Politics

JOANNA CHERRY

ICON

Published in the UK in 2026 by
Icon Books Ltd, Omnibus Business Centre,
39–41 North Road, London N7 9DP
email: info@iconbooks.com
www.iconbooks.com

ISBN: 978-183773-347-7
ebook: 978-183773-346-0

Typesetting by SJmagic DESIGN SERVICES, India

Printed and bound in the UK

Appointed GPSR EU Representative: Easy Access System Europe Oü, 16879218
Address: Mustamäe tee 50, 10621, Tallinn, Estonia
Contact Details: gpsr.requests@easproject.com, +358 40 500 3575

For the late Professor Nina Hallowell. To know her was to love her.
And for the late Alex Salmond, whose dream shall never die.

CONTENTS

Here's freedom to them that wad read,
Here's freedom to them that wad write!
There's nane ever fear'd that the truth should be heard,
But they whom the truth would indite.

Robert Burns

PROLOGUE

I decided to write this book in the summer of 2023 and started while on holiday. I made quite a bit of progress, but the life of a busy constituency MP who is also a committee chair at Westminster doesn't allow for much free time. I didn't return to it properly until February 2024, when I rented an apartment in the south of France with the idea of working on the book for a week during the parliamentary recess. The conditions for doing so were perfect: the weather was unexpectedly dreadful and friends who were travelling down from London to join me were delayed by car trouble and marooned in northern France. But while I had plenty of time on my hands, I found it hard to write. It was not so much that I had writer's block as that what I found myself thinking about and writing about was fundamentally very unsettling.

The more I thought and wrote about what had happened to the SNP over the past decade, the more I asked myself why on earth I was considering standing for a fourth term as an MP for a party with which I was deeply disillusioned, and which in many ways I had grown to despise.

I had reached the view that the chances of furthering the cause of independence at Westminster – the reason I went into elected politics – were very small. I was disappointed by the failures of Sturgeon and Blackford's leadership and disgusted by much of what I had witnessed behind the scenes. I was ashamed of the party's record in government in recent years. I was exhausted by fighting off attempts to smear my character and by the bullying, harassment, threats and abuse I had to endure for standing up for women's rights in the face of the leadership's espousal of gender-identity politics. I was also afraid of having my reputation for integrity tainted by being associated with a party dogged by tawdry scandals.

On the other hand, I knew that there were many in the independence movement who still had faith in me as someone who might be part of reforming the SNP and delivering their dream of independence. I also knew that many women, particularly lesbians, valued my parliamentary advocacy for their rights in the face of identity politics. I was proud of the work I had done during the Brexit years, halting the unlawful prorogation of parliament and the work I had done to help save the Human Rights Act, working cross-party and as Chair of the Joint Committee on Human Rights. I also knew I had the respect of the House of Commons and of my constituents.

Nevertheless, I could see the writing was on the wall for the Westminster SNP group, who were going to be first in line to take the electoral fallout for the Scottish government's policy failings, the scandals bedevilling the SNP and the dropping of the ball on independence. I had reached the view that we would be getting a kicking and that the Liberal Democrats would be restored to the position of third party. I wasn't sure I could face another five years as a backbencher in the fourth party, particularly when I had come to so dislike that party in its current incarnation.

Throughout 2023, the Labour Party made several overtures to me to defect, and many in the Alba Party were keen for me to defect to them, but neither option appealed. I also thought about running as an independent. But although I was used to feeling isolated within my own party group, the thought of being a one-woman band in parliament also did not appeal.

I came very close that month to deciding to announce my retirement from parliament at the next election. The more I thought about, analysed and articulated what had gone wrong with the SNP under Nicola Sturgeon's leadership and the more I thought about the likely future of the SNP at Westminster, the less I wanted to continue doing a job I had once loved. But external pressures made it difficult for me to give up.

My primary concern was my staff and my constituency office. It is little recognised that when an MP resigns or loses their seat, their staff are made redundant. I'd had my ups and downs over the years with staff, but I had been blessed with a gifted chief of staff, Fraser Thompson, and in recent years he had put together a strong, dedicated and loyal team. My office was effectively running as a welfare and immigration advice bureau, and I knew how long it would take any incoming MP to be able to replicate the service that we had built up over years. I felt that by resigning I would be letting down my staff and breaking up a very effective team.

Another factor which weighed heavily on my decision to stay and fight on was the thought that throwing in the towel would give an undeserved victory to those who had attempted to grind me down with a steady diet of smears, bullying, harassment, social-media abuse and threats, ever since I had first dared to question the Sturgeon orthodoxy.

SNP internal polling showed that my seat was one of the twelve safest SNP seats in Scotland, and if I stood down it was likely to be lost. Friends and family counselled that I should stay and fight. My book would have to wait as I decided to stand in the General Election.

The end, however, came much sooner than I had anticipated. The good people of Edinburgh South West made my decision for me, so now I am free to tell the story of the dramatic rise and fall of the SNP at Westminster and to chart the journey from the hope and optimism of the Yes campaign to the malaise that gripped the party, Scotland's government and the independence movement under Nicola Sturgeon's leadership. It is not a pretty story, but it's a story that needs to be told both for the sake of the SNP and, more importantly, for the sake of probity and integrity in public life in Scotland and the future of my country.

INTRODUCTION: BEFORE POLITICS

In the run-up to the 1978 referendum on a Scottish Assembly, I attended an SNP meeting with my dad at Flora Stevenson primary school in Comely Bank, Edinburgh. Gordon Wilson, MP for Dundee East and the then leader of the SNP, was the speaker. I was twelve years old. At the end Dad took me to the front to speak to Gordon. He asked me what I wanted to do when I grew up. I replied that I wanted to be an SNP MP like him. He told me to go away, get a profession and work at it till I was in my forties, then bring that experience to parliament and the party, by which time I would be of more use to them than if I was fresh out of university. This is the sort of advice we hate when we are young, and I left a little disappointed.

It would be 37 years and a career in the law later before I was elected to parliament as an SNP MP at the 2015 General Election. I was 49 years old. Edinburgh always declares late on election night, and when the results started to be announced at about 4am, my seat came first. So it is that I can say I was the first SNP MP ever to be elected in Scotland's capital city. I would love to also be able to say that the experience was one of unalloyed joy. But it wasn't. Although I would feel elation in the days and weeks to come, on the night of my election, despite my pride and my defiant clenched-fist salute, I felt decidedly ambivalent.

My campaign had been marred by some of the most unpleasant and boorish behaviour I had ever encountered, from two male SNP activists. Earlier that night at the count, they'd had me in tears with their shouting and bullying. I like to think I am a pretty tough cookie, but this was not the first time they had reduced me, or the young woman who had tried to organise my campaign in the face of their resistance to modern campaigning methods, to tears. Later that night they would arrange to cut us both out of the celebratory photographs of the campaign team. However, what upset me most of all was not their behaviour, but the total lack of appetite to do anything about it on the part of SNP HQ, despite my complaints.

At that time Nicola Sturgeon had only been leader of the SNP and First Minister for six months. She had not yet styled herself the 'first feminist', but she was making a lot of her status as the first woman to hold the role and of the importance of encouraging other women into public life. It did not seem to me that the behaviour of these men was conducive to encouraging women into politics, yet when I complained I was told to indulge them because they were 'just old men who were upset at losing the referendum'. This was to be my first taste of the mismatch between the rhetoric and the reality of Sturgeon's leadership.

However, when I got home from the count, after champagne and bacon rolls with my closest supporters, I began to absorb the enormity of the result. The SNP had won 56 of Scotland's 59 seats at Westminster – and I started to feel the elation I ought to have experienced when the result of my seat had been announced.

On the Saturday morning after the election, the newly elected SNP MPs met up at South Queensferry beside the Forth Bridges for an iconic photo opportunity. I am in the middle of the back row with Alex Salmond's hand on my shoulder. At that stage I was only just getting to know him. He had been my hero for years and I was flattered by his attention. Most of the other 56 were unknown to me. I had met Angus Robertson, Michelle Thomson, Hannah Bardell and Dr Philippa Whitford during the campaign. Tasmina Ahmed-Sheikh was already a friend from Lawyers for Yes, the campaign group I had set up during the independence referendum. I had known Ian Blackford as a teenager in the late seventies when he, John Swinney and I set up the Young Scottish Nationalists in Edinburgh. The others were strangers to me, as was Nicola Sturgeon.

On Saturday evening I staggered exhaustedly though a series of celebratory parties. First at the home of a friend from the Yes campaign, then at Tanners in Juniper Green, the pub where my local SNP constituency association were celebrating, and finally at the famous Diggers pub at Slateford, which was packed with SNP and Yes activists from across the city. I bought everyone in the pub a pint.

The next morning, I was up bright and early to be interviewed on Sky News. I'd received the usual briefings from the SNP media operation about the party's key lines but was adjudged to have gone a little off-piste by suggesting that the SNP would lead a cross-party campaign to save the Human Rights Act, which David Cameron had pledged to repeal. At the time I could not understand why this should have annoyed the SPADs (special advisers). My interview and my promise received wide and positive coverage, and it was in line with our stated policy. Later, I would come to understand that in Sturgeon's SNP showing initiative was not welcome, particularly if it gained headlines which might upstage the leader.

On Monday morning the full SNP MP contingent travelled to Westminster and converged at London City Airport. Mhairi Black, who was causing a stir having been elected at the age of just twenty, was whisked away in a taxi by *Channel 4 News* while us lesser mortals boarded first the Docklands Light Railway then the Jubilee line surrounded by a swarm of media. We were even filmed buying our tickets.

At that time we were a united group and a united party. United in our determination to make Scotland's voice heard at Westminster and to hold unionist parties to their independence-referendum vow of more powers for the Scottish Parliament. Our victory signalled that, despite the short-lived triumphalism of the unionists at the referendum result and that of the Tories with their unexpected election victory (in England), so far as Scotland was concerned, it was not to be back to business as usual at Westminster.

The SNP had become the third party at Westminster, vanquishing the Liberal Democrats from the place their party had held for nearly a century. I was to be appointed as the SNP Spokesperson for Justice and Home Affairs and to make my maiden speech from the frontbench on the second day of the Queen's Speech debate, following on from such seasoned politicians as Yvette Cooper and Theresa May.

Not in my wildest dreams could I have imagined that such a thing would come to pass. And it seemed Gordon Wilson had been absolutely right in his advice. My career as an advocate (barrister) meant the House of Commons chamber did not intimidate me as it might have done in my youth. No one who has appeared in the bear pit of Scotland's Court of Criminal Appeal could be intimidated by much. The letters 'QC' after my name commanded respect and opened doors that might otherwise have been closed in my face as a rebellious Scot. Cross-party lawyers welcomed me cordially; Michael Gove invited me to his office to chat with him about prison reform, and Lord Hope of Craighead, the former Lord President of the Court of Session and Deputy President of the UK Supreme Court, summoned me to the House of Lords to discuss amendments to the Scotland Bill.

I was proud to represent the SNP and the Yes movement. My impression was that many at Westminster, particularly on the left, had been misled as to our character and intentions. I enjoyed being the face of measured, considered, respectful nationalism and finally getting to speak in the chamber where I had longed to end up as a wee girl.

However, I never forgot that my long-term goal was independence for Scotland and the chance to change my country for the better. No one who enters politics seriously wants to spend their career in opposition. The real opportunities for effecting change come with government. I won't pretend that I did not sometimes look enviously at those standing at the Treasury Bench despatch box, but I saw myself as part of the government of a future independent Scotland in Edinburgh, not at Westminster.

I was careful in my maiden speech to be respectful to my predecessor as MP for Edinburgh South West, Alistair Darling. The former Labour chancellor had led the successful Better Together campaign during the independence referendum. I reminded the House that while he might have won that battle, I was confident the SNP would yet win the war.

The decision to run for office had been a leap into the unknown for me, but so far it seemed to be turning out rather well. If I could have seen what was to come I would have been horrified, but for the time being my idealism was intact.

I had been involved with the SNP on and off since my childhood. My father had been a member in the 1970s and nationalist politics were regularly discussed at the family dinner table. I could still remember the depths of despair he and I felt when the 1978 referendum on a Scottish Assembly failed to deliver the pitiful degree of home rule then offered, and when the SNP lost nine of their eleven seats in the 1979 General Election. Now the party had swept nearly all before it, leaving only one representative of each of the other main parties in Scotland standing.

The SNP landslide attracted attention across the world. Friends in Australia, where I had spent a year out in 2006–07, sent me links to coverage in *The Age*, Melbourne's daily newspaper, and in the *Sydney Morning Herald*, accompanied by photographs of myself and Alex Salmond. A French friend in rural Provence texted to say that she had nearly choked on her cereal when she saw footage of me canvassing in an Edinburgh council estate on the French breakfast news. The news was also of interest in a small corner of Ireland, where, in what was once Ireland's poorest county, the *Leitrim Observer* proudly declared a front-page headline: 'Daughter of Manorhamilton becomes Scottish Nationalist MP'.

Manorhamilton is my mum's hometown in the west of Ireland. Although she is a proud Irish woman who has always retained her Irish passport, she fell in love with Edinburgh and Scotland when she came here to train as a midwife in the early sixties. She stayed, married a Scot and had two daughters, me and my younger sister, Alison. She used to say that she tried hard not to bring her daughters up to be raging Irish nationalists and they ended up as raging Scottish nationalists instead. In truth, however, my sister and I are a bit of both, but we are a lot of other things as well.

Mum met Dad at a Catholic coffee shop called the Grail (run by the Catholic women's movement of the same name) on

George Street in Edinburgh in 1964. The Grail was a magnet for liberal Catholics in the sixties, as they discussed the excitement of the Second Vatican Council. It was run by my late and much-loved godmother Nora McGrath, an Australian, and her friend Florence Henderson, an American, who later caused a scandal in Catholic circles when she married the eminent theologian Charles Davis, who left the priesthood to marry her. The friends my parents made at the Grail were lifelong friends not just for them, but for me and my sister.

My parents married in Edinburgh on 5 June 1965 at St Peter's RC church in Morningside, where four years earlier my dad had taken instruction to become a Catholic. Like a good Catholic baby, I arrived less than a year later, on 18 March 1966.

Dad was born in Maryhill, Glasgow. During the war he was brought up by his maternal grandmother in Carntyne, while my grandfather was away in the RAF. My grandmother went to work in London with her older sister as a cocktail waitress at what was then the Lansdowne hotel in Berkeley Square. They led a rather glamourous lifestyle, mixing with stars like Clark Gable. My great-aunt Jessie took over a house in Kensington and my dad fondly recalls wartime visits there and the excitement of visiting an American-style milk bar on Kensington High Street.

After the war, my grandparents moved into a new council house in Watford and my dad and his older brother, David, joined them there. David hated it and went back to Glasgow, but after a difficult period of adjustment my dad thrived at Watford Grammar School. He excelled at his studies and went up to Oxford to read History at St Catherine's. Dad's cousin Ronnie (Great-aunt Jessie's son) had gone up a few years before him to Magdalen, where Dad celebrated his twenty-first birthday party. They were the first generation of their family to go to university and they did it in style.

Both my parents were independent thinkers who did not necessarily take the easy route in life. After university Dad was eligible for national service, but as a conscientious objector he was put through two tribunal hearings before he went off to do psychiatric nursing instead. His experiences at the Quaker-run Retreat in York shaped his outlook on life and he went on to take instruction to become a Catholic. Moving to the Royal Edinburgh Hospital in 1961, he completed his Catholic instruction long before he met my mum. I often tease him that he is one of the mad people who have actually chosen to become a Catholic rather than having it thrust upon them.

Suffice to say his Glasgow Protestant parents were not best pleased, but they got over it. I have very happy memories of visits to my paternal grandparents in the hot summers of the 1970s, with lunchtime picnics in Soho Square, near to the office where my grandfather worked as a clerk at the London Electricity Board. To this day I cannot go into Selfridges or onto the Underground without thinking of them.

My mother had a very different childhood in the west of Ireland, where she lived with her parents and younger brother in Manorhamilton. Their happiness was blown apart by the unexpected death of my maternal grandmother from a heart attack when my mum was aged only eleven. My mum was sent away to boarding school in Carrickmacross in the north where she was very unhappy. Later she transferred to a small convent school in Bundoran in Donegal which she adored. Her teacher there, Sister Melanie, remained a lifelong friend who used to visit us in Edinburgh in the seventies. She was always accompanied by a younger nun, Sister Annunciata, and they started a craze for shell craft among the little girls in our suburban street. They wore navy blue habits and veils, and I remember one of my friends asking her mum if she could lend them some of her summer dresses.

Mum was part of that generation of Irish women for whom university was not encouraged. She has a lifelong love of literature and would have been more than able for it, but instead she was sent to domestic science college in Dublin. She went on to qualify as a nurse in Dublin, before she travelled to Edinburgh to train to be a midwife. She fell in love with Scotland on her first bus tour to the Highlands and has never looked back. Later in life, after taking early retirement from her nursing career, she studied first at the Open University, where she graduated with a BA Hons in General Arts, and then at the University of Stirling, where she took an MPhil in Modern Scottish Literature, graduating with distinction.

The devout Catholicism of my parents dominated my childhood. I began my primary schooling at Flora Stevenson primary, near where we then lived. I moved to Holy Cross primary on Ferry Road after my mum passed her driving test in 1973 and was able drive me to and from school, a journey which otherwise would have meant at least two buses either way. Later, I attended St Margaret's Convent school in Edinburgh, the oldest Catholic girls' school in Scotland. We were a family who prayed together at night and went to mass every Sunday.

As I entered adulthood and realised that I was attracted to women rather than men, my sexuality made it difficult for me to continue to feel welcome in the Catholic Church and sometimes also in my family. Until later in life, my parents struggled to accept my sexuality, which was the source of a lot of pain for me when I was young. I have been fortunate that my sister, Alison, has always been 100 per cent in her support of my right to be who I am.

However, I cannot say the same of my Church. Later, during my legal practice, I acted for survivors of physical and sexual abuse in Catholic-run institutions and was appalled by the lack of compassion shown by the Church and its refusal to accept responsibility. The hypocrisy inherent in the contrast between the strictures placed upon gay and lesbian Catholics and the licence that was granted to those who had sexually abused children disgusted me.

While I am no longer a fully practising Catholic, I am still a believer. My Catholic upbringing instilled in me the values of integrity, caring for others, and striving for justice and peace. I feel this has served me well in adult life, both in my legal career and particularly in politics, where I have tried to live up to those important values.

During the 2017 General Election campaign a man turned up at my campaign office asking if I was Alastair Cherry's daughter. He had worked with my father at the National Library of Scotland as a very junior member of staff, and my dad, who was in a considerably more senior position, had always treated everyone equally and with respect, unlike some of his colleagues. This gentleman was a serious left-winger (Dad used to call him 'Red Rab'), but he was also an independence supporter, and he wanted to campaign for me because he had so admired my father.

Nationalist politics as well as religion was a major influence in the Cherry household. We were steeped in the history, culture and literature of both Scotland and Ireland. In the same way that my mother had fallen in love with Scotland, my father fell in love with Ireland. Most of our childhood holidays involved visiting family in the west of Ireland, where we enjoyed long glorious days on sunny beaches followed by evenings of storytelling about Irish history, the famine and the events that led to Irish independence.

My mum's home is in Yeats country – after the poet W.B. Yeats – in the west of Ireland, and she encouraged me to learn many of his poems by heart. Once at primary school when, for being opinionated and cheeky, I was set a punishment exercise of learning a poem and reciting it off by heart, I astonished and no doubt irritated the teacher by reciting 'The Fiddler of Dooney' from start to finish on the spot. My mum sadly has advanced dementia now, but she can still recite from memory Yeats's great poem 'The Lake Isle of Innisfree'.

When we weren't holidaying in Ireland, we explored the Western Highlands of Scotland. My mum always said that she was going to write a book called *Castles, Tea Shops and Public Toilets of Scotland*. My dad was an avid Scottish historian, and these trips were accompanied by erudite lectures largely about the Stuart dynasty, particularly Mary Queen of Scots and the Jacobite risings. Long before Scottish history was properly taught in our schools, my sister and I were well versed in it. These history lessons, which helped instil a love of my country and an appreciation of its culture, were central to my childhood. As was my parents' passionate interest in politics and current events.

Dad had grown up a Labour supporter, but after Winnie Ewing's Hamilton by-election victory in 1967 he embraced Scottish nationalism as his natural home. Like Mum, he was an idealist. She had run beside John F. Kennedy's motorcade in Dublin when he visited Ireland in 1963 to try to shake his hand. My mum insists that one of my first words was 'Czechoslovakia', as my parents followed avidly the events that led to the Prague Spring in 1968. When

Nixon resigned in 1974, we were staying in a hotel in Wicklow full of Americans who gathered around the television each night to watch events unfold. As a little girl of eight I joined them, intrigued by the political melodrama and the sense of being a witness to history.

The Troubles in Northern Ireland had a profound effect on our family. While my parents supported the civil rights movement, were appalled by Bloody Sunday and internment, and longed for a united Ireland, they could not support the violence of the IRA, particularly against innocent civilians. My dad marched with the Peace People when they came to Edinburgh in 1976. The Troubles also made getting to the west of Ireland to see family a great deal more expensive, as my parents didn't want to drive through the North. We had to fly to Dublin and hire a car. This was long before the days of cheap air travel.

In the early seventies my parents argued over the swingometer on election night when Grail friends would come round to stay up late to watch the results. A couple of years after my election as an SNP MP in 2015, I received a letter from a fellow party member which included my dad's membership card from the 1970s. He asked if I was the little girl who used to answer the door when he came to collect my dad's subscriptions and wondered if my dad or I had ever envisaged that I would grow up to become an SNP MP.

We hadn't. By the end of the 1970s the SNP, which had achieved a third of the popular vote and eleven MPs in 1974, were in serious trouble. After their 1979 General Election rout the party moved to the right, and, like a lot of other young people, I felt alienated. Around that time, along with John Swinney and Ian Blackford, I was one of the founding members of the Edinburgh branch of the Young Scottish Nationalists. However, after the expulsion of members of the 79 Group, a radical caucus that wanted to move the party to the left and which included a young Alex Salmond, the SNP seemed an inhospitable environment for those of us who thought that left-wing progressive policies were required to combat Thatcherism. I wasn't the only member of the Edinburgh Young Scottish Nationalists to give up on the SNP and join the Labour Party, which I did in 1983.

I was impressed by the leadership ticket of Neil Kinnock and Roy Hattersley. I remember the front cover of the *New Statesman*, to which I had a weekly subscription (along with *Smash Hits*): they were pictured with the headline 'Can They Stop the Rot?' I believed that they could and that the Labour Party was the best way to fight the Thatcher government and its malign influence on Scottish society.

People often assume that, because I am an advocate and went to a small girls' private school, I am very middle class. Class is not such a big issue in Ireland, but in Scotland my family are very decidedly first-generation middle class, thanks to the opportunities afforded to my grandparents and my father by the post-war Labour government. My parents drove around in second-hand car and eschewed foreign holidays in order to pay the fees to send me and my sister to our convent school, and I am not ashamed of it.

In the Labour Party I continued to argue for home rule, and I was active in the campaign for a Scottish Assembly. In my experience, with a few honourable exceptions, such as Dennis Canavan, most Labour parliamentarians only paid lip service to the notion of devolution. While, in fairness, the Labour Party ultimately came good on their promise to hold a devolution referendum when elected to power in 1997, what won that referendum was a cross-party campaign in which the SNP played a leading role.

I never felt that home rule was that important to most Labour activists, and in truth my active support for the campaign for the Scottish Assembly led them to regard me with suspicion. They were probably right to do so. By the early nineties I had become deeply disillusioned with the Labour Party, particularly because of their failure to protect Scots from the iniquity of the poll tax. The Scotland United and Democracy for Scotland cross-party movements for home rule were gaining momentum after the 1992 General Election, when the Tories had unexpectedly won, again. I marched with them to the Meadows in Edinburgh in December 1992 for a rally where I was particularly impressed by speakers from the Scottish National Party. I left the Labour Party and became an SNP supporter again, although I was as enthused as most people by Labour's 1997 victory and did not actually rejoin the SNP until 2008.

My legal career was consuming me in the 1990s. While at Edinburgh University I had been involved with student politics, but even then, as a young woman, the endless virtue signalling and posturing irritated me. I decided that perhaps a political career was not for me after all and chose to concentrate on the law. No one was more surprised than me when I got a first in my LLB Hons in 1988, together with the Constitutional Law essay prize and a scholarship for postgraduate study. I toyed with the idea of an academic career and planned to do a PhD, but instead, having completed an LLM (masters degree) I decided to qualify as a solicitor.

My traineeship interviews in Edinburgh in the late 1980s were an interesting experience. Those were very different times. At least two firms expressed surprise that a Catholic lefty thought that they might give her a job. During the Diploma in Legal Practice, which all those wanting to be a solicitor must take before leaving university, I and some of my female fellow students were appalled by the sexism of some of the instructors from the legal profession. We formed a feminist society – the Women's Legal Network – and, as a result, were blackballed by many of Edinburgh's leading law firms.

Some of those who most hated what we were doing were men who could not understand why they should be excluded from 'women only' meetings, but we also made enemies of some of our fellow female students who were terrified that they might be tarred with our brush, unable to get a job or a boyfriend and, heaven forfend, be suspected of lesbianism. This was a foretaste of what was to come when I challenged gender-identity orthodoxy in later life.

Despite all this nonsense and prejudice, I secured a traineeship at Brodies in Edinburgh, who appointed their trainees on merit. But I found that office life was not for me. What I really wanted to do was work for myself and be an advocate – the Scottish word for a barrister.

My parents thought I was mad to leave the salaried position of solicitor, which I had secured after the end of my traineeship, and to go to the bar, where I would be self-employed without the benefit of any legal connections in our family or friendship circle, apart from the family solicitor. At that time there were only 25 women at the Scottish bar and no female judges in Scotland. However, I was determined to proceed and was called to the bar in December 1995 at the age of 29, after becoming the first person to have two female devil masters, the Scottish word for pupil masters.

In truth, I did not struggle to get work as much as my parents had feared. I had made some good connections while working as a solicitor at Brodies; the company itself gave me some work and both my devil masters ensured that more was passed my way, including an interesting spell junioring to Donald Findlay QC.

I went on to become both a Standing Junior to the Scottish government from 2003 to 2008 and Advocate Depute from 2008 to 2011. While I was serving in the Crown Office, I successfully applied to become a QC and took silk in September 2009 at the age of 43.

Holding these public appointments precluded me from political campaigning, but I was an enthusiastic observer. My election night parties in my first flat in Iona Street in Leith were legendary, when twenty or so people would be crammed into my small living room. On the night of Labour's victory in May 1997 and on the night of the devolution referendum that followed in September 1997 we went wild, popping champagne corks out into the street from the top-floor window.

I was utterly elated by the election of a Labour government after eighteen years of the Tories and by the advent of the Scottish Parliament. I voted SNP in the first elections to the Scottish Parliament and was a little disappointed by their showing – 35 seats to Labour's 56 – but at least they were the official opposition. On the beautiful June day in 1999 when the Scottish Parliament opened, I was there in the street, observing the parade to the opening ceremony with the hair on the back of my neck standing up. I felt change, real change was in the air for my country.

That evening there were two free concerts in Princes Street Gardens, one in the West Gardens by the rock band Garbage and one in the East Gardens by Scottish Opera. I was only 33 but I felt a little middle-aged as I elected to attend the opera concert with my friends. We brought a picnic, and as I lay back on the grass listening to a soaring aria, I started to think that I wanted to be part of the change that was happening.

The Scottish legal profession has always contained a healthy proportion of nationalists, and a group was brought together to see what we could do to support the new SNP parliamentarians. When I arrived at the first meeting, I was surprised to see a rather patrician and haughty QC, whom I had assumed was a conservative. A colleague explained that we were a broad church, and this gentleman was a supporter of the restoration of the Stuart dynasty.

Nevertheless, it wasn't until after what was for me the unexpected victory of the SNP at the 2007 Scottish Parliament election that I decided I must rejoin the party.

In the run-up to the 2007 Scottish election, I was in Australia having decided to take a gap year for my fortieth birthday. But I was keeping an eye on what was happening at home. I could see that the SNP under Alex Salmond, in his second spell as leader, were pressing the Scottish Labour government hard as the 2007 Scottish Parliament election approached.

In the end it was a close-run thing. The SNP ended up with 47 seats to Labour's 46, but Salmond seized the initiative, declared himself the winner and secured the support of parliament as First Minister of a minority administration. Most people did not think it would last six months. In the event it lasted four years, governed effectively and provided the springboard to an unprecedented outright SNP victory at the 2011 election.

I was home from Australia by the time of the 2007 election and back at the bar. The celebrations at my house were wild. I remember being up all night and sitting with a calculator in front of the television in the late afternoon while on the phone to my friend and colleague Gail Gianni, with whom I would later set up Lawyers for Yes in 2014. When we worked out the SNP had succeeded, we did a quick phone around and convened an impromptu party at my house. The attendees included a Court of Session judge. Once again champagne corks were popped out the window into the garden, this time for an SNP victory.

I was delirious but still working in a public appointment as a Standing Junior to the Scottish government. I made inquiries and established that it would be acceptable for me to be a member of a political party but not to be active, so I rejoined the SNP in 2008.

I won't pretend that my relationship with the SNP was always a happy one after that. I remember feeling uneasy at the total adoration of Alex Salmond I witnessed at the 2011 SNP conference in Inverness – it seemed to me that he could have read out the local phone directory rather than give a speech and the audience would have swooned and clapped like seals. I was to remember this in the years to come when so many of his erstwhile friends and admirers deserted him when he was in trouble.

More importantly, I was alarmed at the SNP government's approach in areas of policy where I had some expertise, including criminal law reform, which seemed to me cavalier both in its lack of respect or understanding for unique aspects of Scots law and for the importance of human rights, even when protecting those rights makes life difficult for the authorities or the government.

A prime example of this came in 2008, when the Grand Chamber of the European Court of Human Rights delivered a landmark judgment in the case of Salduz,[1] a seventeen-year-old Kurdish boy who had been taken into custody by Turkish anti-terrorist police on suspicion of having participated in an unlawful demonstration in support of an illegal organisation. The court ruled that it was a breach of his human rights for him to have been denied access to a solicitor while in custody and before he was interrogated about the alleged offence, to which he had confessed.

Despite contesting the accuracy of the statement he had made to the police without the benefit of legal advice, it was relied upon to convict him. The court held that this was a clear violation of his right to a fair trial under Article 6 of the European Convention on Human Rights.

This decision was to have momentous consequences for the Scottish legal system. While historically there had been a right to legal assistance while in custody in Scotland, this had been abolished in the 1970s and it had long been a talking point that the decision to do so would not survive a challenge under the European

---

[1] Salduz v Turkey [2008] ECHR 3693/02 [Grand Chamber] (27 November 2008)

Convention on Human Rights. Now that the Convention had been incorporated into the domestic legal systems of the United Kingdom in the Human Rights Act 1998 and the Scotland Act 1998, it was inevitable there would be a challenge to the legal position in Scotland from an accused person who found him or herself faced by a prosecutor who intended to use a confession procured without the benefit of legal advice. And indeed such challenges followed thick and fast.

A bench of seven judges in Scotland's Criminal Appeal Court held that the practice of not affording access to a lawyer before interrogation in Scotland did not breach Article 6 because, unlike other countries, it is not possible to be convicted solely on a confession in Scotland because of the requirement of corroboration.[2]

The UK Supreme Court disagreed in the landmark case of Cadder[3] and the Scottish Parliament had to introduce emergency legislation ensuring that accused persons would be afforded the right of access to a solicitor before they were questioned by the police.

To understand the politics of all of this it is important to appreciate that the Act of Union between Scotland and England in 1707 protected Scotland's separate legal system. In criminal justice matters the Scottish Criminal Court of Appeal is a final court of appeal. However, because of the incorporation of the ECHR into domestic law, accused persons can raise an issue as to the safety of their conviction on human rights grounds at the United Kingdom Supreme Court.

Many Scottish nationalists resent this, as do many of my colleagues in the legal profession who are not necessarily political nationalists, but who jealously guard the independence of the Scottish legal system.

There was uproar as a result of the Cadder decision. Members of the Scottish government including Alex Salmond and Kenny

---

[2] HM Advocate v McLean [2009] HCJAC 97

[3] Cadder v HM Advocate [2010] UKSC 43

MacAskill, who as a lawyer ought to have known better, made the cardinal error of attacking the judiciary.[4] It was not the SNP government's finest hour.

It was obvious to me from the moment I first read the Salduz decision that the Scottish legal system was in trouble and that we were out of step with many other countries, and now importantly the European Convention on Human Rights, in our failure to afford accused persons the right to legal advice. Indeed, this had been obvious for some time. While it is true that the requirement for corroboration means that an accused person in Scotland cannot be convicted solely on his unadvised confession, in my experience as a prosecutor it takes very little additional evidence to corroborate such a confession and therefore the requirement of corroboration isn't all it's cracked up to be.

The government decided it was going to abolish corroboration under Scots law. This led to further uproar in the legal profession because it was rightly pointed out that corroboration is central to the criminal law of Scotland and that you can't simply remove the central plank of any system without replacing it with other checks and balances or safeguards.

While working as an Advocate Depute, a Scottish government SPAD phoned me to ask if I would speak out in favour of the SNP stance on the Cadder judgment and their plans to abolish the Scottish requirement for corroboration. They wanted the weight of a nationalist QC behind their position. I explained that I could not because it wouldn't be appropriate for me to make a public contribution in my current role, and in any event I strongly disagreed with the policy. They were not best pleased. The following year, 2012, when I had left the Crown Office, I was moved to write to the *Herald* newspaper stating my opposition.[5]

---

[4] https://www.theguardian.com/uk/2011/jun/01/alex-salmond-scotland-supreme-court

[5] 'Justice for victims and accused is the priority in corroboration argument', *Herald*, 24 October 2012: https://www.heraldscotland.com/opinion/letters/13078146.justice-victims-accused-priority-corroboration-argument

Shortly before I completed my time as an Advocate Depute, I represented the Lord Advocate in one of the further appeals which arose as a result of the Cadder decision, commonly referred to as the 'Sons of Cadder'. It was my first time appearing at the UK Supreme Court and was judged to be something of a triumph, particularly as we won.[6]

At that time I was nearing the end of a three-year appointment where I had been promoted to Senior Crown Counsel and led for the Crown in some of the most important criminal appeals of recent years. After the 2011 SNP election victory, the law officers were changing and there was a round of appointments to the role of Principal Advocate Depute and his/her deputies. I had a very good reputation and everyone in the profession expected me to be promoted to one of the top roles in the Crown Office. I wasn't, and I have often wondered whether my private views expressed to the SPAD in that phone call might have affected my chances of promotion.

My hopes for further promotion within the Crown Office having been dashed, I returned to private practice in the autumn of 2011. Now that I no longer held a public or government role, I was free to be actively involved in politics. However, my misgivings about the policy direction of the SNP government in some areas were such that I felt reluctant to pursue this freedom.

I busied myself with getting my private practice up and running again and chaired the Faculty of Advocates law reform committee, which became closely involved in consultations to make sure that if corroboration was to be abolished, sufficient replacement safeguards would be put in place. In the event this reform never happened, but at the height of what I consider to be the Scottish government's mishandling of the matter there were moments when I seriously thought about cutting up my SNP membership card.

I am glad I did not. The unexpected attainment of an outright SNP majority at the 2011 Scottish Parliament election meant that an independence referendum was on the cards. From a distance

---

6 Jude v HMA [2011] UKSC 55

I watched with admiration Alex Salmond's skilful negotiations with David Cameron's government, which resulted in the Edinburgh Agreement. This was an agreement very much to the SNP's advantage because crucially it allowed the Scottish Parliament to decide the date of the referendum, the question, and the franchise. This meant that Alex Salmond was able to choose a date that would enable a long campaign, a question that begged the answer yes – 'Do you agree that Scotland should be an independent country?' – and a franchise that included sixteen- to seventeen-year-olds, who were known to be very pro-independence.

Two years later, during Scotland's 'Summer of Love' in the last six months of the referendum campaign, I was to become one of the Yes campaign's most enthusiastic proponents and a well-known face as the spokesperson for Lawyers for Yes, one of the many grassroots groups that emerged in support of the Yes campaign.

When the referendum was lost, it might have been prudent to pause and take stock. Clearly, there were issues that should have acted as a warning to me that there were aspects of the SNP's approach that were alien to my values. My misgivings included the party's unquestioning support and adoration for its leader, a tendency towards authoritarianism, and a sometimes cavalier attitude towards human rights protections and the rule of law. These were anathema to me.

So why, then, did I put myself forward as a representative of the party? The answer lies in my burning desire to ensure that the spirit of the Yes campaign, particularly during its last six months, be kept alive. It was a spirit of hope and optimism. A collective effort to make a better country. Above all, it was about debate and ideas for reform. I was an idealist who entered politics because of a cross-party campaign for radical change, not a party-political careerist.

In this book I set out to explore how the spirit of the Yes campaign was crushed and replaced with an authoritarian leadership which encouraged a cult-like adoration that went far beyond anything that had troubled me during the Salmond years. I will reveal why Salmond and Sturgeon became enemies and how crucial opportunities to further the independence cause were squandered.

I also want to look at what can be done to recapture the spirit of hope, optimism and intellectual inquiry that lit up Scotland in the summer of 2014 and how to ensure that our polity can never again be so dominated by a small leadership cabal's ambition and hubris.

I was privileged to play a part in the extraordinary upheavals in the British constitution that followed the Brexit vote in 2016. I'm proud to have been the only member of the SNP who scored a significant hit against Boris Johnson when the case I led against the unlawful prorogation of parliament triumphed in the Supreme Court. What happened in the wake of the Brexit vote – the fact that a charlatan like Johnson was able to become British Prime Minister and behave as he did during the Covid crisis – and the terrible disappointment that is the Starmer government have simply underlined for me that Scotland could do better as an independent country. Unfortunately, in their current incarnation, the SNP are a hindrance rather than a help to that notion.

I decided to write this book to give my perspective on why, despite the turmoil of the last decade, the SNP has failed to advance the cause of independence. I want to give an insider's perspective on what went wrong and what was going on behind the scenes. It is vital to address what has gone wrong in order to lay the groundwork for the future. Lessons must be learned in order for the SNP and the independence movement to progress. I love my country and I share the internal optimism of an idealist who wants to shift the status quo. I believe the dream of independence can be kept alive and that the dream could be made real. However, in order for that to happen we need an honest appraisal of what has gone wrong before addressing how we might do things better in the future. In the chapters that follow I shall endeavour to do both.

FROM REFERENDUM TO LANDSLIDE 1

'Get me the name of that woman from Lawyers for Yes'

On a miserable, cold Friday evening in early November 2014, I came home from working in the Advocates Library, got straight into my pyjamas and poured a gin and tonic. The clocks had just gone back and it was dark already. It seemed a long time since the summer of love which had preceded the independence referendum. I had no plans to go out and was savouring a solitary night in with a takeaway listening to *Any Questions?*. Then I looked at my emails and saw a message from a contact at SNP HQ warning me to 'expect a call from the FM'. His email was the last in a long email trail and I scrolled down. The first email was from Alex Salmond, and it simply said, 'Get me the name of that woman from Lawyers for Yes.'

At that stage, although he had announced his resignation the day after the referendum, Alex Salmond was still First Minister (FM). Nicola Sturgeon was due to take over on 20 November. I had met Alex only twice before: once while I worked in the Crown Office at Lord Advocate Elish Angelini's leaving party, and the other during the referendum campaign when I was campaigning as the co-founder and leader of Lawyers for Yes. I was still very much in awe of Alex, so I was impressed, excited and a little daunted.

When the phone call came it was from an aide who invited me to a drinks party at Bute House, the official residence of the

FM, the following evening. I asked what I should wear. She said smart casual and that there would just be a few people there. When I arrived there were only seven other guests: Michelle Thomson of Business for Scotland; Jeane Freeman, the former Labour SPAD who had campaigned with Women for Independence; Kate Higgins, an SNP stalwart who later became a SPAD to Nicola Sturgeon; Michael Stewart, the footballer who had played for Hibs and Hearts and been capped for Scotland; Brendan O'Hara, a TV producer and SNP stalwart; Jim Spence, the football commentator; and Rab Wilson, the Scots poet and NHS whistleblower.

It was an odd but very enjoyable evening. Alex plied us with drink, canapés and entertaining chat. It wasn't until late in the evening that he explained his purpose in inviting us all there. He wanted us to consider standing for Westminster at the General Election, which was due in May 2015. Some of us, including me, were members of the SNP; others, like Jeane, were not. But at that stage Alex had it in mind to have some sort of Yes alliance at the General Election and to allow non-aligned members of the Yes movement to stand under a broader banner in place of SNP candidates in some constituencies.

He told me that he would like me to consider standing in the Edinburgh South West constituency against the incumbent Labour MP, Alistair Darling. I'd had a fair bit of champagne to drink and replied that if he hadn't been the First Minister of Scotland, I would have told him he was off his head. It seemed unthinkable to me that there would ever be an SNP MP in Edinburgh, much less that it would be me, and that I would gain a seat by defeating Alistair Darling, who had successfully led the Better Together campaign. He had also on at least one occasion bested Alex Salmond in debate, so I didn't fancy my own chances against him.[1]

I was, of course, immensely flattered. Alex Salmond had been my political hero for many years, so to be asked by him to do this was a big deal for me. And I was not completely unprepared. The idea of standing as a candidate for the SNP had already been

---

[1] In the event he retired before the election so I did not have to face him.

raised with me by colleagues and friends in law and politics. Having developed an appetite for frontline politics during my involvement in the referendum campaign, I wanted to remain involved, but the prospect of becoming an MP seemed remote and daunting.

That night at Bute House was a magical evening for me, and I walked home in the early hours of the morning with my mind made up. It was a decision taken on instinct rather than on rational analysis. I just knew it was the right thing for me to do, and from there, despite all the ups and downs that were to come, I never really looked back.

This decision would have been wholly unforeseeable to me at the start of 2014, when I was suffering from anxiety and depression. Since my late teens I have been prone to episodes of depression, but on this occasion it was combined with a level of anxiety I had not experienced before. My mood was worsened by the break-up of a relationship that I felt had shown promise, but in truth my depression had contributed to that break-up.

My ex had told me that she thought I was unhappy in my life and my job. She said that when she asked me where I saw myself in ten years' time, I replied that I would be a judge, but I said it with no enthusiasm. When she said this I was annoyed, but I immediately realised she was right. Over time I was to come to realise that, while I enjoyed advocacy, joining the judiciary as part of the natural career path for a successful advocate did not necessarily appeal to me. I am not really an establishment person – more of a natural rebel. For fulfilment I needed to do something I was passionate about and to use my advocacy skills to crusade for a cause I really cared about.

With the benefit of hindsight, I can now see that part of my depression was caused by a lack of satisfaction in my job. When I worked as a prosecutor, I had a real sense of purpose, and, after leaving that position, up until the autumn of 2013 I had been very focused on a big mental health appeal I was conducting in the Supreme Court. When that case was over, I think I had a huge sense of anticlimax.

To make matters worse my closest friend, Nina Hallowell, to whom this book is dedicated, was heading off on sabbatical to

Australia. My family and other close friends were very supportive, but I was unsettled by Nina being so far away.

I decided that it might be good for me to get as far away as possible from my everyday life, to try to get over my depression and gain some perspective on my situation. So I followed Nina to Australia, spending a month travelling there. While down under, I realised I needed a greater purpose in life and resolved to get properly involved in the independence referendum campaign on my return.

After contacting an old friend from my university days, Susan Stewart, whom I knew to be working for Yes Scotland, I soon became active in Women for Independence (WFI), the grassroots group which had been established by Susan's partner, the late Jeane Freeman, among others, to make sure that women's voices and interests were put centre stage in the campaign.

It was April 2014 and the referendum was still more than six months away. I had little idea that I had started on a course that would completely change the direction of my life and give me the sense of purpose I needed.

The independence referendum campaign

It's a curious feature of the Scottish referendum which reflects badly on our media that only one newspaper supported the Yes side, despite almost half the country voting Yes. The *Sunday Herald* announced its support for Yes on 4 May 2014 with a beautiful front page designed by the late Alasdair Gray. Yes supporters were ecstatic to finally have one newspaper on our side. My Yes-supporting advocate colleague Gail Gianni arrived at my front door with a bottle of champagne to celebrate. I made us steak and chips while we discussed the current situation. We knew that there were many other lawyers who supported independence, and we decided to set up a group called Lawyers for Yes. We felt that contributions to the debate from a professional group who could speak with expertise on what the constitution of an independent Scotland and accession to the EU would look like might increase the appeal of independence. Gail is a skilled networker and gathered over a hundred supporters within a short period of time.

On 23 June 2014 we held a press event to launch the group. Gail encouraged me to be the group spokesperson and so my frontline political career began. Lawyers for Yes joined the many other grassroots groups which had been set up such as WFI, NHS for Yes, and Business for Scotland. Our group, like most others, had been set up completely independently of the SNP and the official Yes Scotland campaign, but both were soon in touch to ask if I could cover TV and radio bids for the Yes campaign. I found myself appearing regularly on radio and television and travelling Scotland to take part in debates, from Glasgow (a bastion of Yes) to St Andrews (a bastion of No-voting upper-class English students). I was told by Yes staffers that Peter Murrell (then the chief executive of the SNP and husband of Nicola Sturgeon) was impressed with my communications skills and wanted me to be utilised by the campaign.

As well as becoming the spokesperson for Lawyers for Yes, I did a fair bit of doorstep and street campaigning, and met Fraser Thompson, the coordinator of the Yes campaign in Edinburgh Central, who was later to become my chief of staff, as well as a close friend and a rock in difficult times.

Much has been written about the unpleasantness and division allegedly generated by the independence referendum. Those with an agenda blame it largely on the Yes side. I don't dispute that some of the cybernats, as they came to be known, went too far, but I had equally unpleasant experiences at the hands of some of the more vitriolic supporters of the unionist campaign. These went beyond social media attacks and extended to some very deliberate attempts to try to malign my personal integrity and my professional standing as a member of the Scottish bar. This continued after I was elected and got worse.

By early 2017, research by Amnesty International showed that I was one of the top five most-abused female MPs in the UK.[2] At

---

2 https://medium.com/@AmnestyInsights/unsocial-media-tracking-twitter-abuse-against-women-mps-fc28aeca498a

that stage I had not yet reared my head as a gender-critical feminist and most of the abuse was related to my support for Scottish independence and my support for the UK remaining in the European Union. In addition, some of the sectarian troglodytes who take an interest in Scottish politics had uncovered the fact that I was a Roman Catholic.

The Scottish independence referendum was a vicarage tea party compared to the Brexit referendum, both in terms of vitriol and in terms of the lies told. We must never forget that a Member of Parliament was murdered at the height of the Brexit referendum campaign. The most violent incident that happened during the Scottish referendum was the throwing of an egg.

My experience was one of a festival of democracy, a flowering of debate and ideas. By and large my relations with representatives of the Better Together campaign were good. Annabel Goldie, the former Scottish Tory leader, and I held a spirited but ultimately very civilised debate in front of an audience of young lawyers in Glasgow. I often found myself head-to-head in television and radio debates with Professor Adam Tomkins, lately a Tory MSP and now the John Millar Professor of Public Law at the University of Glasgow. We developed a mutually respectful relationship and remained in touch after the referendum.

For all the sound and fury, it was clear to me that some at least in the Better Together campaign were making plans for how things might be handled if the Yes campaign won. A senior representative of the campaign told me privately that if Yes won, the British government would negotiate in good faith and would want to get things done and dusted within six months. This may seem hard to take seriously in the light of the tortuous negotiations which followed the Brexit referendum, but these were very different times.

As the referendum approached and one poll showed Yes ahead, there was panic on behalf of the British establishment, with even the late Queen recruited to urge caution.[3] Viewing matters from

[3] https://www.bbc.co.uk/news/uk-scotland-scotland-politics-29200359

my standpoint in middle-class Edinburgh, I never really expected Yes to win, but my hopes were raised.

On the night of the referendum count, the die was cast from the first results from Clackmannanshire, which heralded the No campaign's triumph with 55 per cent of the vote. In the early hours of the morning, I attended what was meant to have been the Yes victory party at Dynamic Earth, Edinburgh's Science Museum, where the mood was sombre.

It was hard to get a taxi, and I walked part of the way home in the misty, rainy dawn feeling very sad. The next day I attended the opening ceremony of the Faculty of Advocates biennial conference, joined by lawyers from across the world. I was touched by how many colleagues, some of whom were clearly not Yes supporters, expressed their sympathy and in some cases remorse for the result.

The weather continued to reflect what seemed to be the national mood, and I headed across the meadows to the home of my former devil master, Laura Dunlop QC, who had invited me for supper and to commiserate. We sat in the kitchen and discussed the outcome. Later in the afternoon, Laura's husband, Ron, came through from the living room where he was watching the television to announce that Alex Salmond had resigned. I burst into tears. I didn't want Alex to resign. I did not think it was necessary, and I did not see how we could have a better leader to take us forward. To me he had not failed, but rather the country had failed in the sense that Scots had had a crisis of confidence. My Irish uncle had telephoned me in genuine puzzlement and asked, 'What kind of country votes against its own independence?' That was very much how I felt, and Alex's resignation unleashed my pent-up emotions of frustration, disappointment and sorrow.

However, as the weekend progressed, social media was alive with reports of a surge in SNP membership applications. My spirits started to lift and there was a very real sense that the argument about Scotland's constitutional future was going to continue and, as Alex Salmond had promised, the dream of independence would never die.

The 2015 General Election campaign

It is hard now to recall the incredible optimism that followed the initial slump in the spirits of the Yes movement after we lost the independence referendum. The exponential rise in SNP membership was quite extraordinary. The first meeting of Edinburgh Central SNP, my local branch, in October 2014 was so oversubscribed that it had to be moved from its usual location at the SNP club near St Andrew Square, which can only take about 60 people, to the gym of Tollcross primary school. Fraser Thompson was the convener of the branch, and he arranged the meeting carefully into discussion groups so that all the new members could explain why they had joined the SNP and what they wanted to achieve. Again and again, we heard from people who had left the Labour Party because of its involvement in the Better Together campaign and who wanted to keep the dream alive.

People are inclined to forget that the extraordinary rise in SNP membership after the independence referendum happened while Alex Salmond was still leader. It was prompted in part by his dignified response to the result and the grace with which he delivered his resignation speech. While I now agree with others that resigning at that point was probably the biggest mistake of his political career, there was no doubting the star quality that was starting to emerge in Nicola Sturgeon.

At this time I had still not met Nicola Sturgeon, but I had watched her political progress with interest. She wasn't particularly popular in the party, and I had always found her manner rather dour. However, it was widely thought that she had been a good health minister, and nobody could deny that her media and debating performances during the 2014 independence referendum campaign were very impressive. In particular, she had shone in the famous debate on 11 September 2014 before an audience of about 7,500 sixteen- and seventeen-year-olds who were first-time voters at the referendum. I believe this made a very strong impression upon her and influenced her future strategy, when she embraced gender-identity politics at least in part as an attempt to court the youth wing of the party and shore up her position as leader.

As a result of her distinguished service on behalf of the independence cause during the referendum, Nicola garnered considerable respect and admiration within the Yes movement and the SNP. Back in 2014, the general view, which I shared, was that if Alex Salmond wanted to resign and if Alex Salmond wanted Nicola as his successor, then Nicola should be his successor.

On 22 November 2014, I went to the final event in a triumphal SNP tour marking Nicola's ascent to power at the Hydro in Glasgow. It was the largest indoor political rally ever staged in Scotland and saw a capacity crowd of 12,000.[4]

I was rather taken aback by the rally. The adulation of not just Nicola Sturgeon but also the somewhat less charismatic figures of Angus Robertson, the SNP Westminster group leader, and Stewart Hosie, the party's deputy leader, puzzled me. I've never been to an evangelical or religious revivalist meeting, but I imagined this was what one must be like, and it made me feel uneasy. It was not so much Nicola and her supporting cast as the audience that troubled me. I just did not get where this near hysteria and cult-like worship of Nicola was coming from. I didn't want to seem churlish, so I kept my own counsel. In any event it was hard to be immune to the sense of mounting excitement in the party that the victory in the 2015 General Election predicted by Alex Salmond might well come true.

I heeded the advice Alex had given me at the Bute House drinks, and I entered and won the nomination race to be the SNP candidate for Edinburgh South West against stiff competition in December 2014/January 2015.

As the 2015 General Election campaign proceeded, nobody could doubt Nicola Sturgeon's abilities both on the campaign trail and in the television studios. Her incredibly assured performances in the TV election debates made voters south of the border wish that they could vote for her. An English Labour activist told the story of how he was picking up support for the SNP while canvassing in Ealing, in West London.

[4] https://www.bbc.co.uk/news/uk-scotland-30157986

Peter Murrell was a shrewd political operator, and I think he saw the chance to build on this adulation. Creating the cult of Nicola filled the void left by Alex Salmond, who had been adored by independence supporters in a way Nicola never had, at least until now. The cult of Nicola would become central to the SNP's approach to campaigning and governing throughout her leadership.

As well as having huge shoes to fill, Peter and Nicola must have been aware that prior to the independence referendum campaign and her unchallenged ascent to the leadership, Nicola had not been very popular in the party or with the public. Although that had clearly changed, not everybody was convinced. A close friend from the bar who was a natural Labour supporter, but who had generously offered to help me leaflet in Edinburgh South West, was horrified when the pictures on the leaflets were of Nicola and not me. I explained that most people did not have a clue who I was unless they were an ardent Yes supporter, but Nicola was a vote winner.

From there on in Nicola was front and centre of everything the SNP did. I was desperate to get her to come and campaign on my patch. A plan was made but fell through due to no fault of Nicola or her people. Later, during the 2017 local government elections, she visited the Whale Arts Centre in Wester Hailes in my constituency, and I was really impressed with the way she interacted with my constituents. While in private she was cool and reserved, she certainly had the common touch when dealing with the public.

Alex Salmond's plan of a broad Yes coalition for the 2015 General Election was knocked on the head by Sturgeon and Murrell, and the campaign proceeded conventionally along party lines. Party HQ were keen for candidates and their teams to knock on as many doors as possible so that we could collect data and identify our supporters and get them out to vote. Anyone in political campaigning will tell you that's the way to win elections. However, the local activists in my constituency were not keen on door knocking and wanted to conduct the campaign by leaflet only. I had to fight quite a battle behind the scenes to persuade them that door knocking was necessary and made myself rather unpopular with some of the older men who ran the show and did not appreciate what they saw as a younger woman telling them what to do.

In the end Fraser Thompson's fiancée, Sarah O'Gallagher, a young lawyer with whom I had worked when she was a trainee at the Crown Office, stepped in to help me and organised the canvassing.

The constituency of Edinburgh South West stretches from the city centre out to the village communities of the Pentland Hills. It contains some of the most leafy and affluent suburbs in Edinburgh, including Colinton and Craiglockhart, and also huge former council estates, including Wester Hailes, Broomhouse, Sighthill and Oxgangs. It was previously known as the Pentland constituency, and the history of its representation at Westminster since the 1970s very much marks the progression of modern Scottish politics and, in particular, the politics of our capital city. When I was growing up in 1970s Edinburgh it was represented by the Conservative MP Malcolm Rifkind. He lost the seat to Labour in the form of my colleague Linda Clark QC, now Baroness Clark of Calton, in 1997. Linda was succeeded by Alistair Darling, who had formerly been the MP for the abolished seat of Edinburgh Central, in 2005. Since 2024 it has a Labour MP again, Scott Arthur.

On the first morning that we went door knocking, a small team of us hit the streets in the very typical middle-class Edinburgh suburb of Kingsknowe. Our canvas returns indicated 39 per cent SNP support in that locality. I was stunned and found myself hyperventilating in a suburban front garden. This was not what I had expected, and I knew that if we were getting that level of support in middle-class areas, we would likely be getting closer to 60 per cent in working-class areas and I was going to win the seat.

Across Scotland other SNP campaign teams were getting similar or better results, and it was gradually dawning on everyone that Alex Salmond had been right when he predicted that if the 45 per cent who had voted Yes voted SNP then we would have a landslide on our hands.

On International Women's Day in March 2015, I was invited to an event at Westminster together with other SNP female candidates. We took the opportunity to have a look around and to meet with the existing SNP group. We were warned by Angus Robertson not to look as though we were 'measuring the curtains', but shortly after we left his office and walked across Westminster Hall, we bumped into Torcuil Crichton, then the Westminster correspondent of the *Daily Record*, now a Labour MP, who promptly tweeted, 'I see some of the SNP candidates are down measuring the curtains.'

Alex Salmond was also visiting, and he invited us for lunch at a restaurant about ten minutes' walk from the Palace of Westminster. However, the journey there took about 40 minutes because Alex was being constantly waylaid by passersby who wanted a selfie. These insistent selfie takers included tourists who had seen the massive Conservative campaign billboard at Piccadilly Circus that featured a picture of Alex Salmond with Labour leader Ed Miliband in his suit pocket. Alex was as much a celebrity in London then as he was in Scotland.

There was huge interest in the General Election campaign across the constituency, and I attended no fewer than seven local hustings. At one husting, held in Juniper Green, an affluent middle-class suburb of Edinburgh, an irate unionist in the audience demanded to know why I continued to support independence despite the result of the referendum. I answered by quoting the words of Charles Stewart Parnell, 'no man can stop the march of a nation', and received a rousing round of applause. When you get that sort of a reaction to quoting an Irish nationalist in suburban Edinburgh then you know something unusual is happening.

Polling done by Lord Ashcroft predicted that I would win the seat with 43 per cent of the vote to Labour's 28 per cent, which turned out to be almost 100 per cent accurate. I was taking part in a debate organised by the *New Statesman* at the London Welsh Centre on 'Our Disunited Kingdom' when Jason Cowley, then the editor of the *New Statesman*, announced the poll result to the audience to rapturous applause. The newspapers were full of headlines like 'Cherry to take Darling seat' and the rather predictable 'Cherry on top'.

It was heady stuff, but the miserable old men in my campaign team were determined that it should not go to my head and continued to make my life difficult, despite my complaints to HQ. They subjected both Sarah and me to angry tirades, and sometimes we had the sensation that they were deliberately trying to undermine our ground campaign. My abiding memory of the election count is being shouted at by one of them.

Late on the night before I was due to go to London to take up my seat, one of them sent me a 'parting shot' email in which he implied that I would rather spend more time with women – and I assumed he meant Sarah – than him. I read that as a nasty insinuation about my sexuality. It was pretty desperate stuff. Fraser and Sarah had got engaged on the night of the referendum, and I was looking forward to attending their wedding on the anniversary of that day. The behaviour of these men cast a pall over the first few months of my career as a Member of Parliament, because they went out of their way to undermine me in the constituency. The author of the email had taken a very strong dislike to me and never lost an opportunity to cause me trouble as the years went on.[5] I was shocked at the lack of help I received from the SNP hierarchy when I complained to them about it.

The 56

Despite all the excitement that surrounded the SNP landslide, my experience had left me with an ambivalence that stayed with me for a long time. In Scotland the new SNP MPs were colloquially referred to as 'The 56', the SNP having won 56 of Scotland's 59 seats. The press interest and razzmatazz around our arrival at Westminster was exciting. The reality was a little less glamorous.

Most MPs will say that they found the months immediately after their election a challenge. There are very few jobs where you arrive on your first day to find you have no office, no desk, no equipment, not even a paper clip, and no staff. At the same time, one finds oneself assailed by literally thousands of emails and letters not just from constituents, but from all sorts of organisations, including charities,

---

[5] https://www.scotsman.com/news/politics/snp-veteran-quit-party-after-bitter-clash-with-mp-cherry-1417620

NGOs, lobbyists and a sizeable proportion of eccentric timewasters. It was almost impossible to know where to start.

I was, however, fortunate that towards the end of the election campaign Sarah had indicated her willingness to work for me, and we agreed that she would step back from her legal career for a couple of years to get my office up and running. I don't know how I would have managed without her.

Then there was the weekly commute to Westminster, down early on a Monday morning then back up on a Thursday to be in the constituency on Friday and at weekends, and the living out of a suitcase. I also found the intense media focus on 'The 56' alarming, and although I enjoyed the challenge of being a frequent media spokesperson for the new SNP Westminster group, it was daunting.

When, later in 2015, Alex Salmond published his bestselling memoir of the independence referendum campaign, *The Dream Shall Never Die*, I threatened to publish a memoir about the first six months of being a Member of Parliament entitled *Will the Nightmare Never End?*.

I faced an additional problem in that I was starting to develop a significant disability caused by severe pain in my left hip joint and leg, which eventually led to me having to have a hip replacement in December 2015. I had been born with dislocated hips, which meant I had developed severe osteoarthritis despite being only in my late forties. Problems had started to manifest during the campaign, and as the spring and summer progressed I was often unable to straighten my leg or to walk. I experienced a throbbing pain at night which made it very hard for me to sleep.

However, I was determined to dance at Fraser and Sarah's wedding on 18 September, the anniversary of the referendum. It led to me spending the following week in bed barely able to walk to the bathroom. There was no question of me getting to London, but the negotiations in one of the pre-Brexit skirmishes on EU co-operation on law enforcement were at a crucial stage.[6] I took

---

[6] https://www.theguardian.com/uk-news/2015/nov/23/mps-vote-joining-european-police-dna-fingerprint-database

phone calls from Theresa May, who was then Home Secretary, in my pyjamas lying on my bed, with Sarah sitting at the end of the bed taking notes on her laptop.

When the new SNP MPs arrived at Westminster, we were astonished by how little preparation had been done by the previous Westminster group for our impending victory. Matters were not helped by the fact that the longstanding chief of staff of the Westminster group left to take up a job in the private sector almost as soon as we arrived.

While many individual staffers worked hard, our Westminster press operation seemed entirely incapable of dealing adequately with the onslaught of press attention, some of which quickly turned very hostile. Early on it was left to Alex Salmond to spike a particularly prurient piece that one tabloid had prepared concerning the fact that both Mhairi Black and I were lesbians. He suggested to them that having run a puff piece on the Scottish Tory leader Ruth Davidson and her girlfriend recently, it would look pretty bad if they made insinuations about lesbians in the SNP.

The inability of the press team to deal adequately with the field day the press were having was part of the wider problem of a lack of strategic direction. In our naivety, MPs like me, Tommy Sheppard and Philippa Whitford, all middle-aged people who had held senior positions in roles outside of politics, expected that the group of new MPs would together devise a strategy and approach not just for dealing with the press, but also for dealing with the incredible opportunities afforded to us by having become the third party at Westminster. This did not happen.

Instead, decisions and announcements were taken very much on an ad hoc basis by Angus Robertson, who continued as the SNP Westminster group leader, and those close to him. Despite having been the MP for Moray since 2001, Angus made some decisions that were politically inept. So, for example, when the usual press uproar about the latest award of a pay rise for MPs kicked off, Angus announced that all SNP MPs would be donating their pay rise to charity. None of us were consulted on this decision and his announcement meant that we then received an avalanche of emails and begging letters, not to mention persistent press queries asking to which charities we were donating. This put all of us in a very difficult position.[7] (It later emerged that Angus was receiving an additional £33,000 per annum from Westminster group funds because he was the group leader. Despite being on the group executive, I was unaware of this at the time.)[8]

Angus had set up a group executive, of which I, as Justice and Home Affairs spokesperson, was a member, but it very quickly became clear to me that it was there just to rubber stamp Angus's decisions. Now that we were the third party, we were entitled to frontbench speaking rights and the prized roles of the chairpersonships of two of the cross-party select committees that exist to scrutinise government. We were assigned the Scottish Affairs Committee and the International Trade Committee.

As a result of reforms which had taken place in the previous parliament these chairpersonships were now elected by backbench MPs, unlike at Holyrood where the chairs of the committees are selected by the party whips. In the Conservative and Labour parties these posts are much sought after and result in keen competition. MPs seek selection and nomination as candidates from their fellow party members, and then backbenchers of all parties can vote for the candidates. However, Angus decided that the SNP would not approach matters in this way; instead, he would give the chairs of the Scottish Affairs Committee and the International Trade Committee to Pete Wishart and Angus MacNeil – the MPs for Perth and Kinross, and the Western Isles respectively – who had been part of the SNP group in the last parliament. To be fair, each of them had considerably more parliamentary experience than any of the newly elected MPs. However, I felt that this was a fundamentally undemocratic way of approaching matters and challenged

---

[7] https://www.scotsman.com/news/politics/snp-mps-urged-to-donate-big-pay-rise-to-charity-1499770

[8] https://www.standard.co.uk/news/politics/times-scotland-scottish-government-angus-robertson-nicola-sturgeon-b1076071.html#:~:text=Angus%20Robertson%20received%20the%20salary,for%20independence%20campaigning%20was%20spent.

Angus's decision, asking why we wouldn't follow the same process as the other parties. He told me he had no choice but to do it this way, and besides, as they had so many friends cross-party, Pete and Angus would win any election against the rest of us unknowns. My impression was that he felt he had to placate them – or that someone else had told him to do this.

I found my new position as Justice and Home Affairs spokesperson challenging. It was a big brief to get across. On most days in the House of Commons there are topical statements or urgent questions, for which one receives at most about an hour's notice, and because Justice and Home Affairs covers such a wide range of issues, frequently these fell within my portfolio.

I vividly remember the first urgent question I had to deal with, which concerned a question from a Labour MP directed to the Home Secretary Theresa May about the Mayor of London Boris Johnson's decision to requisition German water cannons for crowd control. I was completely flummoxed and could not have managed to get on top of the material and craft a politically savvy response without the assistance of Stephen Noon, one of Alex Salmond's most valued SPADs, who was seconded to the Westminster team for the first few months after the election. Without his assistance, and that of Tom French, one of our savvier press officers, and Anne Harvey and Christopher Mullens Silverstein in the whips' office, I would have struggled more than I did.

I tag-teamed with Alex Salmond, and by preparing some bullets for Theresa May to fire at her old adversary on the water-cannon issue, I made an early friend of her. She was somebody I came to respect and admire, despite our radically different political positions. So it was that when she feared not having a majority among her own Eurosceptic backbenchers to support the Prüm Convention, she approached me to see if I could guarantee that the SNP would vote for it, and we did.

I always found Theresa May very approachable and professional to deal with, despite the fact that there were occasions both in public and in private when voices were raised as we discussed matters such as the Investigatory Powers Bill (better known as the Snooper's Charter). I also found Michael Gove, then the Justice

Secretary, charming when he invited me to his office to discuss prison reform and other shared interests. However, both Labour and the Liberal Democrats were initially very sore losers when it came to the SNP landslide.

Now that the SNP has suffered the humiliation of losing the position of third party, with all the privileges and opportunities that holds, I am a little more sympathetic to the Lib Dems who, in 2015, took an inordinate length of time to vacate the coveted suite of third-party offices, close to the chamber, which they had occupied for most of the last century.

However, there was a little more to their antipathy towards the SNP than the fact we had usurped their position as third party. Their erstwhile leader Charles Kennedy, who had been the MP for Skye, Ross and Lochaber, had lost his seat to my SNP colleague Ian Blackford. There were rumours that it had been a particularly unpleasant campaign. Kennedy had a self-confessed drinking problem and was, at the time, grieving the death of his parents and best friend. The hashtag adopted by Ian Blackford's campaign was 'Where's Charlie?'. Kennedy was called a 'quisling'[9] among a barrage of social-media abuse, and unpleasant anonymous messages were allegedly left on his car and pushed through his letterbox. According to reports at the time, Liberal Democrat activists complained to the police about the behaviour of Ian Blackford, claiming he had arrived at the Kennedy campaign office shouting at them and threatening revenge for alleged personal attacks on him.[10] The police said no crime had been committed. Apparently, when Kennedy returned home from the count having lost his seat, his bins had been emptied across his driveway.[11]

---

9 A traitor or collaborator

10 https://www.sundaypost.com/fp/close-friend-of-charles-kennedy-says-she-witnessed-snps-ian-blackford-being-aggressive-and-threatening-during-election-campaign/

11 https://www.dailymail.co.uk/news/article-3112992/Hounded-SNP-hate-mob-weeks-lonely-death-Charles-Kennedy-endured-vile-campaign-bullying-abuse-separatist-fanatics-deeply-wounded-vulnerable-man.html#:~:text=Early%20on%20May%208%2C%20a,'

There was very strong feeling about all of this among Kennedy's Lib Dem colleagues, and at a parliamentary dinner in the National Portrait Gallery, a Liberal Democrat peer reduced one of my female colleagues to tears through haranguing her about the allegations. At the time I defended Blackford and my party, thinking the allegations about how the campaign had been run were exaggerated. Due to my subsequent dealings with Ian Blackford, now I'm not so sure. The thought that there was a nasty personal element to Kennedy's last election campaign and so close to his tragic death is troubling particularly given his considerable contribution to public life both in Scotland and at Westminster.

During the tributes to Kennedy in the House of Commons, I ended up sitting next to Tim Farron and holding his hand because he was so upset. I felt a little ashamed on behalf of what had allegedly been done in the SNP's name.

If the Lib Dems were less than friendly, the hostility SNP MPs encountered from some Labour MPs was off the scale. Sometimes it verged on the comic. Once I saw Dennis Skinner gesticulating at one of my colleagues, saying, 'That's the wee lassie who stole Jimmy's seat.' But other times it was rather more unpleasant. Labour did not want to concede the SNP's rightful place to their left on the opposition frontbench. There was much childish scuffling, which came to be known as 'The Battle of Buttockburn', until a deal was reached.

During these confrontations, one of my colleagues was spat on. On another occasion a Labour MP forced his way onto our benches, sat down between two female SNP MPs and then loudly passed wind.

My impression was that a lot of the English Labour MPs had been led to believe that we were a bunch of ignorant hillbillies or 'fascists', and I took great pleasure in correcting this assumption whenever I spoke in parliament. Particularly during my maiden speech when I was gracious about my predecessor, Alistair Darling.

Not all MPs were hostile to the SNP. I was made very welcome by lawyers in other parties, particularly Dominic Grieve KC and Sir Edward Garnier KC on the Tory benches and Keir Starmer KC on the Labour benches, who like me was a new MP catapulted onto the opposition frontbench. Later, Keir and I worked together when each of us led for our parties on parliamentary scrutiny of the Investigatory Powers Bill, and in fact we were jointly nominated for an award for the work we did in that regard. I found Keir polite and professional to deal with and warm in personal interactions in a way that does not always come across now that he is PM.

It was particularly challenging to get on top of parliamentary procedure, and I found myself turning to Alex Salmond for advice and support. I was not alone in this, and I noticed that Angus Robertson and the other original members of the SNP group very much looked to Alex for advice and were content to leave major strategic decisions to him. I remembered this later when so many of them were prepared to turn on him and disown him when he was in trouble.

Alex played a pivotal role in our approach on budget days, during the passage of the Scotland Bill – designed to deliver the Vow (a joint pledge made by the UK party leaders to deliver extensive new powers to the Scottish parliament in the event of a No vote) – and to our approach to the EU Referendum Bill, which we tried to amend to say that a majority of the four constituent parts of the UK must vote for Brexit.

Alex became a firm friend and, together with Tasmina Ahmed-Sheikh, then the SNP MP for Ochil and South Perthshire and latterly Alex's business partner, we had a regular Tuesday evening dinner date. We did not always see eye to eye, but in fairness Alex listened when I chided him about what were, from my point of view, his past misdemeanours in relation to the Cadder case and the UK Supreme Court.

Alex and I crossed swords again in January 2016, over the issue of Julian Assange. Late in the evening of my first day back after my hip replacement, I was walking to my hotel across Westminster Bridge with Sarah, still using a stick and making a very conscious effort not to slip on the rain-sodden pavements, when Alex called. He was abroad on business and wanted me to go to see Assange in his stead. At that time, Assange was living in the Ecuadorian embassy, where he had sought refuge in June 2012 after he breached bail while Sweden were trying to extradite him from the UK to stand trial on rape charges. He was granted asylum in August 2012 and lived there until April 2019, when his asylum was withdrawn and UK police entered the building to arrest him.

Back in January 2016 he had been living in the embassy for four years. Assange had asked to see Alex because he said he had important information he wanted the SNP to raise in parliament. Alex could not make it and wanted me to go in his stead. It was agreed that I would do so on the Wednesday morning in time to take any information back to Westminster to be used at PMQs if necessary.

There was much discussion about the security aspects of my visit, as Assange had warned Alex that someone might want to steal the envelope he was going to hand me when I left the embassy. I was also told that the embassy was under surveillance.

The Ecuadorian embassy is on a side street behind Harrods. As instructed, we got out of our taxi a few doors away and walked up to the embassy. Once inside, we were asked for our phones, which were placed inside a bag then a drawer at the desk at reception. Sarah sat in the entrance hall keeping a close eye on that drawer, while I spent over an hour with Assange in one of fewer than half a dozen rooms in the embassy, which had clearly once been a residential flat.

I was not allowed to take anything in with me, so I had to make notes on an envelope that he provided. What he told me I promised to keep secret. I found him a little odd but charming, engaging and persuasive, but of course he was flattering me because he wanted to recruit the SNP to his cause. I did not think what he told me was particularly useful to us, and Angus Robertson agreed when I left and got safely back to Westminster without any cloak-and-dagger activity outside the embassy.

Within a matter of days, a UN committee ruled that Assange was subject to arbitrary detention. Alex wanted me to take up Assange's case in parliament. I refused to do so. The committee's opinion was being presented as something akin to a court judgment, when it was no such thing, and I felt his incarceration was voluntary and therefore disagreed with the opinion. Most importantly, I did not want to be presented as an apologist for a man who was perceived to be trying to evade justice on a charge of rape. I had no doubt that recruiting us to his cause had been the real reason for Assange's invitation to the SNP to visit him. When I told Alex this was not a cause I would be championing, he was not happy with my decision, but he respected it.

However, one area where Alex and I were on the same page was in our concern at the quality of briefings produced for SNP MPs. With all the short money[12] we earned as the third party we were able to employ a big research team. There were some bright people in that team (and also some who really were not up to the job), but it was not at all focused or well led. This on occasion led to SNP MPs being briefed with information that was incorrect, as happened to both Alex and me in January 2017 when we faced the *Today* programme and Andrew Neil with figures on Scotland's trade with Europe and the world which were not wholly accurate. I have never seen Alex so angry. It was symptomatic of a wider malaise.

After the 2017 election, Ian Blackford asked Roger Mullin, the former MP for Kirkcaldy, to prepare a detailed review of the research operation with recommendations for reform. To my knowledge these recommendations were never implemented, and indeed as time passed some of the research team had enough time on their hands to become involved in attempts to smear me as a bully, even when I hadn't worked with them, and to abuse me on social media for my sex-realist views.

One of the reasons I became so fond of Alex Salmond was that he was someone who could be relied upon in a crisis. Early in the autumn of 2015 one of my colleagues was to find herself in a very severe bind – and learn that in Nicola Sturgeon's SNP, when you were in trouble there wasn't much support.

In September 2015 a scandal engulfed Michelle Thomson, one of the 56 SNP MPs. Michelle had come to prominence through her work with Business for Scotland during the independence referendum. She was an effective campaigner and communicator and appealed to the sort of middle-class voters we were keen to win

[12] Public funding paid to opposition parties to help them with their costs.

over. She was among the people that Alex Salmond invited to Bute House shortly before he left office in November 2014. She accepted his challenge to stand for parliament and was elected alongside me in May 2015 as the MP for Edinburgh West.

When the SNP became the third party at Westminster after the election, Michelle was chosen by Angus Robertson to be the group's Business, Innovation and Skills spokesperson. The *Sunday Post* described her as one of the twelve SNP MPs to watch in the new parliament.

During the General Election campaign, she had had several campaign visits from Nicola Sturgeon. I remember my campaign team being rather jealous of how much time Nicola had spent in Michelle's constituency. There had been a particularly photogenic campaign visit in South Queensferry, and social media was full of pictures of Nicola and Michelle shopping and having coffee together. In the long term this close association was not to Michelle's advantage, because when the scandal broke Nicola and her operatives moved quickly to distance themselves from her.

In late September 2015 the *Sunday Times* published a story raising questions over Michelle's business affairs before she entered parliament, and Police Scotland announced it was launching an inquiry into 'alleged irregularities'. Ultimately, the police inquiry came to nothing and was dropped – but too late to save Michelle from the SNP reaction to the media storm that engulfed her.[13]

It wasn't long before it was announced that Michelle was resigning the SNP whip, which also meant that she was resigning from the party. At that time Michelle and I were both working out of the same serviced offices on Morrison Street in west Edinburgh while we looked for permanent constituency offices. She told me how she was visited there by Derek Mackay, the party's internal business convenor, and Mike Weir, the SNP Chief Whip. Together

---

[13] https://www.thetimes.com/best-law-firms/profile-legal/article/solicitor-in-snp-mps-house-deals-struck-off-8zxz900cvdc#:~:text=Mark%20Macaskill,stated%20she%20was%20a%20partner.

with Peter Murrell and Liz Lloyd, Nicola's chief of staff, they put her under insurmountable pressure to resign.

Michelle had no doubt that they were acting on Sturgeon's orders, and she has suggested that as a relatively inexperienced leader, Sturgeon panicked when she saw someone to whom she had been so close under such fierce media attack.[14]

I was shocked by the rapidity of Michelle's defenestration. I felt that it was setting a very bad precedent which would mean in future as soon as a serious accusation was made, no matter how baseless it might ultimately prove to be, it could prove to be the death knell for any of the new MPs' political careers. I was not alone. Alex Salmond railed against Michelle's treatment, and many of the other SNP MPs were equally angry and concerned. On two occasions the SNP Westminster group voted to have her reinstated, but that was overruled by the national executive committee of the party.

In a manner reminiscent of Operation Branchform (the police investigation into SNP finances between 2021 and 2025), this police investigation dragged on for nearly two years before it was dropped in August 2017.[15] By that time Michelle's career as an MP was over. She was ineligible to be an SNP candidate at the June 2017 election and stood down. The Liberal Democrats won her seat, and the SNP have never regained it. The whole situation was a massive own goal for the party, but Nicola had been protected and that was all that seemed to matter.

Interestingly, not all SNP parliamentarians whose financial affairs have come under police scrutiny have been treated quite as harshly as Michelle. Neither Nicola Sturgeon nor Colin Beattie lost the whip while remaining under police investigation during Operation Branchform. Yet in their case matters progressed well beyond Michelle's inquiry. Unlike Michelle they were actually arrested and interviewed under caution. Even more significantly, not long after the harsh treatment meted out to Michelle, Chris

---

14 https://www.heraldscotland.com/news/15456354.michelle-thomson-breaks-silence-my-two-years-hell/

15 https://www.bbc.co.uk/news/uk-scotland-scotland-politics-40788469

Law, the SNP MP for Dundee West, also came under press scrutiny for his financial dealings, having been detained and questioned by police in September 2016.[16] He was exonerated of any wrongdoing in January 2017, but at no point in the interim period did he lose the whip or his position as a frontbench spokesperson.[17]

Perhaps he was fortunate in that he was not as close to Nicola Sturgeon as Michelle had been during the 2015 election campaign. Whatever the reason for his different treatment, it speaks to the lack of due process in the party and a failure to treat like with like, which I was to find increasingly troubling.

My first personal experience of being thrown under the bus came in early 2016, when I woke to Sunday papers full of stories about how I had been reprimanded by Nicola for supporting independent press regulation in the Commons. I was initially puzzled, as it was SNP policy to support independent press regulation. The press had never been much of a friend to the SNP or the nationalist cause, and the thought that when complaints were made they should not get to mark their own homework appealed to the SNP membership.

Now Nicola had given an interview to one of the big Sunday newspapers in which she expressed support for IPSO (the Independent Press Standards Organisation, which is owned and controlled by the very newspapers it is supposed to regulate), and it was being presented as an attack on me for getting too big for my boots.[18] It was humiliating for me and infuriatingly unfair, as I had done nothing wrong.

---

16 https://www.theguardian.com/politics/2016/sep/29/snp-mp-chris-law-police-dundee-west

17 https://www.bbc.co.uk/news/uk-scotland-scotland-politics-38782007

18 https://www.thesun.co.uk/news/2596792/nicola-sturgeon-slams-dangerous-press-gagging-laws-as-government-confirms-it-wont-implement-them-in-scotland/; https://www.dailyrecord.co.uk/news/uk-world-news/nicola-sturgeon-slams-uk-government-9606315. https://www.heraldscotland.com/news/15020700.nicola-sturgeon-odds-mps-press-regulation/#:~:text=12th%20January%202017,Crime%20and%20Courts%20Act%202013.

With the benefit of hindsight, I believe that this was a decision taken by Sturgeon and those close to her to get the press on her side. It certainly might provide an answer to those who feel that some newspapers have been less than thorough in their scrutiny of Sturgeon, particularly in relation to the Salmond affair.

For me, as a loyal and hard-working frontbencher, it was a shock to be treated in this way. From then on, I was rather wary of Nicola, but I was prepared to put my experience down to 'that's politics'.

My concern about Nicola's unilateral volte-face on independent press regulation was shared by many other SNP MPs. If the issue of independent press regulation had come to a vote at that time, she would have faced a considerable rebellion, as many of my colleagues were prepared to break the whip on this issue. It played to a considerable unease in our group about the lack of protection afforded by the party when we came under attack in the media. The level of scrutiny of the new SNP MPs was unprecedented and has never been repeated.

I was not the only SNP MP who raised repeated concerns about the SNP media operation at Westminster group meetings. However, the substance of our concerns was never addressed, and efforts were made by Angus Robertson and those close to him to try to misrepresent our legitimate concerns about the lack of protection given to us as an attack on those who staffed our press operation rather than an attack on our strategy. This was something that would come back to bite me hard after the 2017 election.

A diverting upside of my continued support for independent press regulation was that later in 2016 I was invited for dinner by Hugh Grant, in his capacity as a member of the board of Hacked Off, the press standards campaign group. He was as utterly charming in person as he is on the stage and very warm and witty. It was to be the start of a working relationship which would encompass Brexit as well as press regulation.

Allied to concerns about the lack of support for the newly elected MPs was a very strong feeling among the Westminster group that we were not being well led. While the public persona of Angus Robertson was of a competent performer at PMQs and in the media, behind the scenes he was a remote leader who was very reluctant to engage in discussions about political strategy or policy.

Frequently at group meetings when such a discussion threatened to happen or something difficult was being raised, his phone would ring or he would find himself called away on urgent business.

My sense of being treated unfairly over the issue of independent press regulation was considerably offset when, after the SNP were returned to power in the Scottish parliamentary elections in 2016, albeit having lost the outright majority gained by Alex Salmond, Nicola Sturgeon seriously considered making me Lord Advocate, the top law officer position in Scotland. In the end she decided that if I were to take up the position it would mean a by-election, and she was worried that we might lose it. She also thought I might be open to the accusation of political bias. I was disappointed but fully understood her reasons. In retrospect, given what was to come with the Salmond affair, I dodged a bullet.

Salmond once described the group of SNP MPs elected to Westminster in May 2015 as one of the most talented groups of people he had ever worked with. However, as time progressed, many members of that group became very disaffected with the SNP leadership. There was a strong sense that the group was not being led well and that we needed to make more of the opportunities afforded to us. In the run-up to Theresa May's unexpected snap election in June 2017, Alex and I were plotting to challenge Angus Robertson for the leadership of the group. We went on a charm offensive, inviting different groups of SNP MPs to dine with us at our regular Tuesday night out to discuss how they saw things and what they wanted. In the end our efforts were thwarted by the election.

THE 56 BECOME 35

2

The Brexit referendum, its immediate aftermath and the 2017 General Election (2016–17)

Brexit and Scotland

In the early hours of the morning of Friday, 24 June 2016, I stood at the entrance to SNP HQ in Edinburgh and rang the doorbell for a long time before anyone answered. I had come from the Brexit referendum count at Meadowbank Stadium where, as expected, 75 per cent of voters in Edinburgh had voted to remain in the European Union. After rather a long wait, given that I knew HQ was full of staffers and activists, to my surprise the door was opened by Nicola Sturgeon herself. She was wearing jeans and an open-necked shirt, and her feet were bare. Her mouth was hanging open and her face wore an expression of astonished disbelief. While I had been driving the short distance there, David Dimbleby had announced the overall result of the referendum. Across the UK 52 per cent of people had voted to leave the European Union. In Scotland only 38 per cent had voted to leave; 62 per cent had voted to remain.

Once she had recovered her composure, Nicola's first words to me were, 'How would you like to be my legal adviser on indyref2?' I was overjoyed. Although I never knew Nicola well, at this point we were on cordial terms, and earlier that month we had discussed whether she should appoint me as Lord Advocate.

The UK-wide result came as a total shock to those who had spent most of the campaign in Scotland, although not to those of us who had spent time in England. In Scotland the consensus of all the main parties was pro-Remain. Despite the proportional representation system at Holyrood, which tends to enable smaller parties to make a breakthrough, UKIP had not succeeded in doing so. There were no UKIP councillors in Scotland and only one UKIP MEP. Those who had been on different sides during the independence referendum were pretty much on the same side in this referendum. The Scottish Tory leader Ruth Davidson played a major part in the Remain campaign, as well she might having promised Scots during the independence referendum that the way to ensure their European Union citizenship was to remain in the United Kingdom.

The Brexit referendum campaign in Scotland had nothing like the intensity of the independence referendum campaign, and to be honest I think people were still a little bit worn out by that. However, certainly in Edinburgh, there was still quite a lively Remain campaign. I took part in lots of hustings and events and was out knocking on doors, leafletting and doing street stalls. It was clear that the overwhelming consensus was that Scotland should remain in the European Union.

Spending time in England, I sensed a very different atmosphere, particularly when I took part in *Question Time* or *Any Questions?* across the country. This was brought home to me when I was asked to speak for Remain at a lawyers debate in the Inner Temple. Dominic Grieve QC and I were teamed against Michael Howard QC and Martin Howe QC. After the debate the audience held a vote, which came out two-thirds Remain and one-third Leave. That alarmed me, because in a gathering of lawyers in Scotland, it would have been at least 90 per cent Remain. It seemed to me that if a third of barristers and solicitors in London were Leavers, it was likely that the percentage of Leavers would be much larger in the general population.

Nicola Sturgeon was clearly one of those who were deeply shocked by the overall result, but ever the consummate politician, she could see the opportunities presented by the disparity between the result in Scotland and the overall result in the United

Kingdom. In 2014 it had been a central promise of the Better Together campaign that voting to stay in the UK was the best way to guarantee Scotland's continued membership of the European Union. The spectacular breaking of this promise was a material change in circumstances which would justify a second independence referendum.

On 24 June 2016, standing at the entrance to SNP HQ and learning about the Leave vote, I still believed in Nicola Sturgeon as the inheritor of Alex Salmond's legacy and the SNP leader who would take Scotland to independence. I would have been proud to do whatever I could to assist her in extracting Scotland from the unwanted disaster of Brexit and using the result of the EU referendum as a springboard to a second independence referendum.

One of the main issues Lawyers for Yes had campaigned on during the independence referendum was an independent Scotland's continuing membership of the European Union. The constitutional battle which now lay ahead was the reason I had entered politics, and I was keen to use my legal expertise to further our joint cause. I felt excited and energised. Later that morning, as the sun rose over Edinburgh Castle, I stood on a balcony outside the penthouse suite of a hotel in the Grassmarket, being interviewed by CNN, with an incredible sense of anticipation. There was tremendous international interest in what this vote might mean for Scotland, and a lot of sympathy for our predicament. I thought the independence cause was about to be reborn.

Over the months to come I would speak with many people who had voted No in 2014 but were now open to voting Yes if it meant a way back into the EU. There was everything to play for. I really believed that Nicola Sturgeon wanted me by her side, plotting the way to ensure Scots got a second vote for an independent Scotland in the EU. I was ready and willing to serve her, drawing on the skills I could offer as an experienced QC.

In June 2016, the SNP was still a relatively happy family. After letting me in to HQ, Sturgeon disappeared into an office with her advisers and emerged later in a smart suit ready to face the press. Later that morning she made an impressive and statesperson-like speech announcing that a second Scottish independence referendum was now 'on the table'. The Brexit referendum result represented a significant and material change of the circumstances in which Scotland had voted against independence in 2014. The SNP manifesto on which she had been re-elected the previous month gave her a clear mandate to request another referendum in the event of such a change of circumstances.

Section 30 – the 'gold standard'

Nicola Sturgeon wanted a repeat of the Edinburgh Agreement, brokered between David Cameron and Alex Salmond in 2012, whereby power was transferred from Westminster to the Scottish Parliament under Section 30 of the Scotland Act to hold the 2014 referendum. She wrote to Prime Minister Theresa May requesting such an agreement, but May famously replied that 'now is not the time'. This phrase was to be repeated whenever subsequent requests for a Section 30 order were made, which was often. It came to infuriate independence supporters, but it is a little-recognised fact that the phrase actually came from Nicola's letter, a strategic misstep that was perhaps a warning of what was to come.[1] Perhaps if those advising Sturgeon had been less focused on the extremely photogenic pose she adopted while writing the letter (famously barefoot and elegantly poised on a sofa in Bute House) and more focused on the actual content, this mistake would not have been made.

Over the years that followed, Sturgeon would repeatedly announce that a second independence referendum was imminent, without being able to deliver on her promises due to the veto on a further Section 30 order imposed by successive British prime ministers. This impasse was what later led me and others to argue that she should have a plan B – a route to holding a further Scotland-wide vote on the issue of whether we should become an independent country that did not depend on the co-operation of the British government.

---

[1] https://www.bbc.co.uk/news/uk-scotland-scotland-politics-39456681

The Scotland Act 1998 is the founding statute of the devolved Scottish Parliament. It sets out the areas of competence which are reserved to the UK Parliament. Section 30 provides a mechanism whereby the UK Parliament may give permission to the Scottish Parliament to pass legislation in areas that are normally reserved to the UK Parliament. A Section 30 order cannot happen without the consent of the UK government.

Until the UK Supreme Court ruled on the matter in 2022 (see chapter 7) it was thought that the Scotland Act was not entirely clear as to whether it would be competent for the Scottish Parliament to hold a referendum on the question of independence. The position of successive British governments was that the power was reserved. However, there was a respectable body of legal opinion in Scotland that the Act was sufficiently vague for a carefully crafted bill to be within the Scottish Parliament's competence.[2]

When Alex Salmond had achieved an unprecedented outright majority for the SNP in 2011 and a mandate to hold an independence referendum, he adopted the position that it would be open to the Scottish Parliament to hold a referendum but that it would be preferable to put the question beyond doubt by reaching agreement with David Cameron and getting a Section 30 order. As a result of skilful negotiations, he achieved what he wanted, partly because Cameron was under the misapprehension that there was no question of the referendum being won by the pro-independence side.

However, this was not going to happen a second time round. The fact that the Yes side came so close to winning in 2014 had shocked the British establishment and meant that they were unlikely to grant another order, particularly when they had arguments available to them that it was too soon or that there was too much else going on. Unfortunately, these were arguments that had been reinforced by the unwise wording of Nicola Sturgeon's letter.

---

[2] https://ukconstitutionallaw.org/2012/01/31/gavin-anderson-et-al-the-independence-referendum-legality-and-the-contested-constitution-widening-the-debate/

As time passed it became clear that in repeatedly seeking a Section 30 order, Nicola was banging her head off a brick wall. However, undaunted, she told anyone who would listen that a referendum sanctioned by a Section 30 order was the 'gold standard'. I was worried that this would have the effect of thoroughly cementing in the minds of people at home and abroad that a second vote could not be held without the permission of the UK Parliament and that without such permission there was no other route to Scottish independence.

This seemed to me unwise, as Section 30 is a creature of the devolved settlement that has been in place for less than three decades, whereas the union between Scotland and England is over 300 years old. It seemed to me an illogical proposition that the union between Scotland and England could only be ended by a mechanism created by a statute barely 25 years old. I also thought it was unwise to encourage other countries, particularly other members of the European Union, to believe that any referendum that wasn't sanctioned by a Section 30 order would be an 'illegal' referendum. Of course, it didn't help that the Catalan referendum intervened, but, unlike the Spanish constitution, there is nothing in the unwritten British constitution to say that a part of the union may not secede. On the contrary, there is a clear precedent in British constitutional history, Ireland having left its union with England ultimately by agreement and as the result of a negotiated treaty.

Had I been in the Sturgeon inner circle, these are all things that I would have urged her to consider. However, despite her offer to make me her legal adviser on 24 June 2016, I was never consulted on the political or legal strategy and instead found myself in the political wilderness for daring to question it.

England's difficulty was Scotland's opportunity

The great Irish politician and campaigner for Catholic emancipation Daniel O'Connell coined the phrase 'England's difficulty is Ireland's opportunity'. On various occasions in Irish history, nationalists took advantage of crises in England to launch rebellions. It was plainly the case that the turmoil caused at Westminster by the Brexit vote offered an opportunity for the nationalist movement in Scotland: not to launch a rebellion as such, but to advance the interests of Scottish independence, which included advancing Scotland's relations with the EU. However, it was one that needed to be pursued with a careful strategy which balanced a number of factors, including the fact that it is sometimes necessary to work with one's political enemies to get what one ultimately wants.

David Cameron had, of course, resigned in the wake of the Brexit vote and was replaced as Prime Minister by Theresa May. Theresa May and Nicola Sturgeon held high-profile meetings in Edinburgh, Glasgow and London. Sturgeon and her team were very good at the choreography of such meetings. At the first, which was in Edinburgh, Sturgeon greeted May on the steps of Bute House like a visiting foreign leader, and they were photographed sitting side by side with the Union Jack and the Saltire as if they were equals. But, of course, they weren't. Sturgeon was the leader of a devolved administration; May was the leader of the parent parliament that held all the power. That did not mean that Sturgeon had not been served a particularly good hand of cards by the Brexit referendum. However, how she played them would be crucial.

An anecdote told to me back in 2019 by Robin McAlpine (writer, independence campaigner, founder of the Common Weal thinktank), if accurate, illustrates my view that Nicola Sturgeon did not play that hand well, and instead of having a properly worked-through strategy, preferred to grandstand. Robin has subsequently written about the incident in his blog. Here is what he said:

> I'm going to share a story with you ... my source for this story is reliable and the original source is reliable but I don't know if there was any 'Chinese Whispers' between the two (and now me) ... After Brexit and the elevation of Theresa May to Prime Minister she arranged a first meeting with Nicola Sturgeon. Her side had a strategy; the civil service had prepared a full package of concessions to Scotland which were sitting in a folder in front of May. They wanted to try and get an orderly Brexit through parliament

> and were ready to make serious concessions in turn for some cooperation from Scotland and some concessions in return. On the way to the meeting Sturgeon was confrontational and outspoken about her contempt for the subject of the meeting. Outside the meeting she did it again. And then in the meeting she opened with another diatribe that could be summarised as 'no retreat, no surrender'. May's civil servant quietly reached over and slid the folder off the table. It was never opened.[3]

I think this incident, if it happened, is most likely to have taken place not at the first meeting in Bute House, but at the last of three meetings that I mentioned above between Sturgeon and May, in October 2017 at Downing Street. The latter meeting took place after Theresa May's disastrous snap general election when she lost her majority, and it is at that stage that I think she would have been most likely to be open to making concessions to Scotland.

In my experience Theresa May was someone you could do business with. I don't believe she really understood Scotland or Scottish politics, but I do believe that she was someone who felt her duty to her country, which of course she would see as Britain, or rather England, very strongly. She wanted to deliver a Brexit deal that caused as little damage to the British economy as possible, and she needed help to do it.

There was significant goodwill towards Scotland in Europe at this time. Whether this would have translated from sympathy to action is, of course, a quite different matter. In June 2016 Nicola Sturgeon went to Brussels and met with Jean-Claude Juncker, the President of the European Commission, who told her, 'Scotland has won the right to be heard in Brussels.' He went on to say, 'I will listen carefully to what the First Minister will tell me, but we don't have the intention, neither Donald [Tusk, President of the

---

[3] https://robinmcalpine.org/in-government-you-need-to-work-with-the-enemy/.

European Council] nor myself, to interfere in the British process, that is not our job.'[4]

However, the opportunity was there for the SNP government to press home our advantage within the British process, in the knowledge that if the British government raised the possibility of a special deal for Scotland this would have fallen on sympathetic ears in Brussels.

Alex Salmond was busy travelling to Brussels and other European capitals trying to get people on side. He and I held a number of high-level meetings in Brussels in August 2016, and in December 2016 Jean-Claude Juncker said again to Alex that 'Scotland had earned the right to be listened to' regarding its demands for a separate Brexit deal. Salmond and Sturgeon were still on good terms at this point and Alex generously attributed the progress being made to 'the diplomatic efforts of the First Minister and her team'.

'Scotland's Place in Europe'

At this stage the diplomatic efforts were proceeding well. On 20 December 2016 the Scottish government published 'Scotland's Place in Europe', a policy paper which put forward the idea of a differentiated deal for Scotland or a compromise for the whole of the United Kingdom.[5]

The foreword to the document, written by the First Minister, emphasised the need to build consensus, including the need to address the concerns of those who voted to leave. However, it stressed that in Scotland there was clearly a desire to be a 'full and active member of the European family of nations'.

Sturgeon said that she wanted to explore not just her preferred option of independence, but all options to protect Scotland's place

---

[4] https://www.theguardian.com/politics/2016/jun/29/nicola-sturgeon-scotland-plea-eu-leaders-sympathy-little-hope

[5] https://www.gov.scot/publications/scotlands-place-europe/

in and relationship with Europe. The Scottish government would, in good faith and in a spirit of compromise, seek to identify a solution that might enable Scotland's voice to be heard and mitigate the risks that Brexit posed to our interests within the UK. At the heart of the document was Scotland's determination to maintain our current position in the European single market.

A number of proposals were advanced. Firstly, that the UK as a whole should remain within the European single market, through the European Economic Area, and also within the customs union.

Secondly, the paper considered how Scotland might remain a member of the European single market and retain some key benefits of EU membership even if the rest of the UK decided to leave.

There are other countries in Europe who are members of the single market but not the customs union, such as Norway, which belongs to the European Free Trade Area (EFTA) and the single market through the European Economic Area (EEA). In December 2016, I joined a delegation of SNP MPs to Oslo led by Alex Salmond in order to explore this option. We met with parliamentarians, academics, NGOS and representatives of the EEA and EFTA. The trip greatly boosted morale, as we realised that Scotland had a variety of viable options for co-operation with Europe.

Sturgeon was at pains to stress that the proposals contained in 'Scotland's Place in Europe' did not prioritise the European single market over free movement and free trade within the United Kingdom. The Scottish government considered that UK-wide free movement and free trade could and would continue if Scotland became independent, just as the UK government believed that free trade and movement between the UK and the Republic of Ireland would continue after Brexit. The proposal was to seek to secure the benefits of the European single market for Scotland in addition to, not instead of, free trade across the UK.

The paper also argued that, in the light of the removal of the rights and protections provided by EU law, and whatever the outcome of the Brexit negotiations, Scotland's interests within the UK demanded that the powers of the Scottish Parliament be fundamentally revisited. If the real and substantial risks that Brexit posed to Scotland's interests could not be mitigated within the UK, the option of choosing a better future through independence should be open to the Scottish people.

Sadly, while 'Scotland's Place in Europe' was well received by the academic community and in Brussels, where Michel Barnier was said to have read it with great interest, it was ignored by the UK government, who went on to cut the Scottish government out of the Brexit negotiations completely. Meanwhile, thanks to skilful diplomacy by the Irish government in Brussels, the question of a differentiated deal for Northern Ireland because of the need to keep open its border with the Republic became central to the Brexit negotiations.

I do believe that the compromise proposal put forward in 'Scotland's Place in Europe' could have worked, but it would have required a significant rebalancing of the British constitution – an approach more akin to Canadian-style federalism. Clearly a differentiated deal is working for Northern Ireland. That only came about because of the insistence of the European Union. Northern Ireland had the Republic of Ireland to advocate for it. Scotland had no one to advocate for it in that way, and the British Conservative government simply did not have the appetite to revisit the British constitution in the way that would have been necessary. Nor did the Labour Party, who were missing in action on these arguments.

Theresa May triggered Article 50, the notice required for the UK to leave the EU at the end of March 2017, then, over Easter, she had a rush of blood to the head and announced a snap General Election.

The 2017 General Election

The lack of strategic direction within the SNP Westminster group and within the wider party became particularly pronounced in the aftermath of the Brexit vote. Alex Salmond and I had planned to challenge Angus Robertson for the group leadership, and we had been on a charm offensive with colleagues to discuss our shared concerns. But Theresa May's snap General Election announced in April 2017 put paid to that.

Some SNP MPs, including me and Alex Salmond, advised against supporting the snap election because we felt it would not have been advantageous to us for Theresa May to strengthen her majority, as all the polls indicated she might do in England. It was hard to see how we could improve upon the tally of 56 seats out of 59 in Scotland. Indeed, the backlash to Nicola's announcement of a second referendum so soon after the first meant that the Tories had a good chance of taking seats off us in areas of Scotland where Brexit was less unpopular, such as the fishing communities in the northeast and rural communities in the borders.

Ultimately, we were proved right. The 2017 General Election campaign was a disaster for the SNP. There was no clear message. The leadership ran scared from their commitment to a second independence referendum and instead grandstanded about Brexit and the Scottish government's record. The Scottish Tories made hay with the widespread antipathy to yet another referendum so soon after the 2014 and 2016 ones, and many independence supporters stayed at home. Support for the SNP fell by nearly half a million votes from the 2015 General Election, and we lost 21 of our 56 seats, including those of Angus Robertson and Alex Salmond.

It was the aftermath of that poor election result that marked the parting of ways for me and Nicola. Already there was concern in her circle about my growing popularity with the membership after a series of strong Commons and media performances in the wake of the Brexit referendum. At Spring Conference 2017, after my appearance on *Question Time* the night before, I received a standing ovation. It was reported to me that this had not gone down well with the Sturgeon or Robertson camps. There was consternation about rumours of my and Alex's plan to oust Angus.

The Tories had identified 15 SNP target seats. We lost 13 of them, including those of Alex and Angus. Pete Wishart survived with a majority of 21 and I held on with a majority of 1,097. My survival was unexpected and was thanks to a fantastic GOTV (get out the vote) effort by my election agent and campaign manager. Pete had had a lot of help from the party establishment. I did not. A friend who was in SNP HQ on the night of the results reported that when my unexpected win was announced at 4.30am, half the room cheered and the other half stayed ominously silent.

At the Edinburgh count the atmosphere was tense. The Tories were confident of taking my seat, but Fraser, who was my election agent as well as my chief of staff, was quietly confident that we had held on by a few hundred votes. I was not so sure, but he turned out to be right. Ruth Davidson, who as an MSP was not a candidate, was at the Edinburgh count poised to bask in the reflected glory of Miles Briggs, the Tory candidate, taking my seat. Instead, I got to bask in the surprise that he didn't.

As my result was not confirmed until after 4am, I had a white-knuckle ride watching so many of my colleagues lose their seats. When I went onto the stage to make my victory speech, I was unaware that Alex Salmond had lost his seat because my phone had mysteriously disappeared for the last 30 minutes or so. I later found out that Fraser had asked Nina to hide it so that I didn't know Alex had lost. When I came off the stage a journalist told me, and I burst into tears. Fraser immediately enveloped me in a bear hug and told me not to cry as I had achieved a great victory. In the midst of his own defeat, Alex found time to text 'Epic hold, Jo.' It was typical of him to be thinking of his colleagues even in his own most difficult moment. His father had died earlier that week.

In the midst of the shock of the loss of so many colleagues, it was hard to see any basis for optimism. However, Fraser and I quickly realised that a considerably weakened Tory government that had lost its majority might prove advantageous to the SNP in advancing our cause, and while the SNP group was also reduced in size it might have considerable bargaining power. Furthermore, the Westminster group would need a new leader, and it couldn't be Alex because he was gone as well. We quickly decided that I should stand for the leadership of the group.

The SNP Westminster group leadership battle

I spent the weekend after the General Election contacting colleagues who had lost their seats to take their temperature. Most were in a state of shock, and many told me they were hurt not to have heard from Nicola. After I had done that, I spent some time plotting with Fraser and a senior SNP Westminster staffer and started to contact the colleagues who had survived. We decided that my campaign would have to be based on an honest acknowledgement of what had gone wrong over the last two years and offer a significant change in the way in which the Westminster group was led.

I was exasperated with the way in which the 2017 General Election campaign was run, and I didn't try to hide it. Little thought seemed to have been given to the campaign strategy, and incumbent MPs felt like we had been left to run 56 by-elections. Fraser was my election agent, and I remember him hanging on the telephone trying to get guidance from SNP HQ as to what the plan was with no joy. I was contacted by Gina Miller on behalf of Best for Britain, the anti-Brexit campaign group. So keen were they to have anti-Brexit voices in parliament, despite their name and aims, they were considering backing SNP candidates with endorsements and campaign donations. They were getting no joy from SNP HQ so they wanted me to ring round SNP candidates in seats where the Tories were a threat to see if they would accept their endorsement and cash. Most, who felt they were fighting a battle with one hand tied behind their backs, were keen. Gina came up from London with her legal adviser to discuss her offer further and took Fraser and me out for lunch, but ultimately nothing came of it.

While opposition to Brexit was a central part of the SNP campaign in Scotland, the campaign largely focused on the record of the SNP government in Edinburgh rather than the record of the Tories at Westminster. It seemed foolish to me for the SNP to allow the election focus to be on the record of a Scottish government that was one year into a new term and therefore was not going to be at its most popular with the public. This was a Westminster election, and I felt that the Westminster group had a good story to tell about the significant difference our presence had made there.

Instead, it looked like the Tories were making headway in Scotland. The major problem, as we all came to realise, was that in the aftermath of the Brexit result Nicola had moved too soon to announce her intention to hold a second independence referendum and had alienated large swathes of the public who could not face yet another referendum. Equally, we had alienated our core support by running scared of Nicola's promise of a second referendum and instead focusing on the (not stellar) record of the Scottish government.

During the election campaign Nicola took part in several set-piece TV debates with the other party leaders from the Scottish Parliament. Although Nicola was still our strongest asset at that stage, I thought it was unwise to have agreed to this debate format, as it inevitably placed focus on the record of the SNP government at Holyrood rather than the record of the Tories at Westminster. I argued that it would have been more sensible to put our Westminster group leader forward for debates and focused on the record of the Westminster government and that of the SNP Westminster group in opposition. My warnings fell on deaf ears.

At one of these TV debates, I was asked by the party to attend in the 'spin room', the designated area for journalists to interview political pundits during and after the debate. I had never done anything like this before and sought guidance in advance from SNP media and the campaign directors about how best to approach things. I was told they were very busy, but they would get back to me. They did not. When I arrived at the venue and asked again for a briefing, I was informed by Jeane Freeman MSP, who was also there as a commentator, and by the SNP media staffer accompanying her that I was there to defend the Scottish government. If there was anything about the Scottish government's record about which I was unsure I could check the newspapers like everyone else. This was typical of the high-handed arrogance from some MSPs and staffers that MPs were getting accustomed to, but I did not find it particularly helpful and said so.

During the televised debate, Nicola, who was usually very adept, was wrong-footed by a question from a nurse in the audience who said that she was so badly paid she had to use a food bank. Sitting in the spin room I started to receive messages from a variety of sources, including other SNP candidates, that this nurse had been in the audience at *Question Time*, which had taken place in

Edinburgh the week before, sitting beside a Conservative councillor to whom she was married.

The spin room was packed with representatives of all the political parties and print and broadcast journalists. The atmosphere was frenetic, to say the least. Because the exchange with the nurse had so discomfited Nicola it was the main topic of conversation. The fact that the nurse had been in the *Question Time* audience the week before, sitting beside a Conservative councillor to whom she might be married, was also being widely discussed. I felt under pressure to defend Nicola, as clearly that was my job, but I didn't think I was being given any clear lines on what to say

After the debate was over, in a pre-recorded interview with Nick Eardley of BBC Radio Scotland, I was pressed on what the nurse had said. I commented that as the wife of a Conservative councillor she ought to have been aware that nurses were in fact considerably better paid in Scotland than they were in England, thanks to the SNP government. This last bit was true; unfortunately, the stuff about her marital status turned out to be wrong.

I was dismayed when I found this out. There had been two SNP staffers sitting beside me as I waited to be interviewed, and I had asked them whether the information about the nurse had been confirmed before I said anything. I was assured that it had been. Whether that was carelessness or a misunderstanding I cannot say, but it was certainly in keeping with the chaotic approach to briefing in advance of the event.

All hell broke loose. Although my interview had not yet been broadcast there was a lot of criticism on Twitter of the nurse, and I was being blamed for it. The SNP staffers present had melted away and I was unable to get any advice on how to handle the situation.

Of course, with the benefit of hindsight, no matter how much reassurance I had received from the SNP staffers, I should not have criticised the nurse who had asked the question. I should have played the ball, not the person. However, I felt it was unfair that I was being blamed for the pile-on that was happening on social media completely independently of anything I had said in an interview that was yet to be broadcast.

Nicola's chief of staff, Liz Lloyd, contacted me and instructed me to tweet in the following terms: 'Sorry I was wrong about twitter rumours. Entirely right that your voice is heard.' I was initially resistant to the wording of the tweet because I felt it ran the risk of being interpreted as an acceptance of responsibility for the abuse the nurse was getting on Twitter. However, it was made very clear to me by Liz Lloyd that unless I put the tweet out and took the heat off Nicola, I would not have the party's support. I was left with no choice but to tweet in the terms she suggested. I continued to be blamed for the whole episode, and the wording of my tweet was interpreted in just the way I had feared. The story was huge and received wall-to-wall press and media coverage.[6]

My seat was one of the Tories' top targets, and I'd had very little backup from SNP HQ to date, so I feared that this incident would seal my fate and I would lose my seat. I was extremely upset and only persuaded to return to the campaign trail by Fraser, who correctly predicted that most members of the public wouldn't be aware of the press storm. I took quite a bit of convincing, and eventually had to be coaxed out of my house by Fraser sticking his phone through the letterbox and playing an inspirational part of the audiobook version of Alex Salmond's *The Dream Shall Never Die* – read by the man himself.

We headed up to Wester Hailes to do some door knocking afterwards. I had spent a lot of time working to get to know people in the Wester Hailes community since my election win in 2015, and, as Fraser had predicted, I got a warm reception on the doorsteps. No one said anything about the nurse.

In fairness to Nicola, while she was critical of the social-media reaction to the nurse, she gave me her backing, saying that I had made an honest mistake and apologised for it. I was grateful. However, the episode that Fraser and I referred to as 'nursegate' dogged me for some time.

---

[6] https://www.bbc.co.uk/news/uk-scotland-scotland-politics-39997155#:~:text=Claire%20Austin%20(L)%20received%20an,that%20your%20voice%20is%20heard.%22

It also made me deeply suspicious of staffers close to Nicola, so I proceeded with care in my Westminster leadership campaign. Unfortunately, I inadvertently blotted my copybook from the outset by arriving late for the photo opportunity arranged with Nicola and what was left of the group on our first day back at Westminster. I did try to attend, but my flight from Edinburgh to London was late and there was nothing I could do about it. Nevertheless, it was taken as a calculated slight.

At that point there were four potential candidates for the leadership: Ian Blackford, Tommy Sheppard, Drew Hendry and me. Nicola wanted to see each of us separately. Her plan was to install Stewart Hosie as a caretaker leader for an unspecified period. I made it pretty clear to her that I didn't think that was a good idea. Part of the reason the group had lost so many MPs had been the lack of leadership, and Stewart as deputy leader of the group had been missing in action in the last two years. She told me that I shouldn't be so personal about people. I explained that it was nothing personal but based on the lack of leadership he had displayed to date, and that the group badly needed a strong leader to get us back on track. Her manner was cold and terse, and I was left in no doubt that she did not wish to see me as leader of the group.

As it turned out, it was the prevailing view of MPs at the group meeting that we needed to get the leadership election out of the way and get on with things, so Nicola was thwarted in her desire to install Hosie as a temporary leader. It was unusual for her not to get her way in the party, and she was very unhappy with me as the ringleader of the antipathy to her plan.

The atmosphere at the group meeting was fractious. People were shocked and upset at our losses. There was a lot of anger at the way in which the campaign had been run. Nicola was very resistant to and stung by the criticism.

As the leadership battle progressed, Tommy and I, the two candidates for change, compared notes carefully. He took the view that he could not win and dropped out to endorse me. The party machine swung in behind Blackford, although in truth Nicola's preferred candidate was Stephen Gethins. However he had held onto his North East Fife seat by only two votes in the face of a strong Liberal Democrat challenge and felt he had to concentrate on his constituency.

In the event Blackford had only one more vote than me on the first preferences, but received all of the second preferences from Drew's four first-preference votes. Notwithstanding this reality, the press were briefed by Nathan Sparling, a staffer close to Angus Robertson, that I had lost by a distance. I was precluded from correcting this because we were told the result was secret, no doubt to save Blackford and Sturgeon's blushes.

Blackford should have had a margin of two votes over me, but his surprise seconder, the left-wing Mhairi Black, turned up too late to vote. I was rather surprised that I had done so well. All the stops had been pulled out to prevent me becoming the leader of the SNP Westminster group, including resurrecting the 'nursegate' scandal in the press. The *Daily Record* ran rather a curious story about a random member of the public accosting the nurse in question while she was having lunch in a restaurant and filming her.[7] The insinuation was that this was my fault, for reasons that were never made clear. I was not surprised. The *Record* had it in for me because of my support for independent press regulation; it was Liz Lloyd's favourite outlet for briefings against those out of favour with the leadership; and Stewart McDonald, Blackford's campaign manager, was close to its then editor, Murray Foote.

Some of the petty jealousies that had festered among the group since the 2015 election came to the fore, particularly between some of the original SNP MPs and those of us elected in 2015. One night, after a few pints, on the House of Commons terrace, Pete Wishart yelled at me, 'You stole all my media!' He was stung when I criticised his efforts as acting Chief Whip in relation to office accommodation for SNP MPs that resulted in many of my colleagues having offices so far from the chamber they were of limited utility, and later I read in the newspapers that I was offering colleagues 'plush offices for votes'.

---

[7] https://www.dailyrecord.co.uk/news/scottish-news/watch-foodbank-nurse-confronted-over-10640525

This wasn't true. Blackford, however, was promising frontbench roles in return for votes. It turned out later that he had made the mistake of promising the coveted (by some) role of Chief Whip to both his campaign manager Stewart McDonald and to Patrick Grady. He gave the role to Grady and kept him there for a long time, despite a staffer's claims of sexual harassment against Patrick, which were covered up for years.[8] All of which ensured Stewart's dangerous enmity.

I tried to appeal to my colleagues' better instincts. I promised that on my watch no one would be thrown under the bus, and where complaints were made or press stories were published people would have a fair hearing and be defended properly where appropriate. It didn't quite work, but it came close.

There was a lot of press interest in the election, no doubt fuelled by the strength of the briefing against me, and as I left the room on the committee corridor where the results had been announced and walked through the journalists assembled outside, BBC Radio 4's Carolyn Quinn said to me, 'Are your colleagues mad?'

I was flattered, but although I was disappointed by the result, I was not as shocked by it as she clearly was. However, I was worried for my future position in the group, and I was right to be. Blackford reappointed me as the Justice and Home Affairs spokesperson, but from that point onwards he and his inner circle, which was largely a boys' club, apart from Kirsty Blackman, made every attempt to undermine me, including a particularly childish ploy to prevent me from sitting on the frontbench at PMQs or in any set-piece debate in which I wasn't down to speak.

This was done by sending Ian Blackford's right-hand man Chris Law into the chamber early in the morning to reserve all the available spaces with prayer cards for the boys' club and Kirsty Blackman. Even a party loyalist such as Deidre Brock was moved to comment on occasions that the frontbench was looking a bit too male.

---

8 https://www.bbc.co.uk/news/uk-scotland-scotland-politics-61926125#:~:text=%22I%20am%20absolutely%20determined%20that,questions%20that%20must%20be%20answered%22.

Philippa Whitford and I found ourselves excluded from the sort of Brexit strategy meetings that had previously taken place under Alex Salmond's chairmanship. To be fair, we were not at all sure that they were happening anymore – there was little sign of any considered strategy – but if they were, we were not invited, even though each of us had a high profile in the Brexit debates in the chamber and served on the relevant select committee.

Frequently when I tried to initiate a discussion about our Brexit or independence strategy at group meetings, I found myself shouted down by male MPs close to Blackford and Blackford himself. Repeatedly, my interventions were mischaracterised as criticisms of staff rather than criticisms of our strategic approach. Both Ian Blackford and Kirsty Blackman, the group leader and deputy, went so far as to insinuate to MPs and staff at the group meeting that staff were complaining about me.

However, it was not just my position in the group that I now needed to worry about. I was told by friendly SNP staffers that there had been very real concern that if I had succeeded in taking the leadership of the Westminster group, I would have used it as a platform to challenge for the leadership of the party. At that stage nothing was further from my mind. In fact, at no stage have I ever planned a leadership attempt. The difficulty for me was that over a sustained period from 2017 onwards this was much speculated upon and led to a level of paranoia that sealed my fate when Sturgeon and those around her decided to move against anyone seen as a threat to her leadership.

The first sign of serious trouble for me came in December 2017, when I was notified of an investigation into my alleged behaviour towards a member of staff. In due course I would discover that the Westminster group had introduced a new complaints process which appeared to be very similar to the complaints process that had been devised by Scottish government civil servants to address allegations against Alex Salmond. In my case the allegations were of bullying; in his they were of sexual harassment.

The processes used against us had a lot in common, including the fact that neither has ever been used against anyone else. In my case this was particularly surprising, given that at the time the Westminster leadership were aware of the existence of complaints of sexual harassment by a Westminster staffer against Chief Whip Patrick Grady, dating back to 2016. Instead of being investigated using the new process, these were covered up for years until the staffer in question went to the Parliamentary Standards Commissioner and the press.[9]

Ultimately, the complaint against me was dropped, but the whole process was decidedly Kafkaesque. For example, in common with Alex, it took me months to find out what the complaints were, and the initial proposal was that the person who had counselled the complainant and carried out the investigation should also be the adjudicator.

It took Alex and me a while to realise what was going on. When we did, he advised me that my enemies in the party would do their best to tie me up in fighting the moves against me in order to weaken my effectiveness as a parliamentarian. I was determined that they would not succeed.

---

[9] See footnote 4, page 37.

3 THE BRITISH CONSTITUTION IS FALLING DOWN

The parliamentary wrangling over Brexit, and the unlawful prorogation of parliament 2018–20

It's the summer of 2019 and I'm sitting in the square of a little town in Provence called Rasteau. I've been visiting friends here for years and attending the local *fêtes du vin*, but this year there is a new guest at our table, former Labour spin doctor Alastair Campbell, who has a house in the region. My hosts, Joanne Delaney and Christophe Link, were beside themselves with excitement when I revealed that I'd got to know Campbell because we were both involved in the cross-party campaign for a people's vote. Former schoolteachers, one Irish and one German, Joanne and Christophe fled the United Kingdom after the Brexit vote to run cycling holidays and *gîtes* while following events in parliament avidly. They insisted I invite Alastair for the evening. While we're sitting there, Alastair takes a call from Michael Heseltine: 'Michael, you'll never guess who I'm sitting here with. Joanna Cherry from the SNP. We're just discussing how we might prevent Johnson from proroguing parliament.'

It was not the sort of company I expected to be keeping when I entered parliament as a Scottish National Party MP in 2015, but adversity makes for strange bedfellows. I remain of the view that it was right for SNP MPs to try to roll back the decision to leave the EU or at the very least ameliorate the impact on Scotland. Many of our critics in the independence movement believe we wasted our time 'trying to save England'. However, Scots voted to remain in the EU, and it was incumbent upon the Scottish government and the SNP Westminster group to do what we could to protect our society and economy from Brexit, which has proved to be the damaging mistake that so many of us predicted.

The strategy set out in 'Scotland's Place in Europe' was the right strategy – to seek compromise and, if that was not available, to do all we could to protect Scotland from Brexit. Ultimately, that included seeking to secure a second vote on the issue across the UK as well as a second vote on Scottish independence.

The setback of the 2017 General Election, in which we had lost 21 of our 56 MPs, could hardly have been presented as an overwhelming mandate for a second independence referendum. Nicola Sturgeon had put her plans for this on hold, and so the focus of SNP MPs at Westminster was necessarily on stopping or ameliorating Brexit.

Independence fundamentalists are often very critical of us for this approach. Not long before he died, I asked Alex Salmond whether he thought I had done the right thing during the Brexit years, and he said to me that I had 'played the best I could with the hand I was dealt'. That is certainly what I tried to do. What many independence-supporting fundamentalists fail to appreciate is that independence would be easier if England stayed in the EU, or at least as close to the single market and customs union as possible. Moreover, supporting the principle that when circumstances change people should have a second vote was clearly advantageous to the campaign for a second independence referendum.

At the end of June 2017, with little choice but to step back from her intention to hold a second independence referendum imminently, Nicola Sturgeon announced a 'reset' of her timetable. Previously, she had called for a second independence referendum to be held in the autumn of 2018 or the spring of 2019, but now she said she was going to delay her plans to introduce the legislation necessary to hold a referendum. However, she claimed that it was still 'likely' that a referendum would be held by 2021.[1]

Alex Salmond told me Nicola had been so shaken by the outcome of the election that it had been her intention to shelve her plans for a second independence referendum altogether, and it was he who persuaded her to instead announce a 'reset'. In June 2017 she was still seeking out and listening to his advice. That would change in the months to come. It would also become clear that her 'reset' was the first step in a strategy of kicking the can down the road, until such time as the road ran out.

Notwithstanding the implacable opposition of the British government to a second independence referendum, and Labour's equivocation on a second vote on Brexit, opposition unionist parties handed the SNP a gift when so many of their membership conceded the need for a second Brexit referendum. As Ian Murray, the Labour MP for Edinburgh South and a leading opponent of Scottish independence, argued, 'Voters have a right to change their minds when all the facts and the consequences are laid bare in front of them.'[2]

At the time Ian seemed not to grasp that the same arguments could be used to justify a second vote on Scottish independence based on the broken promises of the Better Together campaign, including their assurance that the best way to preserve their EU citizenship was to vote to remain part of the United Kingdom.

Nicola Sturgeon was not the only one having to revisit her plans in the wake of the 2017 General Election. Theresa May, who had hoped to bolster her majority in a snap election, instead found herself having to do a deal with the Democratic Unionist Party. Rather than entering Brexit talks with the EU in possession of a strengthened mandate, she was doing so as a lame duck.

The process of triggering Article 50 had already resulted in one of three major constitutional litigations that would mark the period

---

[1] https://www.bbc.co.uk/news/uk-scotland-40415457

[2] https://www.newstatesman.com/politics/the-staggers/2018/01/fanatical-eurosceptics-want-you-think-brexit-inevitable-they-re-wrong

between the referendum and the UK's eventual exit. This first case, known as *Miller I*,[3] was brought by campaigner Gina Miller to challenge Theresa May's proposed use of prerogative powers to trigger the withdrawal process from the EU under Article 50 of the Treaty of the EU. The UK Supreme Court ruled that the prerogative powers could not be used to nullify rights enacted by parliament through primary legislation and that parliament must have its say.

The Lord Advocate, then James Wolffe QC, intervened on behalf of the Scottish government to argue that the legislation notifying the UK's intention to leave the EU required the consent of the Scottish Parliament.

The Sewel convention provides that Westminster will not normally legislate on devolved matters without the consent of the Scottish Parliament. It had been put on a statutory footing in the Scotland Act 2016. However, the UK Supreme Court ruled that the convention was non-justiciable, meaning that it cannot be enforced by a court. Accordingly, we were left with an unenforceable rule which was to be broken repeatedly in the years to come.

Many Scottish academic lawyers were disappointed but not surprised by the Supreme Court's decision. As some have argued, the UK Supreme Court has never really been terribly interested in defending the devolution settlement.[4] Their approach to construing the checks and balances in devolution's constitutional settlement was conservative with a small 'c' to say the least, and in marked contrast to the more expansive constitutional approach that they took later on in the case concerning the unlawful prorogation of parliament.

Insouciance towards Scotland's place in the UK constitution has always been a feature of the British establishment, unless a real threat is perceived. As matters progressed at Westminster, despite any fine words or intentions from Theresa May in the immediate

---

[3] Miller v Sec of State for Exiting the EU [2017] UKSC 5

[4] See for example https://strathprints.strath.ac.uk/62791/1/McHarg_2018_Constitutional_change_and_territorial_consent_the_miller_case_and_the_sewel_convention.pdf

aftermath of the Brexit referendum and perhaps because of the intransigence of Nicola Sturgeon and the perceived weakening of the SNP's position after 2017 election, consultation with the devolved governments became a formality.[5] Although machinery was established for that consultation to take place and meetings were held, my colleagues who participated, such as Mike Russell, said they were very much a box-ticking exercise. Quite often Scottish ministers would learn nothing that they hadn't read in the papers already. If something important was about to happen there was no forewarning, and the Scottish government got sight of white papers and bills at the same time as the general public.

As Brexit proceeded, the UK government regularly forged ahead with legislation that affected devolved matters in the face of opposition from the Scottish Parliament. The arrogance of their disregard was insufferable, but apart from emoting no concrete action was taken by the SNP leadership. Many in the SNP grassroots and wider independence movement became restive. The judgment in *Miller I* and the behaviour towards the devolved governments that followed served to underline the powerlessness of the Scottish government to protect the country from the consequences of Brexit, and the need to find a way to hold a second vote on independence before the UK left the European Union. It was felt that the Scottish government and the SNP Westminster group needed to be more proactive.

However, whereas *Miller I* may have marginalised Scotland, the next two big constitutional cases would put Scotland at the heart of proceedings. I was one of six successful litigants in *Wightman and Others*,[6] which concerned whether the UK's notice to leave the EU could be unilaterally revoked, and I was the lead litigant in Cherry v Advocate General,[7] concerning Boris Johnson's unlawful prorogation of parliament.

---

5 https://www.tandfonline.com/doi/epdf/10.1080/21582041.2023.2197881?needAccess=true

6 *Wightman and others v Secretary of State for Exiting the European Union* (Case C-621/18), EU:C:2018:999, 10 December 2018

7 Cherry v Advocate General for Scotland [2019] UKSC 41

These were very much initiatives in which I engaged as an individual MP rather than on behalf of the SNP. The decision to strike out on my own was prompted by my frustration at the inability of the Scottish government or the Westminster group to get results from its Brexit strategy and a growing realisation that there was not a strategy as such at all. In relation to both litigations the party leadership were either obstructive or mere bystanders, until it looked like I was going to be on the winning side. When I was, they were happy to adopt the wins as SNP victories.

There was no surprise but plenty of outrage when Theresa May was willing to press ahead with the EU Withdrawal Bill without the legislative consent of the Scottish Parliament. Originally known as the 'Great Repeal Bill', this legislation was designed to repeal the European Communities Act 1972 and to end the supremacy of EU law in the UK domestic legal systems and the jurisdiction of the European Court of Justice. However, to ensure a smooth transition and a degree of continuity, it also copied over a lot of EU law to the UK statute book. The idea being that these EU laws would be gradually repealed or altered thereafter, once the 'freedoms' of Brexit had been realised. To do this, the UK government proposed to give themselves sweeping 'Henry VIII powers', allowing ministers to make changes to legislation without having to go through meaningful parliamentary scrutiny. The Scottish government joined the outcry against the assumption of such wide powers by the executive. They described the bill as a 'power grab' that threatened the autonomy of the Scottish Parliament in relation to devolved competences, as well as undermining the ability of the UK Parliament to scrutinise legislation.

The Scottish Parliament voted – with the cross-party support of everyone apart from the Tories and one Liberal Democrat – to withhold consent to the bill. This was, of course, ignored. Then, when the Scottish Parliament tried to pass its own Legal Continuity Bill, dealing with the consequences of Brexit for devolved powers, it was challenged by the British government in the UK Supreme Court. While the hearing of the case was pending before the court, the Tories retrospectively changed the law in the House of Lords by amending the Withdrawal Bill to render large parts of the

Continuity Bill *ultra vires* or outwith the powers of the Scottish Parliament.

When those amendments came back from the Lords to the Commons, Scottish MPs were given just nineteen minutes to debate their implications, and all that time was taken up by the government minister. In response, the SNP staged a walkout from the Commons in June 2018.

The walkout was spontaneous rather than planned. It took place because of an altercation between Ian Blackford and the Speaker, John Bercow, during Prime Minister's Questions. In protest at the lack of debate and the 'power grab', Ian brought Prime Minister's Questions to a halt by moving that the House should sit in private. Bercow seemed unsure about what to do at first, but when Blackford refused to sit back down, he suspended Ian for the rest of the day's sitting. I and the other SNP MPs walked out with him in protest.

On the TV footage I can be seen in a pink jacket gesticulating at the Speaker with a huge bundle of papers in my hand. There was due to be a debate on amendments to the bill later that afternoon and I had been planning to take part in it. My gesticulations were not so much directed at John Bercow as at the whole House. What I wanted to say was: 'Here we are, ready to do our jobs properly and well prepared, and yet we are treated with utter disrespect – that's the reason why we are off.'

Ian was escorted from the parliamentary premises and the rest of us accompanied him out to talk to the media, but then there was confusion about what we should do next. Some, including Pete Wishart and Stephen Gethins, who, like me, were due to speak that afternoon in the debate on amendments to the bill, indicated their intention to return to the chamber. I felt that this would look weak and silly (and indeed those who did return were mocked and chided by other MPs) and I declined to join them. I was exasperated because it was clear to me that although Ian and the Chief Whip had contemplated a walkout in advance of PMQs, they had no plan about how to take things forward thereafter.

Our actions were very popular with the public. We received a rousing reception in a Westminster pub when the group met up with Ian later that evening, and when I returned to Edinburgh that weekend many constituents told me that they thought we had done the right thing. However, like so many SNP initiatives during the Brexit saga, it was a short-term tactic that was not part of an overall strategy. There was no plan to capitalise on what had happened, so the excitement around it fizzled out quickly and business returned to normal.

As time progressed the movement for a second vote on Brexit, 'the people's vote' had been gathering momentum. I had been working behind the scenes for months to try to persuade the SNP leadership of the wisdom of supporting this position. Various leading lights of the people's vote campaign were desperate to speak to Nicola Sturgeon and, not unsurprisingly, given my high profile as an SNP spokesperson, assumed that I would be able to set up such a meeting. They found the door shut in their face on numerous occasions – even when they came up to Edinburgh specially to try to see her. Internal pressure behind the scenes also failed to prompt proper discussion or a decision, so prior to the party's autumn conference in 2018, Tommy Sheppard and I prepared an emergency motion urging the party to adopt support for a second vote as party policy. A head of steam was clearly building up behind the position despite one or two vocal opponents in the party, including Pete Wishart and Angus MacNeil.

How I found out that the SNP were finally going to officially support the policy typifies how the party was being run at that time and the lack of communication between the leadership and mere mortals such as myself and Tommy. Nicola Sturgeon could not possibly allow policy to be achieved or dictated by an initiative that was anything other than her own, and so it was that when I was driving to Glasgow along the M8 for the conference I heard it announced on the radio that the party would be supporting a second vote. Nicola had moved to pre-empt the inevitable result of the motion lodged by Tommy and me, and, after months of dithering, she had decided to make the policy her own.[8]

---

[8] https://www.bbc.co.uk/news/uk-scotland-scotland-politics-46044517

While Nicola subsequently basked in the adulation of English Remainers, unusually for the SNP, colleagues who were unhappy about the decision were allowed to rail against it without consequence to the extent of breaking the whip.[9] This was in marked contrast to what occurred to those of us who later opposed Nicola's policy on self-identification of sex. However, the concerns of the critics were not without foundation. There was quite a lot of uneasiness about opening us up to the possibility of a confirmatory vote after any pro-independence referendum. That said, those of us in favour of a second EU vote were alive to the risks for the independence strategy (such as it was) and worked cross-party to try to alleviate some of the concerns.

Philippa Whitford, the MP for Central Ayrshire, and I got involved in a cross-party group, which began to meet daily in autumn 2018. The group included prominent backbenchers from across the House: Chris Bryant and Ben Bradshaw from Labour; Dominic Grieve, Anna Soubry, Justine Greening, Jo Johnson (brother of Boris and far more reasonable) from the Tories; Tom Brake from the Lib Dems, Liz Saville-Roberts from Plaid Cymru; and Caroline Lucas, the sole Green MP at that time.

It was very collegiate, and a lot of work went into ensuring we could achieve as broad a coalition as possible. A huge amount of time was spent on discussing parliamentary tactics. On the question of a second vote Phillippa and I urged the group to get the wording of any amendment right so that the SNP group could live with it.

For me it was an instructive experience working with seasoned parliamentarians such as Dominic Grieve and Chris Bryant, and I learned a lot. I saw how business was done at a high level between different parties, and I got to better understand some of the issues faced by Conservative and Labour colleagues in dealing with the Brexit morass. Both of their parties were hopelessly divided over

---

9 https://www.heraldscotland.com/news/17533645.snp-mps-rebel-nicola-sturgeon-peoples-vote/#:~:text=The%20option%20is%20seen%20as,resentment%20and%20reverse%20the%20result.

the UK's relationship with the EU, but there was at least a degree of communication between those on either side of strong internal party disagreements. In the Conservative Party, Remainers and Leavers managed to maintain personal friendships across the bitter divide. It was not thus in the SNP.

I also could not but help notice the contrast between the detailed strategic discussions that took place in the cross-party group, which met very regularly, and what went on at the SNP weekly group meeting. There, particularly after Alex Salmond lost his seat in June 2017, no such discussions took place, and we proceeded on the basis of diktats handed down by Nicola Sturgeon and communicated to the group by Ian Blackford. Debate and dissent were strongly discouraged.

I once complained to a friend who was a Cabinet Secretary at Holyrood that it was hard to know what our Brexit strategy was, and he said that I should find out in the same way that he did, by reading the newspapers. The same Cabinet Secretary, frustrated with the intransigence of the Lord Advocate, James Wolffe QC, on the competence of the Scottish Parliament to legislate for another independence referendum, asked me if I would put together an informal group of lawyers to give the government alternative advice. This put me in a very difficult position, as it could have been interpreted as undermining or usurping the role of the Lord Advocate. So, I replied that if the Cabinet were dissatisfied with the advice they were getting, perhaps they should reconsider the First Minister's choice of law officer.

There were plenty of lawyers who thought an argument could be constructed that the Scottish Parliament could competently pass a bill. Had Nicola prioritised this issue she could have asked potential candidates for Lord Advocate about their position on the question before appointing them, to ensure they were on side. That she either did not do so or did so and proceeded with the appointment of two law officers in a row notwithstanding their scepticism on the issue is telling.

There was also quite a bit of discussion in legal circles about whether the notice to quit given by the UK government under Article 50 of the EU treaty could be revoked. *Miller I* had proceeded on the understanding that it could not. Gina Miller's counsel David Pannick QC drew an analogy with the impossibility of recalling a bullet that had left the barrel of a gun. However, many prominent lawyers with an expertise in EU law thought that this was both wrong in law and a tactical error.

My own view was that there was no point in planning for a people's vote with the aim of halting or reversing Brexit if it wouldn't be possible to unilaterally revoke the Article 50 notice. I'd had discussions about this with some prominent QCs in London, many of whom were nervous about bringing court action to establish the position, lest it result in an outcome that was unfavourable to the holding of a second vote.

I had also had discussions with Aidan O'Neill QC, an eminent Scottish silk with an expertise in EU law, and with Jolyon Maugham, an English tax silk who had become a campaigner against Brexit. They both felt the bullet analogy was wrong.

The decision was taken to litigate in Scotland. The English judges who had delivered the judgment in *Miller I* had been attacked in the press as enemies of the people and widely reviled not just by members of the public who had voted for Brexit, but also by members of the ruling Conservative Party, including some very close to the government. Liz Truss, who at that time was occupying the post of Secretary of State for Justice and Lord Chancellor, declined to defend them. There had been no similar criticism in the Scottish media or by Scottish politicians, and it was felt that the Scottish judiciary might find it easier to make a ruling given the very different atmosphere surrounding the Brexit debate in Scotland.

Our decision to proceed was not tactically popular among some London-based Remainers. Both Jolyon and I were leaned on quite heavily not to be part of the case. On one memorable occasion I was invited to a lunch of high-flying female lawyers and businesswomen clearly designed to talk me out of it. Nevertheless, I persisted.

A group of MEPs and MSPs led by the prominent and widely respected Green MSP Andy Wightman was put together. In addition to Andy there was his Green MSP colleague Ross Greer, Labour MEPs David Martin and Catherine Stihler, and the SNP MEP Alyn Smith. Jolyon Maugham, who was organising the group, felt it needed two MPs, and he persuaded me, together with Lib Dem Christine Jardine, MP for Edinburgh West, to join the group. Our solicitor dubbed us 'the magnificent 7', but when the case fell at the first hurdle we became 6 – sometimes known as 'the Scottish 6' – when Christine Jardine decided to pull out.

Given the presence of an SNP MEP in the original group, I assumed that there would be no objection from the SNP to my taking part. Still, I thought I had better check first. I messaged Mike Russell, Nicola Sturgeon's Minister for UK Negotiations on Scotland's Place in Europe, someone who until then had been very supportive and whom I viewed as a personal friend. To my surprise he was lukewarm to say the least. His advice was that I should not do it as it was 'not seen as a worthwhile thing in terms of the overall strategy'. I queried why Alyn was involved and was told that he didn't ask first.

I remained of the view that it would be extremely useful to clarify the position in order to assist the democratic process. My view was reinforced when, on 13 December 2017, Dominic Grieve joined forces with opposition MPs to secure an explicit legal guarantee of a 'meaningful vote' for parliament on the terms of any Brexit deal.[10]

I spoke with Mike again, and he was clear that while he did not think it was worthwhile, it was up to me to choose whether to do it. I decided to get on board and texted Mike to tell him of my decision. I was rather taken aback at the vehemence of Mike's response: he disagreed with the decision and said it would add weight to the idea that I was 'not a team player'.

I was very annoyed by the team player comment. It seemed rather unfair to me, as I had put in quite a shift covering major bills and debates in the Commons and media bids while other SNP MPs were taking a decidedly more relaxed approach to parliamentary life in the bars of Westminster. Plus, I felt I had taken one for the team regarding the 'nursegate' affair. I replied stating as much and telling him that I intended to proceed.

---

10 https://www.bbc.co.uk/news/uk-politics-42346192

Despite the spiky tone of these exchanges, Mike and I remained on good terms at this stage. A couple of months later, when, as a member of the Exiting the EU Select Committee, I was afforded access to the controversial Brexit impact assessments, which the UK government had tried to withhold from parliament, I took detailed notes and passed the information on to Mike after the British government had refused to let him see them.

The Article 50 litigation got off to rather a shaky start. The petitioners sought a reference to the European Court of Justice for a ruling on the question of whether Article 50 could be revoked. In February 2018 the judge at first instance refused to let the application for judicial review proceed, ruling that the issue was hypothetical because there was no evidence that the UK government intended to revoke the notification. He also considered that the matter was not justiciable.

I thought long and hard about whether to stay and support an appeal, given the financial and reputational risks, but was persuaded to do so out of loyalty to the other petitioners and a feeling that the judgment at first instance was wrong.

If there was to be a meaningful vote on the terms of any withdrawal agreement struck between the UK and the EU, it seemed clear to me that in the absence of an acceptable withdrawal agreement parliament might contemplate revoking the notification. Accordingly, the question was not hypothetical. In the event my presence as the sole MP among the remaining group proved to be important for that very reason. The appeal court remitted the case back for a fresh application for judicial review. Again, it was refused as too speculative. However, by the time we appealed that judgment the EU Withdrawal Bill had passed into law and was now an Act of Parliament. Section 13 enshrined the requirement for a meaningful vote in law. On that basis it was held that the question was not hypothetical, and the petition was competent at least at the instance of an MP, because MPs who would be required to vote needed to be properly advised as to their options. The Inner House referred the question to the Court of Justice of the European Union.

I flew to Luxembourg for the hearing before the Grand Chamber on 27 November 2018 feeling optimistic about the outcome.

The UK government had got themselves into the ludicrous position of refusing to argue the case on its merits. All their counsel could do was harp on about the issue of admissibility, arguing that because the UK government had no intention of revoking the Article 50 notice, the issue was purely hypothetical. Their approach clearly irritated the court. By contrast, Aidan O'Neill, in a virtuoso performance, had the court eating out of his hand.

Barely two weeks later, on 10 December 2018, the Grand Chamber ruled unanimously in our favour. Now there was no doubt that both the parliamentary vote and any second referendum on Brexit would be meaningful votes. The victory breathed new hope into those of us who thought that stopping Brexit was possible.

Naturally the SNP welcomed the win, despite Mike Russell's criticism of me for embarking on the case at all. Alex Salmond took Fraser and me out for dinner to the Delaunay in London to celebrate, and I also held a party in my house in Edinburgh. It was attended by an interesting cross section of nationalists, Remainers and legal figures including the Lord Advocate. Andy Wightman was the guest of honour. One guest, the late David Gow, a distinguished journalist,[11] opined privately that he thought this was the start of my campaign for the SNP leadership. Another SNP friend remarked excitedly that you knew you were at a good nationalist party when on your way to the bathroom you saw Lesley Riddoch, the influential broadcaster, activist and journalist, in the study writing her newspaper column.

As 2019 dawned there was increasing chaos in the Tory government, marked by some extraordinary ineptitude over ferry procurement that came to be known as the Seaborne Freight scandal. Matters came to a head at the Brexit Select Committee where I got the opportunity to cross-examine one of the hapless ministers in the frame.

The Select Committee for Exiting the European Union had been set up in October 2016 with Hilary Benn as chair. Angus Robertson decided that I should be appointed as one of the two SNP

[11] https://www.theguardian.com/media/2025/nov/03/david-gow-obituary

representatives, the other being Peter Grant, MP for Glenrothes. At that stage the SNP had a standing Brexit subcommittee chaired by Alex Salmond which was dictating our strategy. Alex thought I should put myself forward as deputy chair of the select committee. A plan was agreed but was not carried through, because Peter, whose support was vital, arrived too late at the committee to propose me, having managed to lock himself in his hotel room. In the event the Conservative Leaver MP John Whittingdale was elected deputy chair. This was probably the correct and inevitable move to reflect the divisions on the committee.

Fellow members of the committee over its lifetime included Michael Gove, Christopher Chope, Jacob Rees-Mogg, Andrea Jenkyns, Dominic Raab, Craig Mackinlay and Sammy Wilson, so it was lively to say the least. Hilary Benn as chair had the patience of a saint and is to be credited with navigating the committee through some very difficult times.

Through repeated visits to Brussels, Paris, Dublin and Berlin, I got to meet with and understand the positions of parliamentarians from across Europe. It was also a great opportunity to get the SNP government position across and to emphasise Scotland's pro-EU credentials. Throughout these visits, and in other unconnected visits to the West Bank, Rwanda and Strasbourg, I was greatly impressed by the support afforded to visiting British parliamentarians by the British diplomatic service. I also got to know the Irish, French and German consuls and ambassadors well and to gain an appreciation for the importance of the work done by diplomatic services in general. One of the highlights of my time as an MP occurred on a committee visit to Paris, where we dined and stayed overnight at the Hôtel de Charost, the British Ambassador's residence, just a few doors down from the Élysée Palace. Built in 1720 by a senior courtier of Louis XV, the Hôtel de Charost was bought by Napoleon's sister in 1803 and sold to the Duke of Wellington on behalf of the British government. I don't think I will ever dine in such splendour again, and my room in the attics with a very old-fashioned marble bathroom and a note of the famous visitors who had stayed there in the past was like going back in time.

I tried not to let these experiences turn my head, and Philippa and I endeavoured to keep our feet on the ground and amuse ourselves by discussing which prime diplomatic real estate Scotland should bid for after independence. I put the Paris residence at the top of my list.

I remained on the committee throughout its life and therefore had a front-row seat to witness the rudeness of some Conservative Brexiteers towards Michel Barnier and their fury when the Deputy President of the European Parliament, Mairead McGuinness, told us all off in a Brussels hotel for the ludicrous way in which the UK was behaving. Afterwards, Philippa Whitford, the SNP MP for Central Ayrshire who had replaced Peter Grant on the committee, and I were walking up to the EU Commission building behind two of the Tory MPs on the committee and overheard them bewailing the mistake Britain had made in 'giving' the Irish their independence and 'bailing them out' in recent years. As women of Irish descent, we were more amused than put out by their arrogance and exceptionalism.

Arrogance combined with incompetence was a recurring theme in the approach adopted by Conservative Brexiteers, including government ministers. In late December 2018 it was revealed that the government had negotiated a £13.8 million contract with a ferry company to cover commercial shipping contingencies in the event of a no-deal Brexit. The trouble was that the company had no ships and no trading history. When parliament reconvened after Christmas on 7 January 2019, a minister was summoned to the Commons to answer an urgent question, during which I raised the fact that the contract had been awarded without a competitive tendering process. The public contracts regulations permitted this only in emergency situations brought about by unforeseeable events. It seemed to me that a no-deal Brexit had been eminently foreseeable for some time. Indeed, the government had had staff working on no-deal Brexit planning for two years. I asked if the government would publish the legal advice that had permitted them to proceed without a competitive tendering process. I did not get an answer.

Two days later, Christopher Heaton-Harris, the Parliamentary Under-Secretary of State at the Department for Exiting the

EU (DEXU), appeared before the Brexit Select Committee and I cross-examined him on the justification for the lack of a competitive tendering process, without an answer. The combination of my persistence and his arrogant evasiveness meant that the video of my cross-examination went viral. Andrew Neil tweeted: 'Joanna Cherry should have her own interview show. Magnificent, persistent questioning.'

I was pretty chuffed, and more so when my concerns about the tendering process were vindicated. On 9 February the contract with Seaborne Freight was cancelled. Eurotunnel sued the UK government for their breach of competition law and the case was settled out of court for £33 million.

In the normal course of events, any other SNP MP who had come up with such a coup would have had praise lavished upon them at the group meeting. Instead, MPs close to Ian Blackford complained that I had stolen the thunder of Alan Brown, the then SNP Transport spokesperson, and a rather unpleasant scene ensued at the SNP Westminster group meeting where I was harangued by him and other members of the boys' club. This was a typical example of how petty jealousies and egos prevented the group from working effectively as a team. It was also typical of the misogyny that was allowed to flourish under Blackford's leadership. A good leader would have tackled this problem. Blackford did not and was happy to take the side of my critics.

It was exasperating to face such internal antagonism when I was already dealing with a good deal of hostility from Leave campaigners due to the high-profile role I was playing in parliament. Throughout the parliamentary Brexit turmoil, the atmosphere outwith parliament was also very lively. My own experience of this ranged from a rather posh-looking well-dressed lady in a *Question Time* audience at Bognor Regis who stuck her tongue out at me, to protestors outside the Supreme Court who suggested that I should be hanged from the nearest tree. Tory ministers who had been jostled by Remainers outside parliament were afforded a police escort. SNP MPs were not afforded the same courtesy, and on one occasion, as I walked into parliament, I was accompanied by a Leave campaigner repeatedly shouting, 'You're a fucking disgrace,' in my face. The tension was offset by a Remainer, clearly a fan of the SNP's approach as well as Jacobite history, who shouted encouragement with the words: 'You didn't turn back at Derby after all.'

During a huge Leave rally outside parliament I was horrified to see an Orange Order band from Scotland marching past. The last thing that needed to be added into the mix was the blight of sectarianism. Any Catholic of my generation will have experienced the intimidatory chill of these marches, and it was alarming to see them getting in on the act.

Every time I spoke in the chamber I would receive abusive emails from Leavers. Mindful of the lynching threats, I was alarmed one day to receive an email entitled, 'We've got a tree for you.' I was all set to contact the authorities until Fraser pointed out that it was from climate-change campaigners who were gifting saplings to MPs in exchange for a photo opportunity.

At times I did fear for my personal safety during the Brexit controversies. It didn't help that I was beginning to feel rather isolated within the SNP group. The approach of cutting me out of decision-making by Blackford's boys' club continued. I found this and the antagonism towards me from Blackford and his supporters more difficult to deal with than the abuse I got from the pro-Brexit mob – because it was coming from my colleagues. However, I was determined to keep going because I could see that my work was yielding results.

By the end of March 2019, the hapless Theresa May had not won any of the meaningful votes on the deal she had secured in November 2018. Her party was in open revolt, and she was shedding cabinet ministers. Unable to command a majority, she faced a deadlocked, dysfunctional parliament whose machinations were fast becoming a spectator sport across Europe and the wider world.

MPs decided to take matters into their own hands and hold a series of indicative votes to try to establish if there was a way forward that commanded a majority. This involved an unprecedented move led by Hilary Benn and Tory MP Sir Oliver Letwin to take control of the parliamentary order paper, which is normally the sole preserve of the government of the day.

Two rounds of indicative votes took place on 27 March and 1 April 2019. The first round of options included leaving without a deal; if there was to be no leaving deal, a transition period while a trade deal was negotiated (the 'Malthouse compromise'); the option of EEA/EFTA; the option of keeping the customs union; negotiating a Norway plus deal ('Common Market 2.0'); a Labour frontbench plan; a confirmatory referendum plan (the 'Kyle–Wilson' plan); and my plan of revoking the Article 50 notice to avoid a no deal.

Apart from the Labour frontbench plan, all the options were sponsored by backbenchers. The revocation option was sponsored by me with cross-party support from Tories, Labour, TIG (the new Time for Change group of independent MPs who had defected from Labour or the Tories), Liberal Democrats and Plaid Cymru, including Dominic Grieve, Ben Bradshaw, Sarah Wollaston and Liz Saville-Roberts. It was only possible because of the Wightman case, and I had worked with Jo Maugham to draft it carefully.

These eight options had been chosen from sixteen submissions. It was up to the Speaker, John Bercow, to select the options upon which we would vote, and I worked hard to persuade him to select mine, including chatting with him on the telephone from a café in John Lewis on Oxford Street on the Sunday afternoon before the second round of votes.

After the first round of voting there was no majority for any option. Internal party splits abounded, but the SNP were united in supporting my motion and the pro-referendum option. We voted against the hard Brexit solutions and abstained on the so-called soft Brexit options.

A further unsuccessful vote on Theresa May's deal followed on 29 March, and then we were into a second round of indicative votes. My revocation option made the cut together with customs union, Norway plus, and the confirmatory referendum on any deal option. Again, there was no clear winner. I had worked hard to get Labour MPs to support my option, but their whips were uncooperative, and in the event only 121 of a possible 262 Labour MPs voted for it. I was exasperated, and a hilarious meme circulated of me very clearly mouthing the words 'fucking Labour' to Philippa

Whitford as the results were announced. I also had rather a waspish exchange with Keir Starmer on the floor of the House, after which he apologised.[12]

I wasn't the only MP who became a little tired and emotional as matters progressed. Around this time, it was not unusual to see Conservative MPs drunk or weeping in the lobbies as their internal party drama played out. Others like Ken Clarke were cheerful, and on one occasion he remarked that he was spending so much time in the same lobby as the SNP he might have to become an honorary member.

SNP MPs were much criticised for not supporting his customs union option or the Norway plus option. However, we could not do so because access to the single market and its benefits such as freedom of movement were absolutely central to SNP policy. Membership of the customs union alone was not an option that we could support because it would have been economically damaging for Scotland.

Across the UK the public were riveted and, in many cases, infuriated by the parliamentary drama. At the close of ten days of frenetic activity the parliamentary majority against no deal succeeded in forcing a second extension of the Article 50 period to 31 October 2019.

Cross-party talks

With her back against the wall, Theresa May offered cross-party talks. That didn't work, and after a few other procedural machinations in parliament she finally threw in the towel on 22 May 2019, announcing that she would be formally resigning on 7 June and triggering a Tory leadership election.

[12] https://hansard.parliament.uk/Commons/2019-04-01/debates/196307A6-6E12-45F9-A50D-B8FD8018C9A1/EUWithdrawalAndFutureRelationship(Motions)?highlight=edinburgh%20south%20west#contribution-67A135B9-C17E-4E17-9743-DA9F91AC0287

I have often been asked whether Theresa May made any overtures to the SNP to earn our support for her withdrawal agreement. I do not know whether this occurred because, despite the high-profile role I played in the parliamentary process and the early rapport I had established with her, I was not involved in any talks held between the Tories and the SNP at Theresa May's instigation. These are matters that only Ian Blackford or Patrick Grady, the Chief Whip, could answer. As I have argued elsewhere in this book, there was a time when the SNP could have played our hand with considerably more strength and skill, when Theresa May was open to making concessions to the Scottish government at the outset of the process. The ultimate prize for us would have been to secure for the Scottish parliament the right to hold a second independence referendum at a time of our choosing in return for supporting a soft Brexit for the UK.

Events within the SNP

Notwithstanding my pivotal role in the indicative votes episode, with which the SNP were happy to go along, in the period between Easter and summer 2019, a significant amount of my time and energy was spent fighting off attempts from within the party to smear me as a bully. I believe these were motivated by spite and encouraged by people close to the top of the party who saw me as a rival to Sturgeon.

Alex Salmond warned me that my enemies within the party would do their best to tie me up in knots to limit my effectiveness as a parliamentarian and to quieten a voice challenging the style of Sturgeon's leadership. I was determined that they would not do so, and as well as advancing my work against Brexit I had also decided to stand for election to the National Executive Committee (NEC) of the party. Two positions are reserved for parliamentarians when the elections take place annually at the autumn party conference, and all delegates are permitted to vote. I topped the poll in November 2018 and started to attend NEC meetings.

The way in which business was conducted at the NEC was another significant eye opener for me. It was clear that both Nicola and Peter micromanaged everything that occurred through a few loyal lieutenants in SNP headquarters and among the NEC delegates. Nothing happened without their say so and it was frowned upon to raise matters that were not part of their agenda.

Every meeting started with a political report, which of necessity focused on Brexit. After Nicola had spoken, the chair would turn to me for the Westminster end of things. I took the opportunity to also raise my concerns about our wider strategy on Brexit and independence. This was not well received.

While I was probably the highest-profile SNP MP at Westminster as a harsh critic and tough scrutineer of the UK government's approach to Brexit, behind the scenes, as 2019 progressed, I was facing vicious briefings against me and an attempt by members of the NEC to have me deselected as an MP. It was immensely frustrating as well as very upsetting to have to deal with this, but mindful of Alex Salmond's advice, I was determined to keep going and to face down the petty manoeuvrings of those close to the SNP leadership. The grudge against me was both personal, because I dared to defy Nicola Sturgeon, and also political, because I was asking questions about investigations into Alex Salmond and because my initiatives were having more success than the Scottish government's. By this time I had also stuck my head above the parapet as a gender-critical feminist.

During the Easter recess I went to stay in a cottage belonging to friends on the Isle of Skye, not far from where Blackford lived. Given the state of relations between us I didn't have any intention of looking him up, but I bumped into his wife (now ex-wife), who invited me for drinks and then dinner. As a result of this, and on the advice of Fraser, when I was made an honorary bencher of the Middle Temple and invited to bring three guests to my installation in early July 2019, I invited Blackford. Fraser felt I needed to return some hospitality to him and could do so while showing off the honour I was being given in recognition of my parliamentary and legal work during the Brexit crisis. As Fraser said, it would act as a reminder of the esteem I was held in outside parliament and would perhaps encourage him to lay off me.

It was also meant to be an olive branch. By this time, I had been fully exonerated of any bullying charges after an independent investigation into the complaints against me by the Parliamentary Standards Commissioner, and over the summer of 2019 a period of relative calm within the SNP followed, as we all turned our attention to the internal machinations of the Tory leadership battle triggered by Theresa May's resignation statement on 24 May 2019.

A government of national unity?

On 23 July 2019, as many of us had feared, Boris Johnson was declared the winner of the Tory leadership election. On 24 July he was appointed PM and parliament promptly went into recess to recover from the shock.

Plotting by cross-party grandees to stave off a no-deal Brexit continued. A proposal to hold a motion of no confidence in Boris Johnson's government and to replace it with a cross-party government of national unity received media coverage.[13] The main problem for the plotters was who might lead such a government. The leader of the opposition, Jeremy Corbyn, was unacceptable to Tories who might otherwise come on board. Various other more unifying names, including Hilary Benn and Ken Clarke, were mooted. But, of course, the very idea itself was problematic for the SNP. In the first place, a coalition with even remnants of the Conservative and Unionist Party was unthinkable for obvious reasons. Secondly, even the name itself would have been anathema to most nationalists. When your *raison d'être* is to leave the United Kingdom, participating in a government of national unity makes no sense. The last thing any SNP MP wanted was to be like a latter-day Michael Collins coming home with his treaty to face a vocal body of fury.

Of course, none of this was actually discussed by the SNP Westminster group. Had it been, my view would have been that

---

13 https://www.ft.com/content/00e75fb4-b793-11e9-8a88-aa6628ac896c

we should consider taking part in a cross-party government, provided we got something out of it. To try to pacify our supporters, we would have had to insist it was called a temporary emergency government or something like that, and the price of our support would have been an agreement that a second independence vote should be held by the Scottish Parliament at a time of its choosing.

Instead, the grandees focused on plans for another backbench bill to facilitate a further extension to the Article 50 process, taking us beyond 31 October 2019. When parliament reconvened, it passed what became known as the Benn–Burt Act (after the MPs who co-sponsored it), or, if you were Boris Johnson, the Surrender Act. It was now the law that if parliament had not approved either a deal or a no-deal exit by 19 October, the PM must seek a further extension of the Article 50 process to 31 January 2020.

The unlawful prorogation of parliament

When the Commons reconvened on 3 September, it did so in the middle of one of the biggest parliamentary upheavals in British history. On the advice of Johnson, on 28 August 2019 the Queen had given her consent to parliament being prorogued between 9 and 12 September and 14 October, when a new parliamentary session would start with the State Opening of Parliament.

This turn of events had been anticipated, hence my conversation with Alastair Campbell in Rasteau in August 2019. I had been working with my old friend Jolyon Maugham to put together a group of parliamentarians willing to take legal action in Scotland to obtain an interim interdict (court order) prohibiting any prorogation for an unlawful purpose. Jolyon and I spent a lot of time on the phone while I was on holiday in France, and I had agreed to be the lead litigant. Jolyon had generously offered to afford me and any other parliamentarians who joined in an indemnity against our expenses in the event of losing.

I wrote personally to all my SNP colleagues inviting them to join me. I explained that the upside was lending their name to a very important principle that would be a vote winner in Scotland, while the potential downsides if we lost were modest, perhaps amounting to some mild embarrassment. I also stressed the importance of the indemnity and that Jolyon and I would handle the media. In the end, quite a few colleagues joined in, as well as MPs and peers from other parties, and we ended up with 75 petitioners.

We decided to litigate in Scotland because, unlike their English counterparts, the Scottish courts don't take a vacation over the summer. Litigating in Scotland can also be cheaper, and we thought that the Scottish courts, after *Wightman*, might be more prepared to entertain a hypothetical. At the outset of our litigation Johnson had not yet brought his plan to fruition.

The litigation was up and running, but we hadn't yet obtained an interdict when, on returning on the sleeper from a cross-party event in London, I received a phone call from Ian Blackford telling me that Jacob Rees-Mogg was at Balmoral procuring the Queen's permission to prorogue on the advice of the PM.

I convened a hasty teleconference with my legal team of Aidan O'Neill QC and Balfour and Manson, and we resolved to seek an emergency order to try to prevent the prorogation. We were not successful, and on 4 September the judge at first instance, Lord Doherty, ruled that the matter was non-justiciable. I was undaunted. I thought he was wrong and so did my legal team. Moreover, we had lost *Wightman* at first instance and gone on to triumph in the Inner House (the Scottish appeal court) and the Court of Justice of the European Union.

Parallel action taken by Gina Miller in England was also dismissed. However, on the day the English High Court judges issued their reasons, the Inner House of the Court of Session, Scotland's civil court of appeal, breathed new life into the case with a judgment which ruled that it was unlawful to suspend the UK Parliament for the specific purpose of preventing parliament from scrutinising the Brexit process and holding the UK government to account.

Our investigations for the case had uncovered evidence by way of redacted memos and emails of Boris Johnson's plot to use the prorogation to force through a damaging no-deal Brexit against the will of parliament. His special adviser Nikki da Costa later admitted that this was entirely the case.[14]

Both cases were fast-tracked to the Supreme Court. Many in the English legal establishment assumed we would lose, but they turned out to be wrong and all hell broke loose when the Supreme Court found unanimously that the prorogation was unlawful on 24 September 2019. Millions watched the whole thing unfold on live TV. As soon as the judgment was known, Fraser rushed from the court to secure the prime spot outside as he was determined that the first to speak to the press should be me and Jolyon Maugham, rather than Gina Miller's team, because without our action in Scotland the victory could not have been achieved. He was successful in his endeavours, and when we were interviewed I called for Boris Johnson's resignation.

Ian Blackford, who had declined to be a petitioner in the case, was at the court and very much to the forefront when press photographs were being taken. However, behind the scenes Fraser and I had tried in vain to persuade the SNP to have a strategy ready to ensure that Johnson could be removed from office if he didn't resign. In the event Johnson limped on.

Speaker John Bercow confirmed that parliament would sit again the next day. When it did, proceedings commenced with an urgent question from me to the Attorney General asking him to make a statement about his legal opinion on the advice given to Her Majesty the Queen to prorogue parliament.

Naturally I did not get any straight answers, and there was uproar in parliament as the Tory government's law officer, Geoffrey Cox MP, called parliament a 'dead parliament' which had 'no moral right to sit'. I was inclined to agree with Jonathan Sumption, who said this was 'surely one of the most extraordinary statements ever made in public by a law officer'. All the more so as it flew directly in the face of the Supreme Court's judgment. Perhaps Geoffrey Cox

---

[14] https://goodlawproject.org/accountability-and-the-prorogation/#:~:text=We%20were%20deeply%20sceptical%20at,Prime%20Minister%20to%20the%20Court.

was annoyed that on a BBC profile about him I had criticised his advocacy style, suggesting it was less than persuasive and comparing him to Brian Blessed. Either way, it did not matter too much, as his (incorrect) advice to the PM that the prorogation was legal had already been leaked.

Sturgeon and her cabinet were pictured watching the Supreme Court result being announced live on TV and claimed it as an SNP victory. I was widely hailed a hero and a future leader of the party. Notwithstanding this, my enemies on the NEC attempted to hold a vote on a motion to have me removed from the list of vetted candidates at the September NEC meeting. Sturgeon stepped in to stop them.

By the end of September 2019, I was in a strong position. I had seen off the attempts to smear me as a bully and passed vetting to be included on the list of those eligible to be SNP candidates at the next election, despite the last-ditch attempts to remove me. I toured the TV studios to discuss my victory and numerous newspapers wanted to interview me.

I had a high profile north and south of the border. I was the headline speaker for the SNP at several pro-Remain rallies in London, and in October I was invited to speak at the enormous independence rally that took place in Edinburgh. Nicola Sturgeon did not attend.

In November 2019, at the *Herald* Scotland Politician of the Year awards, while Nicola won Politician of the Year, I won Best Scot at Westminster. One of the judges, Torcuil Crichton, then the Westminster correspondent of the *Daily Record*, quipped that I had committed the cardinal sin of upstaging my leader. Nicola and her close circle avoided me all evening. There was no question of us having our photograph taken together.

By the end of October the Liberal Democrats, who had not been known for their cross-party solidarity throughout the Brexit saga, decided to start pushing for a snap General Election as 'the best way of stopping Brexit'. For reasons best known to herself, or perhaps her advisers, Jo Swinson seemed to be under the impression that she was going to be the next Prime Minister. Parliament had twice stopped Johnson from holding a General Election in the week before the prorogation.

Now the SNP swithered and then decided to get on the bandwagon. As usual, this decision was not preceded by any strategic discussion within the Westminster group or with the party leadership. Rather it was dictated from on high, much to the dismay of some of us who felt it was going to herald a Johnson government, which would clearly not be in Scotland's interests. Boris had secured a new withdrawal agreement that, while flawed, was better than no deal. At a group meeting in late October 2019, I suggested we should consider doing a deal with Boris to get a Section 30 order so that we could hold a second independence referendum. I was slated by some in the group who seemed to prefer to hand him victory on a plate for any sort of Brexit he wanted with the inevitable majority he would win.

I could not believe that, having had Johnson on the ropes barely a month earlier, we were now going to participate in gifting him a general election victory with nothing for us in return. But my warnings fell on mainly deaf ears. With the passage of time – and as I became aware of the SNP's considerable internal financial problems – I have come to suspect that the main motivation behind the SNP push for a general election was to ensure more Westminster short money to keep the party afloat. It was clear that even if Johnson won in England, in Scotland we would win and increase our number of MPs and that would mean increased short money. At the time, however, it was suggested that one motivation was to get the election over before Alex Salmond's trial for sexual offences, which was due in March 2020.

Fellow parliamentarians in the cross-party group beseeched me to try to change the SNP's mind. On the day of the vote Lord Hope of Craighead even came down from the Lords to the Members' Lobby of the House of Commons to plead with me. I had to explain to him and others that this was not my decision and that they would be best speaking to Ian Blackford or preferably Sturgeon, the organ grinder rather than the monkey.

I contemplated rebelling and voting against a General Election, but by that time the result was a *fait accompli* and I didn't want to give Sturgeon and Blackford a reason to remove me from the frontbench. I was confident of holding on to my seat given my record throughout the Brexit crisis and the high profile I had attained as a result of the prorogation case. I knew that the actions I had taken were very much in tune with the views of most of my constituents.

In the event, the SNP abstained on the vote for the General Election and only Angus Brendan MacNeil, the MP for the Western Isles, rebelled by voting against. The vote went through with the overwhelming backing of most parliamentarians on a 438 to 20 vote. The parliamentary Brexit deadlock was finally broken.

The SNP campaigned on a Stop Brexit ticket. My role in the fight against Brexit and the prorogation case was given a whole page in the SNP manifesto. Most of my SNP colleagues wanted a photo with me for their campaign literature. It seemed that I now, like Nicola, was a vote winner...

I was returned with a hugely increased majority (from 1,097 to nearly 12,000). However, those who had counselled against playing into Boris' hands by voting for a General Election in 2019 were proven absolutely right. Although we increased our SNP seats from 35 to 48, in England and Wales Boris was returned with a huge majority, and Brexit was now inevitable. The Stop Brexit bus had been almost as big a confidence trick as Boris Johnson's pro-Brexit bus that had promised £350 million pounds a week for the NHS if we left the EU. I felt a little ashamed, although naturally I'd had no part in framing the election strategy.

One curious feature of the Brexit deadlock in parliament had been that the United Kingdom participated in the May 2019 elections for the European Parliament. The SNP had gained three seats. One of those was held by Alyn Smith, who had now been elected an MP and so in terms of the parliamentary rules the next eligible person on the SNP list of candidates should have taken his seat, at least until the UK finally left the European Union. That person was Heather Anderson, a well-respected SNP councillor who was also an organic farmer who owned a farm shop and butchery in the Scottish Borders. However, in order for her to take up her seat, the UK government were required to formally nominate her. She contacted me telling me that they were refusing – or at least delaying – to do so. I made some enquiries and was left with the impression that the refusal was the result of a standoff between

Michael Gove and Mike Russell, who had developed quite an enmity.

I had always got on well with Gove, despite our huge political differences, so I approached him asking for a personal favour. He welcomed me into the inner sanctum of the Cabinet Office, where he saw me without SPADs or civil servants present. I explained Heather's situation and appealed to his sense of fair play, pointing out that Heather was exactly the sort of successful entrepreneur who might have been a Tory had she lived south of the border. He relented and signed off on her papers, so that she was able to take her seat. This is a good example of what can be achieved by negotiation with one's political enemies rather than by simply shouting at them from a distance.

The new parliament met, and Brexit was finally scheduled to happen on 31 January 2020. Grassroots independence campaigners, who felt that more could have been planned by the SNP to mark the day, organised demonstrations across Scotland, including a big one outside Holyrood, where I spoke along with Lesley Riddoch and others. The mood was defiant. I and others in the SNP and the wider independence movement felt that a way should have been found to hold a second vote on independence before the UK left the EU, and that now there should be an urgency about doing so within the transition period, which was to run to 31 December 2020. I tried to raise spirits in my speech, but the grassroots were very frustrated by the inaction of the SNP leadership – and so was I.

The most important political event of the day in Scotland was a major speech from the First Minister billed as setting out the next steps on the road to independence. In a reflection of the strength of my position within the party at that stage I was asked to sit in the front row for the occasion at Dynamic Earth. I was more than a little trepidatious. Nicola's strategy to date for delivering an independence referendum to prevent 'Scotland from being taken out of the European Union against its will' had failed. She needed to come up with something new, and I knew that the assembled press would immediately want to know my view of what she said.

As it transpired, her speech contained three important announcements. First, she renewed her commitment to securing a second referendum by means of a Section 30 order, but did not rule out the alternative of putting a bill through Holyrood without Westminster's permission, and defending it in court if necessary. She said that she wanted the referendum to be held in 2020 but conceded it was more likely to be held after the Scottish Parliament election in 2021. Second, she outlined a plan to invite Scotland's elected representatives – MSPs, MPs, the MEPs elected in the last UK EU elections in 2019 and council leaders – to come together to endorse a modern Claim of Right for Scotland through a new Constitutional Convention. And third, she promised a series of 'New Scotland' policy papers to provide the detail on how Scotland could make the transition from a Yes vote to becoming an independent country.

It was the first time she had talked seriously about the possibility of exploring the legality of holding a consultative vote, though she did make it very clear that was not her preferred option. I disappointed the press by welcoming her speech, both in the interests of party unity and because I felt that at last she was moving in the right direction, but many party members and Yes activists were bitterly disappointed by it because it contained no concrete guarantee of a second vote on independence in the transition period.

It was hardly surprising that there was no great reveal of a new strategy to deliver a second vote on independence. At the last party conference in October 2019, those who had attempted to have a debate on our independence strategy and a plan B had been booed off the stage by a small but strategically placed group of Sturgeon staffers and loyalists, many of whom were also involved in the efforts to demonise the SNP women's pledge at that conference.[15]

Over the previous two years I had also been vocal in suggesting that there might be a way to hold a second vote on independence that was not dependent on the British government granting a

---

[15] https://www.newstatesman.com/politics/2019/10/snp-leadership-crush-conference-rebellion-plan-b-independence https://www.bbc.co.uk/news/uk-scotland-scotland-politics-50059339)

Section 30 order. I had done so both at NEC meetings and within the Westminster group.

I continued to do so in a major speech at Edinburgh University in February 2019, which received a lot of publicity.[16] My tactic was to put pressure on Nicola to proceed with the course of action I favoured without further delay during the Brexit transition period, which was scheduled to run until the end of 2020. In the event she did not do so.

It is interesting to speculate what would have happened in relation to the independence debate if the Covid pandemic had not intervened, which meant that the plans in Nicola's Brexit day speech had to be paused. I do not believe that Nicola would have been able to hold the line on her gold standard approach for as long as she did but for that pandemic.

However, as I made my speech on 16 February 2020, world health events were closing in on Scotland and the UK. The onset of the pandemic was about to take centre stage, together with the trial of Alex Salmond, which began on 9 March 2020.

---

[16] https://www.thenational.scot/news/18269897.joanna-cherry-scottish-independence---two-things-must/

ALEX SALMOND, THE KING ACROSS THE WATER

4

On a cold Thursday morning in January 2019, I found myself ascending the fire escape at the back of the Principal (formerly the George) Hotel in Edinburgh. I was accompanied by a security man called Gordon, whom I had met up with a few minutes earlier in a coffee shop on Hanover Street. From the fire escape, we joined the back staff staircase and ascended to the top floor, where we entered the residential part of the hotel and made our way to a suite at the front of the building. Inside was Alex Salmond, the former First Minister of Scotland and the most successful leader in the Scottish National Party's history. He had just been released from police custody and was facing multiple charges of sexual assault, including two charges of attempted rape.

An hour earlier I had received a phone call from Tasmina Ahmed-Sheikh, the former MP for Ochil and South Perthshire and now Alex's business partner, informing me that Alex had been arrested, interviewed by the police over many hours, and charged. She told me he was alone in a hotel in central Edinburgh and asked me if I would go and see him. She was in Glasgow and unable to travel due to family commitments. She confirmed that the hotel was the Principal, where Alex had a good relationship with the concierge and staff. She told me that the press were camped outside having guessed Alex might be there, so it wouldn't be possible for me to go through the front door, but arrangements had been made to sneak me in the back. That's how I came to be standing in a coffee shop at 11.30 on a Thursday morning waiting for Gordon, who was readily identifiable as a security man by his professional manner and his regimental tie.

Alex was on his own and he looked tired and upset. He filled me in on the events of the last 24 hours. The charges were worse than he had been expecting and, of course, unlike the public and most readers of this book, he knew the identity of his accusers. He was shocked and stunned. The only other time I saw Alex as upset was when he gave evidence to the Holyrood Inquiry and he described his feelings on finding out how former friends and colleagues had plotted against him in a group chat recovered by police from the phone of a senior SNP official.

We ordered coffee and we chatted for about an hour until Campbell Gunn, a former special adviser and loyal friend, arrived. I can still feel the sense of shock that permeated our meeting. Alex was a very confident man normally, full of good humour and jokes, and it was a shock to see him like this. His eyes were red; he looked shattered. Nevertheless, I was impressed by his dignity under the circumstances. He told me that the custody police had been very nice to him and had apologised for having to take away his tie and shoelaces while he was in the police cells, lest he hang himself.

I left a few minutes after Campbell arrived to enable Alex to speak with him and his solicitor, who was due to arrive shortly. Later that afternoon, Alex would appear in court to face multiple sexual-offence charges. Just over a year later he would be acquitted of all those charges in a trial that would take place in March 2020 on the eve of the Covid pandemic lockdown.

I exited the hotel the way I had arrived – by the fire escape. On the way I passed several members of staff, some of whom clearly clocked who I was. To their credit, none of them alerted the press to the presence of Alex in the hotel. It was a comforting reminder that many human beings are fundamentally decent people.

For while all the dramatic events of Brexit were unfolding, an extraordinary scandal had been engulfing Alex. Most of his friends and comrades of previous years had either turned on him or deserted him. Now he was facing charges of sexual assault from people with whom he had worked closely and had once considered his friends and allies.

Of all the meetings I had with Alex Salmond over the nine years of our friendship, this one is the most memorable for obvious reasons. I had admired him for a long time, but I didn't meet him in person until 2011, and it wasn't until we were both elected as MPs in the 2015 SNP landslide that we became friends.

The first time I met him was at the party held at the Crown Office to mark the end of Elish Angelini's tenure as Lord Advocate. It was the summer of 2011, just after he had won an unprecedented outright majority for the SNP at Holyrood, and he was in his pomp. I was at the party in my capacity as one of the Lord Advocate's team of Crown Counsel. My colleagues knew I was a huge fan, and I was taken over to meet him and was instantly charmed.

This was a common occurrence for those who met Alex for the first time. I've heard many anecdotes about people who were not fans of Alex but then met him and had their heads turned. I even heard a story of one woman who postponed her honeymoon so that she could be at her place of work on the day Alex Salmond was visiting.

He certainly had a charm that was attractive to many women. Tom Collins and Jamie Brotherstone, two outstanding young men who used to work for him, told me that it was not unusual for women to burst into tears on meeting Alex, and certainly I've had the experience of walking through the streets with him or through an airport where he has been constantly stopped by women wanting selfies with him. It would be hard for any man or indeed woman not to have his or her head turned by this, and I think this might have contributed to some of the problems he encountered later.

We worked closely together, and he encouraged me to see myself as a future leader of the party. My heart was never really in this because from about 2017 onwards I began to realise that I was surrounded by people whom I didn't trust or respect. Once, in exasperation, I said to Alex that I could never lead a party that contained so many cowards and idiots, to which he replied, 'What the fuck do you think I've been doing for the last 30 years?' He would often say to me, 'Jo, there are not many people in this party with whom

I would go into the jungle, but you are one of them.' The feeling was mutual, and so it was that when he was in trouble, I stood by him. By then I had seen enough behind the scenes of the SNP under Sturgeon's leadership not to take the allegations against him at face value. Furthermore, I was brought up to be loyal to my friends and to stand by them in times of trouble.

The first hint of trouble

The first hint I had that Alex might be facing allegations of a sexual nature came in early November 2017 – nine months before the allegations came to light in August 2018. I was having dinner with Alex and Tasmina in a small Italian restaurant in London on a Sunday evening. Both had lost their seats at the snap election in June 2017, and now, as business partners, they were pursuing the possibility of producing and delivering a political commentary show on television. They were fresh from a successful run at the Edinburgh Festival Fringe with an 'in conversation with Alex Salmond' show. It hadn't been without controversy, and with the benefit of hindsight I can see in events that summer the seeds of what was to come.

During dinner, Alex and Tasmina revealed to me that their new programme, *The Alex Salmond Show*, was going to be shown on Russia Today (RT). I was dismayed; my understanding had been that they were in conversation with ITV or Sky News to host their show. I could immediately see that there were political and presentational problems with RT as host, even though Alex and Tasmina assured me they were to have complete editorial freedom. I had had serious reservations about RT from the start of my elected political career, and I had decided that I would not appear on the channel for fear of being seen to endorse in any way the Putin regime with its human rights abuses and persecution of its political rivals, journalists and LGB people.

Despite the assurance of editorial freedom, I knew their choice of host channel would cause huge controversy and would be weaponised against them by their enemies both in and outwith the SNP.

This turned out to be correct. The news was not well received within the party leadership or with many in the grassroots. There was understandable concern that it might reflect badly on the party, even though Alex had lost his seat. To this day I cannot understand why Alex agreed to do this, other than that deals with other channels did not materialise and that he and/or Tasmina needed the money. As others among my former colleagues have found over time, it's not always easy for former MPs to find a job.

At the time when Andrew Marr privately asked me what on earth Alex was thinking of, I pointed out that it was extraordinary that the SNP had not found an elder statesman role for him after he left the leadership. Nevertheless, the decision was a major blot on Alex's copybook and one I wish he had never taken.

That night in the restaurant my dismay and unease were heightened by Alex's agitation about a story Sky News were pursuing. Apparently, there was an allegation that he had said something to an air hostess at Edinburgh Airport which was being characterised as sexual harassment. The incident dated back many years, and I could not understand why it was surfacing now. Alex speculated that Angus Robertson may have been behind the leaking of the story to Sky News because he had been the recipient of the complaint.[1]

Alex's irritation with the way in which Angus had led the Westminster group and his consequent plans to topple Angus as leader had caused a gulf to arise between Angus and Alex, who hitherto had been close political allies.

In November 2017, Angus Robertson was not in a happy position. Just as the party had failed to find an appropriate role for Alex Salmond after he resigned as First Minister and left the role in November 2014, Angus Robertson was left to swing in the wind after he lost his seat and position as Westminster leader in June

---

1 https://www.holyrood.com/news/view,angus-robertson-raised-perceived-inappropriateness-with-alex-salmond#:~:text=But%20he%20added:%20%E2%80%9CSince%20the,it%20was%20not%20reported%20further.%E2%80%9D

2017. He and his wife Jennifer visited Westminster shortly after the election. I treated them to dinner, it being my impression that once Angus's redundancy money had run out, he might, like many politicians after leaving parliament, face financial difficulties. With the top-up to his MP salary paid from SNP Westminster group funds he had been earning in excess of £120,000 per annum. He had been an MP for sixteen years.

Nicola had never liked Angus and had resented his high profile between 2015 and 2017. So, in late 2017, it seemed likely that Angus might find himself in the political wilderness for a long time. However, by 2019 the party were pushing his initiative in setting up a new polling company called Progress, and by 2020 they were changing party rules to ensure that he would be guaranteed the candidacy in Holyrood's Edinburgh Central seat, which was seen as likely to be gained back by the SNP in 2021 when popular Scottish Tory leader Ruth Davidson stood down. Quite what caused this change of heart has been the subject of much speculation. What cannot be denied is that Angus's return to favour coincided with Alex's fall from grace.

Back on that Sunday night in early November 2017, Alex was more concerned and agitated about the Sky News probe than I had ever seen him before. He clearly feared that someone was out to smear him. This did not surprise me. By that time, my disillusionment with the party was well established. I had been shocked by the events of the 2017 General Election campaign: the incompetence with which it had been run; the lack of leadership; the lack of support for the candidates; and the cavalier way in which losing candidates had been treated.

I was also extremely shaken by what I now believe to have been a clear attempt by Liz Lloyd and other members of the SNP press team to smear me over the 'nursegate' incident. I was also aware that there had been collusion between MPs close to Ian Blackford and the *Daily Record* during the leadership election campaign at Westminster to try to revive that story and paint me as a nasty individual. This was not the first time, and it would not be the last, that SNP operatives would collude with *Daily Record* journalists to smear their internal political rivals.

In the aftermath of the Westminster leadership campaign and Ian's extremely narrow victory over me, I had sensed growing hostility towards me from the boys' club who surrounded Blackford. They cut me out of tactical discussions – such as there were – about our strategy and even went so far as to try to prevent me from physically sitting on the frontbench despite my role as a frontbench spokesperson. My attempts to question the group's strategy were shouted down at group meetings and mischaracterised as criticisms of staff. The situation became so bad that in December 2017 I made a formal complaint of bullying to the SNP Chief Whip. I was also aware that some of Angus Robertson's former allies among MPs and Westminster staffers never lost an opportunity to brief against me.

I was troubled by the notion that something was fundamentally rotten and wrong in the SNP, and the fear that I had given up my career at the bar to become an elected representative of a party that was a nest of vipers.

Was there a conspiracy to remove Alex Salmond from public life?

My sense of foreboding turned out to be well founded. Although the allegations in which Sky News were interested came to nothing, in the years to come Alex was the subject of an investigation into sexual harassment by the Scottish government and stood trial in the High Court of Justiciary on charges of sexual assault and attempted rape. He left the SNP, set up a new political party and raised proceedings to sue the Scottish government for misfeasance in public office. I believe the immense toll all of this took on him contributed to his premature death of a heart attack on 12 October 2024. It also ruined him financially.[2]

Notwithstanding Scotland's Court of Session finding that the Scottish government's investigation against him was unfair, unlawful and tainted by apparent bias, and his acquittal on all the

---

[2] https://www.bbc.co.uk/news/articles/c4gp43pxr8mo

criminal charges, many people still think Alex was a sex pest. I do not believe he was. Instead, I believe that Alex Salmond was, in his own words, the victim of 'a malicious and concerted attempt to ... remove [him] from public life in Scotland' by 'a range of individuals within the Scottish government and the SNP', who set out to 'damage' his 'reputation, even to the extent of having' him 'imprisoned'.[3]

As David Davis MP commented in the House of Commons when speaking about these matters under parliamentary privilege, they are incredibly grave charges. However, like David Davis and others such as Fergus Ewing and Kenny MacAskill, I believe them to be well founded.

I base my opinion partly on evidence that is already in the public domain and partly on my own experiences. It is quite extraordinary that otherwise well-informed commentators such as journalists David Clegg, Kieran Andrews[4] and Paul Hutcheon[5] have rubbished the notion that there is any evidential basis for a conspiracy or a motive to get rid of Alex Salmond. There is plenty of evidence to suggest that there was both.

Motive

By the summer of 2017 Sturgeon was feeling extremely bruised by the loss of 21 of 56 SNP MPs at the General Election. The party had lost half a million votes and 40 per cent of our seats.

---

[3] https://hansard.parliament.uk/Commons/2021-03-16/debates/03E5E1D7-13F3-4AB3-85F2-214EA9179324/ScotlandAct1998ScottishCivilService?highlight=malicious#contribution-63890067-F842-4AF9-9BFB-AB625A2EFDF4

[4] *Break Up – How Alex Salmond and Nicola Sturgeon went to war*. Biteback Publishing 2021

[5] https://www.dailyrecord.co.uk/news/politics/alex-salmond-trial-witnesses-deserve-21775615

Nicola Sturgeon has repeatedly told us that she suffers from impostor syndrome. It is well known that those who suffer from this complex feel insecure. Alex Salmond had a track record of making unexpected political comebacks and there was plenty of evidence in the second half of 2017 that he had another comeback on his mind.

He had form. He resigned the leadership in 2000, but after John Swinney's disastrous first stint as SNP leader, there was a leadership election campaign to succeed Swinney between Roseanna Cunningham, Mike Russell and Nicola Sturgeon. Roseanna was very popular with activists because of her republicanism and looked like she was going to win. However, after a less-than-successful outing for her on *Question Time* in Ullapool, Alex clearly took the view that this could not be allowed to happen. Despite his previous trenchant denials that he had any intention to stand, Alex famously made a deal with Nicola, who was aged only 34 at the time, that she should step aside to allow him to run in return for which he would make her his deputy and successor.

This time around he wasn't even bothering to deny that he was planning a comeback. When he lost his seat in June 2017, he quoted Sir Walter Scott's poem 'Bonny Dundee': 'Tremble, false Whigs, in the midst of your glee, You have not seen the last of my bonnet and me.'

Just what the nature of that comeback would have been is not clear. But he was clearly hoping to be somebody with considerable political influence. It was known that he planned to transform his Edinburgh Festival Fringe show into a television show. He was also involved in the plans for a buyout of the *Scotsman* newspaper.[6]

And, unlike Nicola, Alex was positively brimming with ideas about how to make the most of the opportunities afforded by Brexit for the independence cause. As the autumn of 2017 progressed it was also apparent that there could soon be a by-election

---

[6] https://www.thescottishsun.co.uk/news/1671479/former-first-minister-alex-salmond-reportedly-involved-in-bid-to-buy-the-scotsman-newspaper/

for the Scottish Parliament in Aberdeenshire because of a scandal involving Mark McDonald MSP, a government minister who ultimately resigned because of allegations of sexual harassment.[7] Aberdeenshire was Alex's home turf. If he stood and got into the Scottish Parliament there would have been nothing to prevent him from seeking to topple Nicola as First Minister and leader of the SNP.

It was not only Sturgeon who had reason to fear a Salmond comeback. There were many others both at the heart of government – politicians and staffers – and in SNP HQ whose positions depended on the patronage of Nicola Sturgeon and Peter Murrell. They knew that if Alex made a comeback to the leadership, they would most likely be out of a job.

In evidence that emerged at the criminal trial, Woman H, who accused Alex of attempted rape, was cross-examined about the circumstances in which she first made a complaint about the alleged offence to SNP HQ. She was forced to admit that when she spoke with the SNP's compliance officer, Ian McCann, it was agreed that no action should be taken and that he would simply 'bank' the information until it needed to be 'deployed', should Salmond look like making a return to frontline politics. Then it would be useful as a 'vetting issue' to see whether Salmond was 'fit for office' if he ever wanted to stand for the SNP again.[8]

This conversation reflects my experience and that of others about the way in which SNP HQ dealt with complaints. They were ignored unless they could be weaponised against someone who was out of favour with the leadership, particularly through the vetting procedure for prospective parliamentary candidates. Complaints of sexual harassment, once 'deployed', would be a powerful weapon against a political rival.

---

[7] https://www.bbc.co.uk/news/uk-scotland-scotland-politics-41872427

[8] https://www.bbc.co.uk/news/uk-scotland-scotland-politics-51817397

How the plan to remove Alex from public life unfolded

For me, the first sign that Alex Salmond was seriously out of favour with his erstwhile protégée Nicola Sturgeon was on 30 August 2017 when I attended the official opening of the Queensferry Crossing, which had been commissioned when Alex Salmond was First Minister of Scotland. The opening ceremony took place near Rosyth where stands had been erected to accommodate the audience. Nicola Sturgeon, her government ministers and invited dignitaries were accommodated in a special VIP stand. Fraser and I had managed to secure tickets, and to my astonishment, when we arrived to take our seats in the stands reserved for the general public, Alex Salmond joined us. He had not been issued with an invitation for the VIP box despite being the former First Minister of Scotland under whom the bridge had been commissioned. Alex brazened the situation out and many of his fellow spectators were delighted to find him among them and to be able to take selfies and chat to him. He was charm personified, but it must have been deeply humiliating for him. At the time I could not understand how it was felt that such a slight was appropriate or could go unremarked.

What possible reason would there be for him to be excluded from his rightful place in the VIP box at this event in August 2017 except for worries that he was about to become an embarrassment to the First Minister? I suspect that plans to sideline him were already being made and that it was thought prudent by senior civil servants and advisers to avoid him being pictured beside Nicola Sturgeon.

Back in June 2015 Alex had been accused of sexism after he had said 'behave yourself, woman' to Anna Soubry MP during a debate in Westminster. (In fact, Alex and Anna got on rather well and had a playful, even flirtatious relationship.) Asked about his comment at the time, Nicola said that Alex was the 'least sexist man she had ever met'. She said she had worked with him for 25 years and that he did not have 'a sexist bone in his body'.[9]

---

9 https://www.huffingtonpost.co.uk/2015/06/09/nicola-sturgeon-defends-alex-salmond-sexist-comments_n_7548840.html

At the beginning of August 2017, at the opening of his Edinburgh Festival Fringe show, Alex made an off-colour joke about female politicians and orgasms. During the ensuing furore Nicola again defended him, saying, 'The first thing I would say is that Alex Salmond is not sexist. I'm fairly well qualified to comment on this because I've worked with Alex Salmond very closely for almost 30 years now, so he's not sexist ... occasionally Alex is not always as funny as he thinks he is and perhaps this is an example of a joke that perhaps belongs more in the Benny Hill era than it does in the modern era.'[10]

A year later, when the allegations against him being investigated by the Scottish government were leaked to the press (*Daily Record*, of course), she professed herself to be shocked. She claimed she knew nothing of any allegations against him until he told her on 2 April 2018, although, at the Holyrood Inquiry, it transpired that she had actually been told a few days earlier, at a meeting on 29 March, and that she had been aware of 'concerns' in November 2017.

In March 2021, during her evidence to the Committee on the Handling of Harassment Complaints by the Scottish government, she said, 'Since an approach from Sky News in November 2017 I had harboured a lingering suspicion that such issues in relation to Mr Salmond might rear their head – so hearing of a potential issue would not have been, in itself, a massive shock.'[11]

In the autumn of 2017, the 'MeToo' movement was at its height. Across the world powerful men were being accused of sexual harassment and toppled from positions of power and influence in disgrace. In October 2017 explosive allegations that sexual harassment was rife in the Scottish Parliament were published in Scottish newspapers.[12]

---

[10] https://www.heraldscotland.com/news/15474388.sturgeon-says-salmonds-sex-joke-throwback-benny-hill-era/).

[11] https://www.snp.org/first-minister-nicola-sturgeons-opening-statement-to-the-holyrood-inquiry/

[12] https://www.bbc.co.uk/news/uk-scotland-scotland-politics-41795013

On 31 October 2017, Deputy First Minister John Swinney told the Scottish Parliament that the Permanent Secretary would be taking forward measures within government to ensure that all staff were protected from sexual harassment. Apparently, it had been decided at the weekly cabinet meeting earlier that day that Scottish government policies needed to be reviewed.[13]

According to David Clegg, the then political editor of the *Daily Record*, that same day, following a tip-off, he submitted a series of questions to the Scottish government in a bid to ascertain if any complaints had been made about Alex during his tenure as First Minister. The tip-off was from a 'Scottish government official', to the effect that if a MeToo scandal were to happen in Scottish politics it would be about Alex Salmond.[14] The answer came back that no ministers had been the subject of an official complaint since the SNP came to power in 2007 and that there were no live investigations. The *Record* kept investigating and would go on to be the recipient of the crucial leak that revealed the investigation against Alex to the public in August 2018.

It would be very interesting to know the identity of the official who gave the initial tip-off. Was it the same person who later leaked the outcome of the investigation that followed to the *Daily Record*? We do not know the answer to that question, but what we do know is that on 31 October 2017, when Sturgeon announced her intention to have a new procedure prepared to deal with 'a culture of sexual harassment that had gone unchallenged in many workplaces for a long period of time', at least one senior Scottish government insider knew that Alex Salmond was likely to be the first subject of investigation under the new procedure.

Work began immediately on the new procedure. On 7 November the issue of possible complaints against former ministers was being considered as part of a 'sexual harassment route map'. A day later,

---

[13] https://digitalpublications.parliament.scot/Committees/Report/SGHHC/2021/3/23/3dc69e08-899e-4d55-aa77-83f08cc4a815#5b561795-53af-4544-971b-5508882c5715.dita at para 133

[14] *Break Up op. cit.*, prologue page xxi

a first draft of the new procedure was produced, covering only former ministers. After discussions, a further draft covering current as well as former ministers was produced on 15 November. We know that the decision to include former ministers had the explicit support of Nicola Sturgeon, who wrote to Permanent Secretary Leslie Evans, the most senior civil servant in Scotland, to this effect on 22 November 2017. Liz Lloyd was involved in this exchange of emails in her capacity as the First Minister's chief of staff.[15]

The timing of the decision to make the new procedure retrospective is important. It was made just days after Mark McDonald, a serving Scottish minister accused of sexual harassment, resigned on 4 November,[16] and after it had become known in civil service circles that Sky News were investigating a historic allegation of sexual harassment against Alex Salmond. This information came to light because Alex had contacted some civil servants who had formerly worked with him in the hope they would counter the allegation.

Nicola Sturgeon also knew because Sky News had contacted the SNP for comment on the Edinburgh Airport allegations on 4 November, and she had been made aware of the press query.

The Committee of Inquiry set up in 2020 found that 'as the procedure was being developed in November 2017 ... at least three individuals raised concerns about the former First Minister'.[17] Alex had reason to believe that two civil servants approached the Scottish government with complaints of sexual harassment against him as early as 6 and 7 November 2017. The inquiry report corroborates this partially with their finding that one woman made informal approaches on 7 November 2017.[18]

Against this background it is easy to understand why Alex and those advising him became convinced that the new procedure was designed specifically to deal with complaints against him.

---

[15] Committee report at p.149 and para 192

[16] https://www.theguardian.com/uk-news/2017/nov/04/scottish-minister-resigns-over-allegations-about-private-life

[17] At para 241

[18] At para 282

The Scottish government investigation

The new procedure was formally signed off by Nicola Sturgeon on 20 December 2017. On 17 January 2018 the first formal complaint of 'inappropriate behaviour' against Alex Salmond was received. The complainer, called Ms A to protect her identity, had been involved in devising the policy, and the civil servant appointed to investigate, Judith Mackinnon, had already discussed the potential complaint with Ms A, despite the new policy specifically providing that the investigating officer 'will have had no prior involvement with any aspect of the matter being raised'.

Shortly thereafter, another woman, Ms B, made an official complaint of inappropriate behaviour against Alex Salmond. She too had been in conversation with Judith Mackinnon while the new procedure was being developed.

As I understand it, Ms A's complaint related to an intimate moment in a bedroom at Bute House that had taken place between her and Alex back in 2013. Her concerns about the incident had been dealt with informally at the time when Alex Salmond made an unofficial apology. Ms B's complaint related to an allegation that Alex Salmond had touched her bottom during a photo shoot at Stirling Castle, also during the referendum campaign.

I am not able to comment on the veracity of the complaints of Ms A and Ms B beyond saying that clearly something happened between Ms A and Alex for which he felt it necessary to apologise. As regards the rest of their complaints, it is important to appreciate first that the Scottish government procedure which found that Alex had behaved inappropriately was subsequently struck down as unfair, unlawful and tainted by apparent bias, and therefore its findings cannot be relied upon. Secondly, none of the complaints were found to have been proven at the criminal trial.

Alex Salmond did not find out about the Scottish government's investigation until 7 March 2018, when Leslie Evans emailed to tell him that an investigation into two formal complaints had been ongoing since 17 January. She did not name the complainer nor give details of the complaints, but she was keen to emphasise that Nicola Sturgeon had not been made aware of the complaints and would only be informed of them when the outcome of the investigation was complete.

Around about the same time, on 6 March 2018, Alex Salmond's former chief of staff Geoff Aberdein met with a government official who asked him whether Alex was planning a comeback and suggested it would be a bad idea because of his RT show.

He met the same official again on 9 March and they told him that the Scottish government had received complaints about Alex's conduct and disclosed the identity of the complainer Ms A. Later, the official concerned insisted that Geoff misunderstood the conversation and that they had no knowledge of any investigations, only suspicions. An independent inquiry preferred Geoff's account of the conversation.[19]

Using parliamentary privilege, David Davis has named the individual concerned as Liz Lloyd, Nicola Sturgeon's chief of staff.[20] He also referred to 'an exchange of messages between civil servants Judith Mackinnon and (Scottish government's Director of People) Barbara Allison, in February 2018 suggesting that the First Minister's chief of staff was interfering in the complaints process against Alex Salmond. Mackinnon complained, "Liz interference, v bad". I assume that means very bad. If true this suggests that the chief of staff had knowledge of the Salmond case in February.'

David Davis went on to say that we must assume Liz Lloyd was acting with the knowledge of her boss. I agree that this is likely, unless one is prepared to believe that Liz Lloyd was on a solo mission to discourage Alex from making a political comeback and told Nicola nothing.

When Alex was informed that there was an investigation against him on 7 March 2018, he was not told of the nature of the

---

[19] https://www.gov.scot/publications/independent-report-by-james-hamilton-on-the-first-ministers-self-referral-under-the-scottish-ministerial-code/

[20] https://hansard.parliament.uk/Commons/2024-07-18/debates/4DC08467-BEE4-414B-B9F5-D99EB190B0AA/AdequacyOfTheScotlandAct1998?highlight=liz%20lloyd#contribution-AFB8C127-26C0-4301-BA0C-0EE57F1CDCE1

complaints against him or allowed to see the evidence. He took legal advice, and his solicitors offered conciliation, mediation and legal arbitration to try to resolve the matters. All these offers were rebuffed by Scottish government officials. Alex's lawyers made it clear from an early stage that he was denying the allegations and that they had concerns over the competency and the legality of the investigation.

The leak

Leslie Evans finalised her report on 22 August 2018 and concluded that Alex Salmond had sexually harassed the two female officials during his time as First Minister. A copy of the report was sent to those advising Alex that day. They identified several glaring procedural flaws in the way the investigation had been conducted, which amounted to unfairness, and advised Alex to raise proceedings to judicially review the report and have it struck down.

At 2pm on 23 August the Permanent Secretary told Alex's legal advisers that she intended to make a public statement at 5pm confirming the existence of sexual harassment claims against Alex. His lawyers moved quickly with the intention of obtaining an interim interdict to prohibit publication of the report. The Scottish government were aware of this and had agreed to a stay on publication pending the court's decision on the interim interdict. However, somebody leaked a full copy of the Scottish government's investigation report to the *Daily Record*, and by 10 o'clock that evening the allegations that Alex Salmond was a sex pest were in the public domain.

In her memoirs Nicola Sturgeon offers the bizarre suggestion that Alex Salmond leaked the report himself. Lawyers for Alex have pointed out how ridiculous this is, as he was on the verge of getting an interim interdict and had secured agreement from the Scottish government not to publish in the meantime.

The well-respected former MSP Andy Wightman was so incensed by Sturgeon's allegation, which he described as 'highly misleading, speculative and partial', that he wrote a detailed blog rebutting it.[21] He forensically dissects her insinuation and sets out what we do know about the leak, including that it was investigated by the Information Commissioner's Office (ICO). Although they could not pinpoint the culprit, the ICO prosecutor said, 'I have sympathy with the hypothesis that the leak came from an employee of the Scottish government and agree that the timing could arguably raise such an inference.'[22]

I would add that, unlike Alex, individuals within the Scottish government had every motive to leak the complaint if the purpose of the whole procedure was to discredit him, and that purpose was about to be frustrated by an interim interdict and legal process which could result, as it did, in the whole investigation being declared null and void. It is remarkable that Nicola Sturgeon did not see fit to mention this any of this in her memoirs.

Under parliamentary privilege, David Davis said, 'I have met a witness who has made a statement that he was told by the then political editor of the *Daily Record* that the story was leaked by Liz Lloyd.'[23] The view that the leaker was Liz Lloyd had been widely held among the chattering classes in Scotland long before David Davis named her. In written evidence to the subsequent Holyrood Inquiry, she denied this.

David Clegg, the editor of the *Daily Record* at the time, has denied that the leaker was Alex Salmond. He has never denied that it was Lloyd.

Liz Lloyd's name crops up again in relation to what has proved to be a very vexed issue in this saga – the question of exactly when Sturgeon first knew there were complaints against Alex. Some might think it stretches credibility that, having commissioned the new procedure, having agreed it should cover former ministers, knowing about the Sky News investigation and given the

---

[21] https://andywightman.scot/2025/08/who-leaked-the-salmond-harassment-report/

[22] https://andywightman.scot/wp-content/uploads/2025/08/ICO_report.pdf, para 4.6

[23] See footnote 12, page 94

knowledge of her chief of staff, Nicola Sturgeon did not know Alex was under investigation until he told her on 2 April 2018. But that was indeed her official position, at least at first.

That is what she told the Scottish Parliament in a statement after the Scottish government conceded the judicial review. However, when Geoff Aberdein gave evidence at the subsequent criminal trial, he said that he had gone to see Nicola on 29 March 2018 in order to persuade her to meet with Alex and that he had told her then about the harassment allegations. This later led to Sturgeon being accused of having misled parliament in breach of the Code. Her position then evolved to accepting that the meeting on 29 March had taken place but claiming that she had simply forgotten about it.

What cannot be in doubt is that at least as early February 2018, Liz Lloyd was aware of the investigation. David Davis has revealed that messages between two civil servants at that time show she was directly interfering in discussions with the accusers ahead of their complaints being made. And yet we are asked to believe that she was acting without the knowledge of her boss, Nicola Sturgeon. This does seem unlikely. Unfortunately, Liz Lloyd's evidence on this matter has never been tested, because for reasons that are not clear she did not give evidence to the Holyrood Inquiry.

The aftermath of the leak

I was on holiday in Provence when the story prompted by the leak broke on the night of 23 August 2018, and I spoke late at night with Alex who was clearly very upset and angry. I could not imagine how he must have felt. I was shocked, in tears and trembling with rage when I heard. I had seen enough in the last year to be pretty sure the complaints process was being weaponised against Alex. The next day the story was all over the Scottish newspapers and beyond.

An anecdote from my colleague and friend Anne Harvey, who was head of the SNP whips' office at Westminster at the time, sheds some light on the reaction of senior SNP staffers and staff at HQ to events. The day after the story broke, Anne travelled to Prestwick to attend the SNP National Assembly, which was to be held at Ayr Racecourse on Saturday, 25 August.

She was staying locally in a bed and breakfast, and on the Friday night by arrangement she walked over to the Western House Hotel, where SNP HQ staff were staying, to join them for dinner. In her own words: 'The staff contingent was large, and the hotel had provided a private dining room. I expected to find people upset and in a state of shock about the allegations against Alex. Instead, the mood was jovial, even celebratory. At one point comments were being made about how much they were looking forward to a ceremonial melting down of the bust of Alex Salmond that stood in the boardroom at SNP HQ. This was not a group of people who had learned of a shock development less than 24 hours earlier. It felt as if some people had been well prepared for this. Some would use the words gloating and complicit.'

Before she arrived, she had planned on having a late night, but she felt so uncomfortable she left early. When she got back to her desk at Westminster, she received an email from another staff member who had been tasked by HQ with compiling a comprehensive list of any staff members who had worked for the Westminster group between 2015 and 2017. This is when she first started to suspect that there was a witch hunt against Alex.

Meanwhile, back at the Scottish government, on the day of the leak, Leslie Evans also referred the matter to the police, despite Ms A and Ms B having both said that they didn't want this to happen when consulted about it earlier that month.

The timing is interesting. Why didn't she do it earlier if she thought to do so was in the public interest? One theory is that she only did it because of the fear that Alex might succeed in his judicial review. A criminal investigation might have superseded the judicial review and would certainly have kept matters going even if the Scottish government lost the civil case.

I wish to make it clear here that I am not suggesting that either the police or the Crown conspired against Alex Salmond. As a matter of fact and law, the police are obliged to investigate complaints made to them and the Crown Office is required to consider any report they produce. People, including Nicola Sturgeon, who suggest that those of us who believe there was a conspiracy against Alex are making accusations against the police and the Crown are wrong, and I believe setting up a straw man to distract people from the true focus of concern.

That focus should be on (a) the Scottish government and senior civil servants' behaviour in devising such a flawed procedure and then trying to cover up what they had been up to during the judicial review that followed, and (b) what was going on behind the scenes in both the Scottish government and the SNP when complaints against Alex snowballed after Leslie Evans referred the complaints to the police in August 2018.

I believe that when Alex Salmond's lawyers challenged the new procedure, there was an attempt to hide what had been going on, which went right to the top of government. It should be remembered that Alex's lawyers were challenging the fairness and legality of the procedure long before they raised the action for judicial review.

I also believe that it was concerns at the top of the civil service that the legal challenge was well placed that led to the decision to report the matter to the police, in the hope that the police investigation might supersede matters. At that stage SNP HQ became involved in seeking out further complainers to bolster the police investigation.

Alex, of course, won his judicial review. The circumstances leading to him doing so and being awarded the maximum possible punitive award of costs are really quite extraordinary. They have only come to light fully over time, and after the Scottish government was forced to reveal the legal advice it had in relation to the proceedings.

The procedure used against Alex differed from the existing Scottish government complaints procedure in that it was retrospective, lacked a mediation procedure and, while it applied to former ministers, did not apply to former civil servants.

At the time it was being drawn up it was shared with the Head of Propriety and Ethics in Whitehall, then Sue Gray, who expressed discomfort with the proposals, in particular that they were designed to apply only to former ministers and not to former civil servants. Her concerns were ignored.

From an early stage, Alex Salmond's lawyers thought the procedure itself was unfair and that's why they ultimately sought a judicial review. The judicial review action was raised at the end of August 2018, and by the end of September 2018 the Scottish government's external counsel, Roddy Dunlop KC, was advising them that the complaints procedure had a real risk of being found unfair by the court and that 'the vulnerability arises from the procedure itself, and not from its implementation in this particular case'.

He reached that view without being given the full facts as to how the procedure had been implemented. By the end of October there is evidence that he was concerned that the Scottish government were not disclosing to him important facts about the implementation of the process and that 'it makes little sense to continue to defend the indefensible'. By early November 2018 he was advising the Scottish government that the 'least worst option' was to concede the case.

The Scottish government tried to hide crucial documentation from both their counsel and court. When that documentation ultimately came to light, Roddy Dunlop and his junior advised the Scottish government that their position was 'untenable' and that they were 'personally horrified' at the lack of candour on the part of the government and the false assurances they had been given. In one instance a critically relevant email was actually removed from a bundle of documents that was going to the court after it had been approved by counsel.

Despite the increasingly damning advice from their counsel, the Scottish government did not concede the case until January 2019, and only after their counsel threatened to withdraw from acting for them. They doggedly pursued a case which they knew was doomed for months and thereby ran up huge costs to the public purse and incurred a punitive award of expenses.

Not only was the procedure itself unfair, but the way in which it was implemented, particularly that the investigator had prior involvement with the complainers, breached the procedure's own rules.[24]

What the court didn't know and what only emerged later was that Leslie Evans, the decision maker in the Scottish government process, also met with the complainants during the process. That information was withheld from the Court of Session in one of the many breaches of the Scottish governmental duty of candour.[25] The subsequent Parliamentary Committee of Inquiry found:

> ... that the Scottish Government was responsible from an early stage for a serious, substantial and entirely avoidable situation that resulted in a prolonged, expensive and unsuccessful defence of the Petition ... this state of affairs is unacceptable by an organisation such as the Scottish Government and that those responsible should be held accountable ... The Committee is conscious that the Permanent Secretary's office was identified as coordinating the supply of information for the judicial review and that the Permanent Secretary was one of a few people who had been aware of the prior contact of the Investigating Officer. It must be questioned why the Permanent Secretary in her role and with her knowledge did not ensure that the relevant information was extracted and processed at a much earlier stage. This individual failing is as significant as the general corporate failing already described.[26]

24 David Davis under parliamentary privilege https://hansard.parliament.uk/Commons/2021-03-16/debates/03E5E1D7-13F3-4AB3-85F2-214EA9179324/ScotlandAct1998ScottishCivilService?highlight=horrified#contribution-63890067-F842-4AF9-9BFB-AB625A2EFDF4

25 https://hansard.parliament.uk/Commons/2024-07-18/debates/4DC08467-BEE4-414B-B9F5-D99EB190B0AA/AdequacyOfTheScotlandAct1998?highlight=leslie%20evans#contribution-AFB8C127-26C0-4301-BA0C-0EE57F1CDCE1

26 see paras 589 and 590 of the report.

In his evidence to the committee, the Lord Advocate conceded that the way in which the Scottish government managed the disclosure of documents during the judicial review was unacceptable and that this included giving inaccurate assurances to the court.[27]

It is extraordinary that no one has been held to account for this mess. The *Times* editorial on 10 January 2019 said in reference to the Permanent Secretary, 'Scotland's most senior civil servant is guilty of an egregious lapse of judgement and should be sacked.'[28] However, she wasn't sacked. Instead, her contract was renewed in January 2020 for two and a half years. She retired from the civil service in July 2022 with a hefty pension, and she now gives keynote speeches on civil service leadership.[29]

While the Scottish government and the civil service were busy covering up what they had been up to, there was also considerable activity being coordinated by SNP HQ. Under parliamentary privilege David Davis has revealed the existence of a group, set up in September 2018, which included SNP politicians, senior staffers and senior staff at SNP HQ.[30] Some evidence about this group was also heard at Alex Salmond's trial and at the Holyrood Inquiry.

According to Davis, in March 2021, a whistleblower gave him a transcript of a download from the phone of Sue Ruddick, then the chief operating officer of the SNP. The whistleblower, whose identity has never been revealed, asserted that the download provided evidence of 'collusion, perjury, up to criminal conspiracy'.

According to Davis, in those communications Sue Ruddick and Peter Murrell 'encouraged and coached complainants into reporting

---

[27] see paragraph 605 of the committee's final report

[28] https://www.thetimes.com/article/03e40c7e-1466-11e9-94cd-1357d20693b3?shareToken=9b3614f223b0fc7ed06146368d7e92b1

[29] https://www.instituteforgovernment.org.uk/event/government-2025-conference

[30] https://hansard.parliament.uk/Commons/2024-07-18/debates/4DC08467-BEE4-414B-B9F5-D99EB190B0AA/AdequacyOfTheScotlandAct1998?highlight=coached#contribution-AFB8C127-26C0-4301-BA0C-0EE57F1CDCE1

Salmond to the police' in the period immediately after Leslie Evans had referred the complaints of Ms A and B to the police.

The download in question was recovered by Police Scotland as evidence in the criminal investigation. As such it had to be disclosed to Alex Salmond and his legal team during the criminal proceedings. Alex Salmond's voice broke with emotion when he gave evidence to the Holyrood Inquiry about the first time he read its contents. These people were his former friends and comrades, or so he thought.

At his trial, the Crown argued, with limited success, that the download should not be admitted in evidence because, they said, it was collateral evidence. It is hard to see how evidence of collusion between complainers and witnesses at a sexual offence trial could be said to be collateral evidence. At the time I advised Alex that were he to be convicted, he should appeal his conviction on the grounds that exclusion of some of the evidence suggesting collusion and conspiracy had robbed him of a fair trial in terms of Article 6 of the European Convention on Human Rights. I am vindicated in this advice by a recent decision of the UK Supreme Court, which found that rape shield laws were being misinterpreted by the Scottish courts to exclude this sort of collateral evidence.[31]

Nevertheless, at the trial, as well as being cross-examined about her exchange with Ian McCann, Woman H was cross examined about a text she sent to one of the other complainers, Woman J, in which she said, 'I have a plan. And means we can be anonymous but see strong repercussions.'[32]

---

[31] Daly (Appellant) v His Majesty's Advocate (Respondent) (Scotland) [2025] UKSC38; https://www.heraldscotland.com/news/25615523.supreme-court-makes-landmark-judgement-rape-shield-laws/

[32] https://www.bbc.co.uk/news/uk-scotland-scotland-politics-51817397#:~:text=A%20text%20from%20Woman%20H,pleas%20to%20all%2014%20charges.

According to David Davis there are dozens of messages contained in the download. He told parliament that 'the messages suggest that SNP chief executive Peter Murrell coordinated Ruddick and Ian McCann, the SNP's compliance officer, in the handling of specific complaints. On 28 September 2018, a month after the police had started their investigations of the criminal case, McCann expressed great disappointment to Ruddick that someone who had promised to deliver five complaints to him by the end of that week had come up empty, "overreached" as he put it. One of the complainants said to Ruddick that she was "feeling pressurised by the whole thing rather than supported".'

It was revealed at the Holyrood Inquiry that on the same day that Alex won the judicial review, Leslie Evans sent a message to a colleague saying that the battle was lost but not 'the war'.[33] As Davis says, this is hardly the language of an impartial civil servant.

David Davis also told parliament that there was evidence of contact between figures in the Scottish government and officers of the SNP, and that the WhatsApp messages revealed that Liz Lloyd had convened a 'council of war WhatsApp group' after Alex won his judicial review in January 2019. He also told parliament that on 'the day following the Scottish government's collapse of the judicial review in January 2019, Ruddick expressed to McCann the hope that one of the complainants would be sickened enough to get back in the "game again". Later that month she confirmed to Murrell that the complainant was now "up for the fight and keen to see him go to jail". Ruddick herself expressed nervousness about what happens "when my name comes out as fishing for others to come forward".'

The download also shows that on the day after Salmond's first criminal court appearance in January 2019, Peter Murrell sent a message that read: 'Totally agree folk should be asking the police questions ... report now with the PF on charges which leaves police

[33] https://www.bbc.co.uk/news/uk-scotland-54707592#:~:text=A%20civil%20servant%20deleted%20a,of%20conspiratorial%20element%20to%20it%22.

twiddling their thumbs. So good time to be pressurising them. Would be good to know Met looking at events in London.'

The second message, which appears to refer to the Crown Prosecution Service (CPS) in London, read: 'TBH the more fronts he is having to firefight on the better for all complainers. So CPS action would be a good thing.'

The Metropolitan Police in London received one complaint in connection with the Alex Salmond investigation in January 2019 but dropped its inquiries after contacting the complainant as part of a case review.[34]

As Davis told parliament, these WhatsApp exchanges took place after the criminal investigation into Alex had commenced, and contact with and influencing of potential witnesses is totally inappropriate once a criminal investigation is underway.

I was unaware of this WhatsApp group at the time; however, I was aware that in September 2018 Sue Ruddick and Scott Martin, SNP HQ's in-house lawyer, came to Westminster ostensibly looking for complaints of harassment or bullying, and interviewed several SNP MPs and staff members. Whatever they were up to they didn't discover any complaints against Alex Salmond. To my knowledge none of the other complaints they uncovered were pursued.

Anne Harvey, who has a legal background and who was already alarmed and concerned about the glee she had observed among HQ staff after the *Daily Record* broke the news of the investigation against Alex, formed the view that HQ staff were suborning evidence against Alex Salmond and raised her concerns at a meeting of the Westminster group in October 2018. I took her view seriously enough to raise it at the SNP's National Executive Committee in January 2019 after Alex had won his judicial review. Davis revealed to parliament that the WhatsApp group messages record consternation that I had done so.[35]

---

[34] https://www.dailyrecord.co.uk/news/politics/alex-salmond-face-no-further-22544834

[35] https://hansard.parliament.uk/Commons/2021-03-16/debates/03E5E1D7-13F3-4AB3-85F2-214EA9179324/ScotlandAct1998ScottishCivilService?highlight=edinburgh%20south%20west#contribution-63890067-F842-4AF9-9BFB-AB625A2EFDF4

The criminal proceedings and subsequent investigations

At his criminal trial Alex Salmond faced thirteen charges of sexual assault and one charge of attempted rape from eight different women. He was acquitted on all the charges.

From the outset I had predicted this would happen.[36] For this my judgement was called into question by fellow parliamentarians and by commentators, and I also received a fair bit of social-media abuse, which I found painful. So it was a great relief when I was ultimately vindicated by the verdict. Of course, it was in the interests of those who wanted to remove Alex from the political scene to denigrate my views on the subject, particularly as they might be given some weight because of my credentials as a dedicated feminist and a former sex crimes prosecutor.

Most people at this stage were unaware of the activity that was going on behind the scenes in senior SNP circles. Moreover, this was at the height of the MeToo movement, and the widespread public assumption seemed to be that there was no smoke without fire, particularly as there were so many accusers. I can hardly blame those who took this approach. I might have made the same assumption without knowing Alex and, more importantly, some of his accusers and their cheerleaders.

By this time, I had spent a lot of time with Alex Salmond and had not seen anything to suggest he was a sex pest, much less a serial abuser. I had also noted a striking contrast between the enthusiastic pursuit of complaints against him with the utter failure to pursue serious complaints against other SNP politicians who were close to the leadership.

It also struck me as decidedly odd that if Alex was a serial sex abuser, as was now being alleged, this had not been noticed by those working closely with him or come to light when he was in his pomp in the run-up to the independence referendum. Alex

---

36 https://www.heraldscotland.com/news/17387910.snp-mp-liked-tweet-calling-salmonds-return-leader-shocked-criminal-charges/

already had a lot of enemies long before his friends and comrades turned against him.

I did not take the decision to support Alex lightly. I have devoted a considerable amount of my professional life to improving the prosecution of sexual crime and making sure those who complain of having been sexually assaulted are treated with dignity and respect. As an undergraduate and postgraduate student, I worked on a research project that monitored how rape shield legislation was working in Scotland and made suggestions as to how it could be improved.

In 2008, I was one of the first prosecutors to be appointed to the new National Sex Crimes Unit, set up to improve the prosecution of sexual crime, by Elish Angelini and Dorothy Bain, who was then the Principal Advocate Depute (and is now the current Lord Advocate). Over my three years as a full-time Advocate Depute I prosecuted many cases of rape and other sexual offences and appeared for the Crown in some pivotal appeals on sexual offences.

Accordingly, I am well aware of the low conviction rates in some sexual offences cases, but unlike many of those who emote about the issue, I have the practical experience to understand what the problems are.

In many sexual offences trials, there are no eyewitnesses beyond the complainer and the accused. The issue is not whether sex took place, but whether it was consensual. Commonly there is little or no forensic evidence to confirm the absence of consent and so the evidence boils down to a 'he said/she said' situation in court. In such circumstances it is understandable that juries are often left with a reasonable doubt. That is why they acquit more frequently than they do in cases of murder or assault, where there are usually eyewitnesses and forensic evidence.

However, in sexual offences trials where the accused faces multiple charges from multiple complainers, a conviction on at least of some of the charges is far more likely because of the corroboration afforded by the Moorov doctrine. This is a principle of Scots law based on a case from the 1930s in which a Mr Moorov was successfully prosecuted for multiple indecent assaults. The doctrine allows the evidence of a witness to one alleged assault to corroborate the evidence of a witness to a separate but connected assault, provided the assaults are sufficiently similar in time, character and circumstance to suggest that they are part of a single course of criminal conduct.

Until Alex's acquittal I had never known a case where more than two women had levelled accusations of sexual assault against a man and he was not convicted of at least some of the offences. The fact that Alex was acquitted on all the charges suggests that the jury did not find the evidence of most of the complainers to be either credible or reliable. In Scotland, at that time, juries could convict on a simple majority. If a majority of the jury had found more than one of the complainers to be credible and reliable in their account of events, then they would have been duty bound to convict on the charges in relation to those complainers.

This is really quite a simple matter of legal analysis if you think about it, and it should not be beyond the wit of lay commentators to appreciate. Nevertheless, many who commented on the acquittals in the public domain, whether deliberately or otherwise, drew on the low conviction rate in single-charge rape cases to cast doubt on the verdict. This was at best careless and at worst disingenuous. The lawyers who did so should hang their heads in shame.

In the aftermath of Alex's acquittal many commentators were unable to hide their disappointment and showed little respect for the verdict of the jury. Most of the press accounts of the trial were extraordinarily one sided, focusing on the prosecution evidence but not that led by the defence.

One gains some insight into the acquittal of Alex Salmond if one looks at the evidence of Woman H, who alleged that she had been the subject of an attempted rape in Bute House. I have already mentioned the evidence about the circumstances in which she first reported her complaint to SNP HQ. Alex's defence team were able to lead credible and reliable evidence from a well-respected businesswoman to the effect that Ms H had not been anywhere near Bute House on the night in question. This evidence was used to great effect in the cross-examination of Ms H by one of the two KCs employed by Alex Salmond, Shelagh McCall.

I do not intend to fall into the trap of jigsaw identification, either deliberately or inadvertently. However, it is already in the public domain that the complainers included at least one SNP politican and a party worker.[37] Knowledge of the identity of the complainers who had a political rather than a civil service background is widespread among the chattering classes in Scotland. If that information were ever to get into the public domain, there would be an enormous outcry and a demand for an investigation. If, as many have called for, there is ever to be a public inquiry into the whole affair, it might be found to be in the public interest to remove the anonymity of some of the complainers. While the rule affording complainers in sexual offence trials anonymity is there to encourage the victims of sexual crime to come forward, it is not there to facilitate conspiracies to pervert the course of justice.

An inquiry was set up by the Scottish government to investigate the handling of the harassment complaints against Alex Salmond. The Committee on the Scottish Government Handling of Harassment Complaints did not cover itself in glory. Nor did many of the witnesses. SNP members of the committee in particular displayed a remarkable lack of curiosity. Several Scottish government civil servants had to correct their statements or apologise for giving misleading evidence on oath. Peter Murrell gave evidence on oath that he later had to correct. Leslie Evans was roundly criticised for the conduct of the investigation and the judicial review. Nicola Sturgeon, whose memory failed her on more than one occasion and whose famous grasp of detail deserted her, was found to have misled the committee. The findings of the final report were leaked, some think by SNP members to distract from the findings critical of Sturgeon.[38]

---

37 https://www.bbc.co.uk/news/uk-scotland-scotland-politics-56028750#:~:text=She%20added:%20%22I%20think%20that,have%20made%20it%20significantly%20harder.%22&text=The%20committee%20was%20set%20up,to%20parliament%20%2D%20which%20she%20denies.

38 https://andywightman.scot/2023/03/cui-bono-who-leaked-the-harassment-committees-conclusions/

In fairness to the committee, it was frustrated in its attempts to get at the truth by what David Davis has described as the evasiveness of the Scottish government and by the threat of legal action by the Crown Office.

How the SNP under Sturgeon dealt with complaints – my experience

I hope the reader will understand from my account of the botched Scottish government investigation, the activities of senior SNP officials behind the scenes and the circumstances surrounding Alex trial why I believe, like David Davis and others, that there is prima facie evidence of a conspiracy to remove Alex from public life.

I do not believe that those who set out to remove Alex from public life ever thought their plans would end up in court. The plan was simply to label him a sex pest after an internal Scottish government investigation. That in itself would have been enough to prevent him from ever making a political comeback. However, because of what others have rightly called the 'trademark ineptitude' of the Scottish government and their civil service in the Sturgeon years, the plan was badly executed and grew arms and legs.[39]

There is ample evidence to suggest that the procedure introduced by the Scottish government was deliberately designed to deal with Alex Salmond and Alex Salmond alone, not least the fact that it has never been used against anyone else.

Following the fiasco of the judicial review, an independent review by Laura Dunlop KC recommended the Scottish government completely overhaul the way in which it investigates complaints against ministers and former ministers. She emphasised the need for much greater emphasis on neutrality and natural justice. The Scottish government promised to review their procedures in 2022, but things have gone rather silent since then.

---

39 https://wingsoverscotland.com/conspiracies-for-dummies/

This does not surprise me. Now, for the first time, I can reveal that at the same time as Alex was under investigation, I was also subjected to a procedure which I believe was modelled on the one used against Alex and designed purely to get me. It is a procedure I know has never been used for anyone else, notwithstanding the existence of complaints against other SNP MPs.

As I understand it this procedure was introduced by Kirsty Blackman, the then deputy leader of the SNP Westminster group, for dealing with complaints against SNP MPs. At that time she was the member of the group executive who had designated responsibility for staff welfare. Modelled on the Scottish government's procedure, it too was retrospective. It was used against me in relation to what I believe was a politically motivated complaint of bullying. It was not used against the Chief Whip Patrick Grady, despite the leadership of the group's knowledge of complaints of sexual harassment against him from a staff member dating back to 2016.[40] Nor has it ever been used to address complaints of bullying and harassment that I made against Ian Blackford and Kirsty Blackman.

The complaint against me came from someone on the party's extensive payroll and cast the concerns I had previously raised about the Westminster press operation as bullying of a particular individual. It was not the first politically motivated complaint this individual had raised against SNP parliamentarians who were perceived to be disloyal to Sturgeon, nor would it be the last. I am prevented from naming the individual concerned for legal reasons unrelated to my case. I first became aware of the complaint in November 2017.

At that time, I had no idea that a parallel investigation was taking place into Alex Salmond's behaviour under the auspices of the Scottish government. However, when I found out, Alex and I compared notes, and it was clear to us that the procedure introduced to deal with the alleged complaint against me at Westminster was

---

[40] See earlier footnote

modelled on the procedure that had been drawn up by the Scottish government civil servants to deal with Alex.

Like Alex, I was not told what the complaints were, who the complainer was or given a copy of the procedure being employed against me until I instructed a solicitor, and even then it took her months to get this information out of the Chief Whip. I have often wondered if one of the reasons they were so reluctant to give me a copy of the procedure was that they knew Alex and I were likely to compare notes.

When my solicitor saw the procedure in spring of 2018, she identified the same weaknesses of procedural unfairness and apparent bias as ultimately led to the Scottish government having to concede Alex's judicial review. For example, the investigating officer and decision maker, Kaukab Stewart,[41] had had prior contact with the complainer.

As a result of my solicitor's intervention, the complaint against me was sent to an independent mediator before any determination could be made by Kaukab. When I gave the whole background to the mediator and supplied her with copies of my own (undealt with) complaints of bullying, she realised that it was a political dispute rather than an HR matter and told me she would report to that effect. The Chief Whip had no choice but to shelve the complaints against me and he did so in the summer of 2018, although, interestingly, he refused to let me see the mediator's report. He told me it would be kept on the whips' files for future reference.

I can only assume the report was favourable to me, because for all the years of attempted smears against me that followed it was never deployed or leaked to the press. I suspect a further reason might be that, for reasons I am not at liberty to elaborate upon here, the press might have been very interested to see the identity of the complainer.

---

[41] An SNP activist briefly employed as the business manager of the SNP Westminster Group who is now an MSP and the SNP Government's Equalities Minister.

In September 2018, when Sue Ruddick and Scott Martin came down to Westminster looking for complaints to bolster the case against Alex Salmond, I met with Sue Ruddick and told her about my complaints about Ian Blackford and asked her to investigate them because the Chief Whip had done nothing. At the time I was working in a particularly poisonous atmosphere, and when I was telling her about my situation I became very upset and cried, which is not something I do often. I have no doubt she would have remembered it. Besides, I followed up with a letter to her at HQ setting out my complaints against Ian Blackford and others. Her response was to do nothing about it. Instead, to the astonishment of my solicitor, she announced her intention to reopen the recently closed investigation into me at a party level. She let that drop after my solicitor protested in the strongest terms.

Sue Ruddick has to my knowledge never taken any steps to investigate my complaints, which is in stark contrast to the assiduousness with which she applied herself to the procuring of complaints against Alex Salmond.

Thanks to the independent mediator, I was out of the woods, although another problem soon reared its head. Alex Salmond had warned me that my enemies within the party would try to tie me up with as many complaints and procedures as possible in order to limit my effectiveness as a parliamentarian and dispirit me.

Not long after the SNP Chief Whip had told me that the complaint against me was to be shelved, trouble kicked off in my constituency office. During August 2018, while I was on holiday, I received a phone call from Fraser warning me of staff problems. When I got back, I discovered I had a full-scale mutiny on my hands from junior staff, whose non-specific complaints mainly seemed to revolve around Fraser reminding them of the requirement to be in the office working between 9 and 5 apart from their breaks, unless leave had been agreed in advance.

Further enquiries revealed the involvement of SNP Westminster staffers who were infuriated at my exoneration on the previously confected charge of bullying and determined to get me another way. Correspondence from a Westminster staffer (with whom I'd had little or no contact) was received to this effect and I was told by friendly staffers at Holyrood that rumours were circulating that I was to be done for bullying one way or another.

It is hard to describe the hostile atmosphere in which Fraser and I had to work thereafter. It felt like we were under siege in my constituency office. All confidential calls, particularly with UK Parliament HR (who were fantastic), had to be carried out from my car in the underground car park opposite my office.

Things settled down a little in the autumn of 2018, perhaps because SNP HQ were busy with other things, but in February 2019 one of the former staff members who had been causing trouble in my office the previous summer decided to make a formal complaint about me to the Parliamentary Standards Commissioner (PSC). I believe she was encouraged to do so by SNP HQ.

I had been elected to the SNP NEC in November 2018, and after that I received a high volume of correspondence from party members concerned at HQ's failure to deal with complaints and at perceived irregularities in the parliamentary candidate vetting procedures. The first NEC meeting of 2019 took place shortly after Alex had won his judicial review against the Scottish government. The atmosphere was fraught, to say the least, but it seemed to me that the issue of maladministration in relation to complaints was particularly topical. I argued that the outcome of the judicial review made it imperative that we reformed our own internal complaints procedure. I also mentioned Anne Harvey's concerns that staff from SNP HQ were suborning evidence against Alex. Finally, I raised the concerns about the candidate vetting procedure.

I believe this is what triggered my former staff member's formal complaint against me with the encouragement of SNP HQ, the plan being to leak the existence of the complaint to the press in order to smear and discredit me.

The investigation that followed fully exonerated me, but not before a considerable press storm. From the first NEC monthly meeting in 2019 onwards, I had continued to make myself unpopular with Sturgeon, Murrell and their circle by pressing my concerns about vetting. My confidential correspondence to the party's in-house solicitor, Scott Martin, and to NEC members setting out my concerns, including those communicated to me by other candidates, was later selectively leaked to the press in such a way as to give the impression that it was only my own vetting that I was concerned about.[42]

The PSC operates a strict policy of confidentiality in relation to allegations. However, unlike me, neither the complainer nor her witnesses observed the confidentiality clause, and on the weekend of 11–12 May 2019 lurid allegations of bullying against me were plastered across the Scottish newspapers.[43] I am not going to set out the allegations here because none of them were ever substantiated. However, that weekend was one of the worst of my life.

When I first heard that the press had got hold of the latest complaints of bullying against me, I learned that journalists seemed to be under the impression that the complaints had been made direct to the SNP as well as the PSC. Fraser and I spent a very irritating 30 minutes or so on the phone to Peter Murrell trying to establish whether there were indeed any complaints about me to the SNP. He refused to give us a straight answer. However, to date – despite dark threats from Nicola herself at an NEC meeting in November 2019 – I have never received any official notification of complaints of bullying made about me direct to the party.

When the story broke, on Saturday, 11 May 2019, the papers were full of the unsubstantiated allegations. It is very distressing to be the subject of such a sustained briefing campaign when one knows it to be untrue and politically motivated. The trouble is, of course, that so many people will think there is no smoke without fire, and once a story is published often the damage is done, as had happened to Michelle Thomson in 2016. I was very conscious of this and looking for a way to limit the damage.

In the eye of the media storm I spent all day Saturday confined to my house fielding calls from journalists, with very little

---

42 https://www.thetimes.com/uk/politics/article/joanna-cherry-snp-mp-in-bullying-inquiry-wanted-to-change-vetting-process-for-candidates-6lsnt8lnr

43 https://www.thetimes.com/uk/politics/article/snp-mp-investigated-after-staff-bullying-complaints-879jv9kg5

constructive support from the SNP press team. It felt like I was fighting to save my political life and my reputation. In a professional career spanning 25 years before I went into politics, working as a trainee, a solicitor and counsel in some very high-pressured environments, I had never been accused of bullying. At the bar I had a reputation of the utmost integrity and was trusted and respected. I knew the allegations against me were lies, and if the full background to them was revealed people would appreciate that, but I was limited in what I could say because of the confidentiality of the parliamentary inquiry process.

I spent a lot of time on the phone to Fraser, who was constructing a climbing frame for his children in his garden, discussing what I should do. The Salmond scandal was at its height. Matters had progressed from the civil action to a criminal investigation, and Nicola Sturgeon was treating anyone who would listen to sanctimonious lectures about the importance of taking complaints of harassment or abuse made by women seriously. One of her favourite refrains was to remind people of how hard this was for her because Salmond had been her mentor, but that such complaints must always be addressed without fear or favour. Yet I knew that my complaints of bullying against Ian Blackford and his boys' club had been sitting with the SNP Chief Whip since late 2017 and with SNP HQ since the autumn of 2018 without being addressed in any way. I therefore had damning evidence of Sturgeon's hypocrisy.

Having watched what had happened to Michelle, I had a pretty good idea how things were likely to play out. I could picture the First Minister appearing before the press on Monday morning. How she would tell everyone how important it was that any allegations of bullying were taken seriously and fully investigated, and then announce my suspension from my role as a spokesperson, the SNP whip and the party, until that investigation was completed. From there, as for Michelle, there might be no way back.

I was determined this was not going to happen. So, on Fraser's advice, I telephoned Nicola Sturgeon. I told her that I knew what she and those close to her were trying to do to Alex Salmond and that I would not let them destroy my reputation in the same way.

I said to her in terms that if she took me down, I would take her down with me.

I gave her an ultimatum: if she did not come out on Monday morning and back me, I would give the story of my undealt-with complaints to the press and call her out for her hypocrisy. I told her that I had a friendly journalist teed up and ready to go. Unless she got back to me within an hour with a promise to back me on Monday, a major Sunday newspaper would publish my story the next day.

It was a stark ultimatum. I did not feel particularly proud of effectively blackmailing the First Minister of Scotland and the leader of my party, but Fraser impressed upon me that I had no choice if I wanted to save my career and my reputation.

It was a very difficult thing to do. I was scared but also trembling with rage. Sturgeon was also furious and astonished at my effrontery. Harsh words were exchanged. We swore at each other. However, an hour later she phoned me back and agreed to do as I said. On the Monday morning, when she faced the press pack on a ministerial visit, she told them I had her confidence.[44]

I have no doubt that my threat worked, and for two reasons. Firstly, had the existence of my undealt-with complaints against Ian Blackford been revealed it would have opened Sturgeon up to the charge of hypocrisy. Secondly, my story would have fed into a narrative of the weaponisation of complaints, which would have been useful to Alex's lawyers, who were exploring what options he might have for compensation in the wake of their successful judicial review of the botched investigation against him. Fraser's advice to confront Sturgeon had proven invaluable.

From that moment on Sturgeon and I did not speak. I think it is fair to say we became sworn enemies.

---

[44] https://www.scotsman.com/news/scottish-news/nicola-sturgeon-defends-mp-joanna-cherry-after-bullying-claims-1417714

By the end of June, I had been fully exonerated by the PSC.[45] As usual, the media did not make such a song and dance about this as they had about the original allegations, but the main thing was that I had survived to fight another day. However, events had taken their toll on me. On the day I went to see the PSC to be informed of the outcome of the report into me I was so stressed that I was physically sick. The weekend of excessive press publicity in May alleging that I was a bully was particularly hard to take. It's hard to explain what it's like to be ashamed in relation to something you haven't done.

It is also hard to describe the degree of stress which I was living under at this time. I had to seek medication from my GP in order to keep functioning. Alex Salmond advised me that he understood somebody at SNP HQ had engaged a private detective to spy on him and I should be alert to the possibility that they might also have a private detective spying on me. Fraser advised me that they would likely go through my bins and I shouldn't put the boxes in which my medication came in the bin in case this was used to smear me. This is perhaps not as fanciful as it sounds know that we know that male SNP staffers spied on female SNP MSPs at Holyrood.[46]

It is at times like these that one falls back on family and friends. My family had rallied round me. On the weekend the newspapers broke the story I had felt too ashamed to leave the house, but I needed to go out and do everyday tasks like grocery shopping. My sister sent over my fourteen-year-old nephew Jamie, with whom I've always been very close, and he accompanied me out to the local shops, where I lurked behind the stacks while he nonchalantly checked through my shopping, including a box of tampons. He was so mature and grown up and I was so proud of him and grateful for his support.

---

[45] https://www.thenational.scot/news/17738144.snp-mp-joanna-cherry-cleared-former-staffers-bullying-claim/

[46] https://www.thescottishsun.co.uk/news/15705778/female-snp-msps-bugged-male-aides-spying-scandal/; https://www.scotsman.com/news/politics/holyrood-bosses-urged-to-launch-investigation-into-bugging-claims-5448975.

My experience and those of others suggests that under Sturgeon's leadership there was a modus operandi in the SNP of using complaints against internal critics to smear them publicly, while ignoring complaints made against leadership loyalists. While a huge amount of time and effort was put into the investigations against Alex Salmond by SNP officials, allegations of inappropriate and indeed in some cases criminal sexual behaviour by other parliamentarians, councillors and party officials have been ignored or hidden by the party. A classic example of this behaviour is the case of Cameron Downing , a former party equalities officer whose tweets about wanting to beat up gender critical feminists were ignored despite complaints and who went on to be jailed for a string of sexual and physical assaults.[47] It subsequently transpired that one of his female victims had contacted the party to warn them of his criminal behaviour and been ignored.

At the opposite end of the scale, complaints of sexual harassment against Patrick Grady the chief whip were ignored for years.

I made serious complaints of harassment and bullying against Ian Blackford in 2017, 2018 and 2021, and against Kirsty Blackman in 2021. None of them have ever been dealt with. However, during the selection process for SNP candidates for the 2026 Scottish election, complaints of bullying against a potential candidate from a local councillor were fast-tracked by SNP HQ through what were ultimately found to have been unfair proceedings in order to remove him from the ballot.[48]

There is ample evidence that just as the Westminster group leadership introduced a new procedure to deal with complaints against me that has never been used against anyone else, the Scottish government introduced a procedure that was deliberately

---

[47] https://news.sky.com/story/ex-snp-equalities-officer-cameron-downing-who-wanted-to-beat-up-terfs-jailed-for-sexual-and-physical-assaults-13178930. https://www.heraldscotland.com/news/24496433.snp-ignored-warnings-cameron-downing/

[48] https://www.heraldscotland.com/news/25398911.snp-national-secretary-provided-one-sided-evidence-complaint/

designed for Alex Salmond and has never been used against anyone else. When Alex's lawyers challenged the procedure there was an attempt at a cover-up, which went right to the top of the Scottish government. When those involved in that cover-up became aware that it was unlikely to succeed, it appears from all the available evidence that steps were taken to ensure that the criminal investigation would supersede the civil proceedings. At that stage SNP HQ became involved in seeking out further complainers to bolster the police investigation. Questions have been asked over whether some witnesses may have perjured themselves at the trial of Alex Salmond and there has been a Crown investigation into allegations of perjury against one of the complainers but with no clear outcome.[49] If I am right and there was a conspiracy against Alex Salmond, then those involved in the conspiracy have been well protected – so far.

Like many of those who admired or loved him, I hope that the full circumstances surrounding the allegations made against Alex will one day come to light, including the identity of the SNP politicians and staffers who pursued him. I exempt from this the civil servants who were complainers at his trial. I have no reason to believe that they were part of a conspiracy, but I believe they may have been used by others who were.

It is possible that Alex's action for misfeasance in public office, if it is to be pursued against the Scottish government notwithstanding his death, may go some way to revealing more of the truth of what happened. However, it will take a criminal investigation or a public inquiry or both to reveal the full truth.

For those of us who care about the civic life of our country, whether we are unionists or nationalists, we cannot have political parties, politicians or civil servants abusing complaints procedures or our criminal justice system in order to pursue personal vendettas, settle scores or rid themselves of competition. Nor can we have

---

[49] https://www.scottishlegal.com/articles/perjury-claims-against-alex-salmond-remain-in-limbo#:~:text=The%20Crown%20Office%20is%20still,under%20oath%20at%20his%20trial.

a situation where senior civil servants are utterly immune from the consequences of their actions.

It was a blessing in disguise for Nicola Sturgeon, Liz Lloyd, senior government officials, and staff at SNP HQ, including Peter Murrell, that on the day of Alex's acquittal, the first lockdown of a pandemic that was to last two years was announced. Without this tragic intervention, I believe the degree of scrutiny that would have ensued in the immediate aftermath of the trial might have been enough to bring Nicola Sturgeon down. Instead, the arrival of the pandemic in the UK was a massive and understandable distraction from what had just occurred. It also gave her the opportunity to shore up her reputation in the wake of the scandal.

THE COVID YEARS

5

On 24 December 2020, I was doing some last-minute Christmas shopping in Stockbridge, masked, standing in a queue outside a shop and observing social distancing, when I noticed I had several missed calls from my SNP colleague Margaret Ferrier, then the MP for Rutherglen and Hamilton West. In October, Margaret had become embroiled in a very public scandal when she confessed to having breached Covid regulations by travelling to Westminster while awaiting the results of testing and then travelling home on public transport having tested positive. The story received the sort of wall-to-wall press coverage that Dominic Cummings's ill-fated trip to Barnard Castle[1] met with in the spring and about which SNP politicians had been highly critical. The press were encamped outside Margaret's house for weeks.

Margaret was roundly condemned, with some of the harshest criticism coming from within the SNP, including from Nicola Sturgeon and Ian Blackford, keen to distance themselves from any charges of hypocrisy, given their vociferous attacks on Cummings.

The first I had heard of Margaret's troubles was when travelling north from London on an almost deserted train (as trains were at that time in the pandemic) on Thursday, 1 October 2020. Former

---

[1] https://www.bbc.co.uk/news/52828076

Labour First Minister Jack McConnell was in my carriage, and we were chatting at an appropriate social distance about what had occurred at First Minister's Questions (FMQs) earlier that day.

The then Scottish Conservative leader, Ruth Davidson, had quizzed Nicola Sturgeon about the Scottish government's refusal to hand over key documents to the Holyrood committee investigating the Salmond affair, and about leaked WhatsApp messages that showed Peter Murrell advising an SNP colleague to pressurise the police in regards to the criminal investigation into Alex in January 2019, after he had won his judicial review against the Scottish government. Sturgeon had refused to comment on the WhatsApp messages and was widely judged to have looked very uncomfortable.[2]

After we had finished gossiping, we both sat down to do some work, when suddenly Jack stood up and said to me, 'It looks like another one of your colleagues is in trouble,' and showed me a tweet from Margaret. In the tweet Margaret made a full confession and apologised unreservedly for breaching Covid restrictions by travelling to parliament while awaiting a covid test, after experiencing mild symptoms, and travelling home after a positive test result. She said that she had reported herself to the police as well as the House of Commons authorities and that she took full responsibility for her actions.

I was immediately suspicious about the very public and detailed nature of Margaret's confession. I assumed it had been done without legal advice and with the party's blessing, but I wondered why, given that it was clearly going to invite a media frenzy rather than shut the story down.

I was familiar from my own experience that Liz Lloyd sometimes 'persuaded' parliamentarians to tweet in a manner designed to take the heat off Nicola Sturgeon when a story threatened to damage her. At this time Nicola was riding high in her role as the nation's 'chief mammy' and revelling in the contrast between

---

[2] https://news.stv.tv/politics/sturgeon-challenged-over-husbands-whatsapp-messages

her perceived competence and integrity in handling the Covid crisis and the incompetence and disarray of Boris Johnson and his administration. Clearly, if Margaret had broken Covid regulations, Nicola would wish to distance herself from her, particularly as she and Margaret had often been photographed together at campaign events.

However, I suspected there was also another factor at play, namely a ploy to have Margaret's story replace the one about the difficult time Sturgeon had endured at FMQs across social media, on the evening news bulletins and in the next day's papers.

I phoned Margaret and established that, as I had suspected, the wording of her tweet had been provided by Catriona Matheson, the former head of the SNP media operation at Westminster who had recently been moved to work directly for Blackford. Margaret had been told what she must say after she was summoned to a Zoom meeting attended by Blackford, Patrick Grady, Matheson and Tom French, who had replaced Matheson as head of the Westminster group media team. Margaret told me that they had even specified the precise time at which she should tweet: 5.45pm – just in time for the evening news programmes.

From that moment on the story was rarely off the headlines. Margaret was suspended from the party and had the whip withdrawn. On the advice of Ian Blackford, she had reported herself to the police and to the PSC. By Christmas both the Metropolitan Police and British Transport Police had said that they would be taking no action against Margaret because the regulations under which she might have been charged were not in effect when she travelled. Whenever the story threatened to die down, it was reignited, usually by a tweet or a media interview from one of Margaret's former friends and comrades, including her former office manager.[3] Someone within the SNP had given the press Margaret's personal phone number, so she was besieged on the telephone as well as in her home.

---

[3] https://www.bbc.co.uk/news/uk-scotland-54379026

I was concerned for Margaret's wellbeing and helped her to get a good solicitor. I was not only suspicious about the nature and timing of Margaret's very public confession, but also about the way in which the story was being fuelled by individuals within the SNP.

On two occasions, when questioned about Margaret's actions, Nicola Sturgeon referred to her as 'Margaret Covid'.[4] She said it was a slip of the tongue, but I suspect it was either deliberate or an unwitting public use of a nickname Sturgeon and her circle were using for Margaret behind the scenes. A journalist had told me I was referred to as 'the bitch' in the Sturgeon inner circle.

There was also a concerted attempt by Blackford and elected members and activists in Margaret's local constituency area , some of whom were close to Nicola Sturgeon to have Margaret resign her seat. I was disgusted by the venom with which Margaret was pursued by her former comrades. She had been one of the most loyal party activists I have ever known. If there was a by election anywhere in Scotland, Margaret would be the first person to get in her car and travel across the country at her own expense to campaign for the SNP candidate. She was also a very hard-working constituency MP and utterly loyal to the party. The viciousness with which her former colleagues turned upon her horrified me and I thought it was out of all proportion to her offence. Of course what she had done was wrong, but I felt she was more than paying for it.

Ian Blackford gave an interview to Radio Scotland's breakfast programme *Good Morning Scotland*, in which he demanded that not only should Margaret lose her seat, but that she should also lose her parliamentary pension.[5] This seemed to be going too far to me and prompted me to text him, asking him to lay off. While Blackford is a millionaire with ongoing business interests and a big pension from his banking career, Margaret is a single divorcee in her sixties who,

---

[4] https://www.standard.co.uk/news/uk/nicola-sturgeon-calls-flouting-scottish-mp-margaret-covid-in-second-briefing-slip-up-a4563911.html

[5] https://www.thenational.scot/news/18774952.snp-thrown-margaret-ferrier-wolves/

without her parliamentary pension, would no doubt have nothing to support her in old age other than the state pension.

It is fortunate that Margaret is a strong individual and a devout Catholic. I think someone without her strength of character and her faith might have been pushed to suicide by the strength of the onslaught she endured from the press and her former comrades.

By Christmas Eve, things had died down a bit, so when I returned her calls that day, I was astonished to find that the police were at her front door seeking to arrest her and bring her in for questioning. Understandably, she was distraught. When she and her daughter initially heard the knock at the door they assumed it was the press. On realising it was the police Margaret had phoned her solicitor, but he was away for Christmas and limited in what he could do.

I could not fathom why the police would wish to do such a thing on Christmas Eve when Margaret had no criminal record, posed no flight risk (she had hardly been out of her house for weeks) and when they must have known that she had a solicitor. The normal thing would have been for them to contact her solicitor and arrange to have her come in voluntarily for an interview. I told Margaret to stay in her house, not to answer the door and I would try to find out what on earth was going on.

As a former Advocate Depute, I was aware that ultimately the police answer to the direction of the Crown, so I contacted somebody senior and well respected at the criminal bar who in turn contacted the Crown Office to see if they might intervene. I hoped that they might stop the police from arresting Margaret on Christmas Eve and tell them instead to arrange through her solicitor for her to attend at a police station for arrest and interview early in the New Year. Thankfully they were successful in this.[6]

It transpired that Margaret had not actually broken any of the many rules and regulations that had been introduced in relation to Covid, so she was charged with the common law crime of 'culpable

---

[6] https://www.theguardian.com/uk-news/2021/jan/04/scottish-mp-margaret-ferrier-arrested-over-alleged-covid-rule-breach

and reckless conduct', to which she pled guilty and received a sentence of a hefty 270 hours of community service.[7] I have always wondered whether she ought to have pled to this charge, but I was not privy to the discussions she had with her legal advisers, and of course she was hampered by the very public confession she had made under orders from the party before she had the benefit of legal advice.

In the meantime, a petition for her recall as a Member of Parliament was pursued with considerable vigour by some of her former colleagues and Margaret was forced to stand down. The SNP duly lost the by-election to replace her in October 2023.

From one point of view the whole episode was a monumental own goal, but at a time when pressure on the SNP government and party was mounting over the Salmond inquiry it served as a massive distraction for the press. That is why I believe that Margaret was deliberately thrown to the wolves by the SNP leadership – to distract from the growing scandal surrounding the Salmond affair.

I also fear that pressure was brought to bear on the police and the Crown to make an example of an otherwise blameless and upstanding parliamentarian in order to protect Sturgeon and her reputation as a paragon of virtue in her handling of the Covid crisis, particularly compared to Boris Johnson, who had protected Dominic Cummings over the notorious Barnard Castle trip.

In the absence of a plausible contrary explanation for the extraordinary behaviour of the police on Christmas Eve, I can only surmise that someone at a high level within the police had been put under political pressure to arrest Margaret at that time to add to the general circus. If I am right about this, it is deeply shocking that such a thing could happen in Scotland.

Understanding why a loyal party servant as Margaret was pursued with such vigour and with no mercy for her misdemeanours is the key to understanding what was really going on when Nicola Sturgeon assumed the role of 'chief mammy' for the Scottish nation during the Covid crisis.

---

[7] https://www.bbc.co.uk/news/uk-scotland-62589375

Unionist commentators assert that Nicola took advantage of the crisis to advance the cause of independence. And indeed, she was cross examined to that effect by counsel to the UK Covid Inquiry. However, I would question whether there is evidence to support this. While opinion polls showed increased support for independence based on what was then perceived to be Nicola's competent handling of the pandemic, her administration did nothing to capitalise on that support. Indeed, despite much huffing and puffing from the same unionist commentators, the preparations that Nicola had announced in January 2020, including a constitutional convention and further white papers on independence, were paused during the pandemic. This was in marked contrast to the Tories' continued pursuit of their Brexit plans.

Instead, I believe Nicola and her close circle took advantage of the opportunities afforded to her by the pandemic to shore up her reputation in the wake of Alex Salmond's acquittal. It should never be forgotten that his acquittal happened at three o'clock in the afternoon of the same day that lockdown was later announced. His acquittal raised many questions for the Scottish government, so the timing of the lockdown was very convenient for them.

I suspect that in the early months of the Covid pandemic, Nicola and her closest confidantes, at that time her husband, Liz Lloyd and John Swinney, spent quite a bit of time discussing how to handle the fallout from Salmond's acquittal. The Scottish Parliament committee on the Scottish government's handling of the harassment complaints against Alex Salmond first met in late 2020, and heard some pretty explosive evidence sessions in February and March 2021 before publishing its final report on 23 March 2021, which concluded that Nicola Sturgeon had misled them in her evidence.[8]

I have no doubt that these events were a cause of great anxiety to Nicola Sturgeon and her closest advisers, something they would have been anxiously engaged in discussing often, on WhatsApp because of lockdown restrictions. I am convinced this is why

---

[8] Report of the Committee on the Scottish Governmen Handling of Harassment Complaints at Page 129 paras 718 and 720

Sturgeon, Swinney and Lloyd deleted all their WhatsApp messages for the first part of the pandemic, despite Sturgeon having promised to keep hers, while other government ministers, such as Humza Yousaf and Kate Forbes, kept theirs, suggesting that the 'government policy' cited in defence of the Sturgeon inner circle's behaviour was not a universal practice.[9] Interestingly, at around this same time, the Chief Whip at Westminster instituted a policy of 'disappearing messages' in the WhatsApp groups used by SNP MPs to keep in touch with events.

The daily press conferences that Nicola held during the pandemic played to her strengths, in particular her mastery of detail and performative announcements. They also allowed her to control the dominant political narrative. Small tweaks or unevidenced differences (as we now know from evidence to the inquiry) of approach to the UK government gave the impression that she was more on top of things than Boris Johnson, a low bar at the best of times.

As Robin McAlpine has pointed out, it is not normal to let a political leader have as much unchallenged airtime as Nicola Sturgeon enjoyed during the Covid crisis.[10] Indeed, many of her political opponents questioned the fairness of this, particularly as the 2021 Holyrood election approached. Scottish Secretary Alister Jack referred to the daily press conference as the 'Nicola Sturgeon show'.[11]

On one occasion the BBC received hundreds of complaints when ten minutes of the briefing were taken up with questions about the Salmond inquiry. It was felt by many that she had used the platform afforded to her to cast doubt over the jury's verdict.

---

[9] https://www.bbc.co.uk/news/uk-scotland-68152037 https://www.heraldscotland.com/news/24074409.liz-lloyd-denies-intentionally-deleting-messages-avoid-fois/https://www.bbc.co.uk/news/live/uk-scotland-68080043

[10] https://sourcenews.scot/robin-mcalpine-what-passes-for-normal-in-scotland-these-days/

[11] https://www.heraldscotland.com/news/19147959.bbc-stands-sturgeon-covid-show---complaints-inappropriate-salmond-commentary/).

It was not just her political rivals in the SNP and beyond who questioned this, but also my own professional body, the Faculty of Advocates, which issued a statement urging politicians to respect the rule of law and the independence of the judicial system and 'perhaps most importantly the verdicts of impartial juries in criminal proceedings'.[12]

According to Robin, Nicola was the only leader in the world who held a daily press conference throughout the Covid pandemic, and I have no reason to doubt that he's correct about that. He also makes the rather forceful point that other leaders spent their mornings battling Covid and the economic crisis rather than preparing for and giving press conferences. Importantly, the press conferences were designed in such a way that journalists weren't allowed follow up questions and to be transparently controlling.

On the other hand, I know from neighbours, constituents and friends that many people found these press conferences comforting during the crisis. Indeed, their popularity can be measured by the increase in Nicola's popularity ratings and in support for the SNP and independence during this time.

Lockdown

The first lockdown in the UK was announced at 8.30pm on the evening of 23 March 2020. Just hours earlier, Alex Salmond had been acquitted by a jury of all the charges against him.

I was already at home in Edinburgh, having returned from London ten days previously with flu-like symptoms, which I suspected might be Covid. On the advice of my GP, I had self-isolated for ten days. That Monday is etched in my memory not just because of Boris Johnson's unprecedented broadcast in the evening, but because of the almost unbearable tension I experienced waiting for the jury to come back with their verdicts

---

12 https://www.heraldscotland.com/news/19118578.frenzied-salmond-debate-risks-irreparable-harm-justice-system/

The jury had been out since Friday afternoon. My self-isolation was coming to an end but I did not leave the house as I anxiously waited for the verdict. Fraser, my chief of staff, was at court with Alex and I knew he would message me when he could, but I spent a lot of time refreshing Twitter. Eventually, I gave up trying to concentrate and resorted to housework, not something I normally bother with if possible. As I dusted, I recited the rosary for a just outcome, again not something I do often. When the verdicts finally came in, I wept with relief.

Shortly afterwards, Fraser arrived at my house and we opened a bottle of champagne. He could only have one glass as he was driving, so I gave him the rest of the bottle to take home to share with his wife. He delivered me my office phone and some other basic office equipment. He had been around all our constituency staff in the preceding days doing the same in preparation for the lockdown we had all seen coming. We were determined to keep our phone lines open so that constituents could speak to us in person, and I am proud that, unlike many offices who had only an answer machine, we did so throughout the pandemic.

I shall never forget the surreal quality of Johnson's television broadcast. It felt like something out of a Hollywood disaster movie, except Boris was no Morgan Freeman. I thought the lockdown would last a few weeks at most. How wrong I was. However, for me the first few weeks of the pandemic were a welcome respite from constant travelling to London and back and around the constituency.

I was one of the lucky ones. I had a nice home to live in with a small garden. Friendly neighbours to talk to in the street or over the garden fence. One of Edinburgh's lovely public parks and the water of Leith on my doorstep for walks.

I was unlucky enough to have Covid on several occasions, but I was never seriously unwell. The first time was about two weeks before lockdown. On the next occasion I tested positive shortly after having attended a Christmas party hosted by Hugh Grant in the crystal ballroom of the beautiful St Ermin's Hotel at St James's Park. It was December 2021, and in England at least parties were permitted. More than eighteen months since the start of the first lockdown, it was the first party many of the people there had attended for a long time, and there was a real sense of joy and excitement. There were many people there I hadn't seen for ages, including Gina Miller, whom I embraced, and of course Hugh himself, who embraced me warmly as he told me he thought I had been treated disgracefully by Nicola Sturgeon. The next day I felt awful and realised it was more than just a hangover. When I tested positive, I had to rather sheepishly contact both Gina and Hugh.

The form NHS England required you to fill out at the time asked you to list anyone with whom you'd had skin on skin contact in the last few days. I had to include Hugh Grant, and I took the precaution of adding a note that I was not a deluded middle-aged woman having bizarre fantasies, but that I really had been kissed by Hugh Grant at a party two days before I tested positive. I always wondered what the official reading that form must have thought.

Notwithstanding these tribulations, I was one of the lucky ones who came through Covid with their health relatively unscathed. So too did my family and most of my friends, although we lost my mum to dementia during the pandemic, and I have no doubt that the social isolation of those first few months hastened the onset of that terrible illness. However, my mum is still here, she knows her immediate family, and there are many happy and loving moments. My dad cared for her at home for as long as he could. Now she is in a care home where she is very well looked after.

Understanding dementia as I do now, and with first-hand experience of the care home sector, I cannot bear to think of those elderly people like my mum who were left largely alone to suffer and die at the start of the pandemic, unable to see their families, nor imagine the suffering endured by relatives and friends unable to visit loved ones. I cannot understand why it was felt necessary to discharge so many old people from hospitals into care homes, without testing, when emergency hospital facilities were built that were never used. It is now accepted that this was a terrible mistake.

I have no desire in this book to second guess the decisions made by those in government during the pandemic, or to suggest what they should have done differently. The task of understanding why they did what they did and how we might approach such matters in future is for the UK and Scottish Covid inquiries.

However, while I am not a public health expert, I am an expert in human rights, and my interactions with both governments during the Covid crisis led me to conclude that politicians of all political hues were too ready to discount the importance of human rights protections in their panic at being faced with a global pandemic.

Clearly both governments in the UK were going to require emergency powers to deal with the pandemic. These were always going to raise human rights issues and challenges for the rule of law, including the proportionality of any measures taken and the adequacy of democratic scrutiny.

It seemed to me that while most of the powers initially sought were probably necessary in the circumstances, the safest thing to do was to grant them for only a short period of time, after which parliamentary approval would be required for their renewal. Although Johnston had a huge majority, I knew that there were many Tory backbenchers such as David Davis who shared my concerns.

I worked cross party to articulate these concerns and kept Mike Russell, the Scottish government Cabinet Secretary, who was going to be responsible for similar emergency legislation in Scotland, advised of what I was doing. He agreed with me that it wasn't safe to give such wide-ranging powers to Boris Johnson indefinitely.

The UK government backed down and accepted an amendment that the operation of the Act must be reviewed by parliament every six months. The Scottish Government also introduced a Coronavirus (Scotland) Bill to grant them emergency powers to tackle the outbreak. It had a six-month sunset clause, but there were other aspects of the bill that were concerning.

The Scottish Coronavirus Emergency Bill included a significant relaxation of Freedom of Information (FOI) regulations, potentially permitting public bodies up to five times the standard response period for addressing FOI requests. There was much disquiet about this, and in May 2020 opposition parties on the Scottish Parliament's Covid-19 committee combined to force the government to withdraw these emergency relaxations.

It was later revealed that the then Health Minister, Jeane Freeman, had wanted to suspend FOI legislation in its entirety during the pandemic. Ironically, this information was itself only revealed after a Freedom of Information request filed by the Ferret, an investigative journalism website, which was itself returned more than six months late.[13]

The instinct to do away with FOI altogether shows a mindset that is hostile to scrutiny and transparency. Had this proposal succeeded, it would have been extremely useful to the Scottish government in their efforts to withstand scrutiny of their role in the Salmond affair. For that reason I suspect it was Sturgeon and Swinney, not Jeane, who were behind the plan to get rid of freedom of information legislation.

The Scottish government also planned to give themselves the power to suspend trial by jury in serious criminal cases if necessary. The Scottish Criminal Bar Association described these proposals as 'draconian' and 'an attack on principles that have been built over 600 years and are at the very cornerstone of Scotland's criminal justice system and democratic tradition'. They also described the proposals 'premature, disproportionate and ill advised'. I agreed. So did most lawyers and all the opposition parties

I argued that the proposals were not necessary. I pointed out that there was no proposal to do away with jury trials in England and there were other options, including postponing some serious trials, jurors dialling into trials by video link or cases being held in larger venues to allow for social distancing, which was what eventually happened.

My public comments were jumped upon by the press, as I was the SNP's Justice spokesperson at Westminster, but I had first tried behind the scenes to try to dissuade my colleague Mike Russell from pursuing this proposal. I said to him that quite separate from the pandemic, there was an agenda shared by Rape Crisis and some in the Crown Office and Scotland's senior judiciary to get rid of jury trials in rape cases, and I feared they were taking advantage of the pandemic to trial their plans. There was also a suspicion that

---

13 https://theferret.scot/health-minister-freedom-of-information-foi-covid-19/

in the wake of Alex Salmond's acquittal, jury trials were not exactly flavour of the month with at least some in the Scottish government. I had spoken with Robert Buckland, the English Lord Chancellor, privately, and I knew there were no similar plans to do away with juries in England.

Mike was not particularly receptive to my concerns, saying that his priority was to save lives. I argued that at this stage there was no need to do away with juries to save lives and that he should not let the senior judiciary and victims' charities pull the wool over his eyes.

Humza Yousaf, who at that time was the Justice Minister, was more receptive to my concerns. At my instigation he spoke directly with several of my senior criminal practitioner colleagues at the bar, and by 1 April the plans had been dropped. Ultimately, jury trials took place during the pandemic at remote jury centres.

The dilemma about what to do about jury trials provides a very good example of the importance of governments not overlooking the centrality of human rights when faced with the challenge of a pandemic. The need to find a solution was not just about protecting public health and preventing an administrative backlog. It was also about protecting the rights of accused persons awaiting trial and the rights of victims and other witnesses.

As the pandemic progressed, and parliament met in person again, the SNP Chief Whip sought volunteers to go to Westminster. Many of my colleagues were reluctant to go, but I obliged with enthusiasm. After the initial novelty of lockdown wore off, I hated being stuck at home and it was a relief to have something to do while so many people were in limbo. When I first returned to London in early June 2020 the city centre was deserted and eerie. Parliament also felt very different with social distancing and, initially, bizarre conga lines to ensure social distancing for voting in the lobbies until voting became electronic. However, the atmosphere was more collaborative and less combative than usual, and there was something of the wartime spirit.

Human rights became the focus of my work, particularly after my colleagues on the Joint Committee on Human Rights (JCHR) voted to make me deputy chair of the committee after I had been sacked from the SNP frontbench in February 2021. In April 2022, Harriet Harman was seconded to chair an investigation by the Commons Privileges Committee into Boris Johnson, whom it was suspected had misled parliament over partygate allegations during the pandemic. The committee reported in the summer of 2023, and while Harriet was busy with this investigation, I became the de facto chair of the JCHR.

As well as scrutinising human rights aspects of the pandemic, the committee also reported on the Tory government's plans to replace the Human Rights Act with a British Bill of Rights. I am proud of the role we played in successfully resisting that misguided ploy.

In relation to Covid, we noted that the blanket use of 'do not attempt cardiopulmonary resuscitation' notices in care homes constituted a systematic violation of individual rights; that there had been a disproportionate impact of some of the measures taken to stop the spread of the disease on certain groups in society, such as children, whose right to education was engaged by school closures, and those in detention with autism and/or learning difficulties who were denied family visits. We also highlighted confusion over the status and interpretation of guidance, and the relationship between guidance and the law in relation to the lockdown regulations.

I am also very proud of the role that the committee I chaired played in calling the UK government to account over many of the more oppressive aspects of the Covid regulations. This is, of course, what parliaments and parliamentary committees are supposed to do. I was therefore dismayed by the lack of similar scrutiny at Holyrood and by the government's hostility towards any efforts to bring this about.

Human Rights were not to the fore of decision making at Westminster, nor at Holyrood. However, for all their faults, some of the more libertarian Tories did at least force the issue of civil liberties at Westminster. At Holyrood, lobbying was largely left to the legal profession and the handful of MSPs and third sector organisations who were not afraid of upsetting the government or being seen as a nuisance.

The former Labour MSP Neil Findlay was one of them, and he has written and spoken about the hostility he encountered from government ministers for asking questions about the situation in care homes, even though his mother was in a care home and his wife and daughter were both NHS workers.[14]

He points out that Human Rights organisations in Scotland were surprisingly uncritical of the government. In his experience, when a bad decision was going to be made he would ask third sector organisations or charities to give him a quote or speak out so he could incorporate that in his campaign or speech, but they were afraid to do so in case their budget got cut or their chief executive got a phone call from somebody in government telling them to be quiet.

I met with the relatives of people in care homes who were distraught at the visiting ban in Scotland, but had to explain to them that they were required to lobby their Holyrood MSPs rather than me, as it was it a devolved matter. After years of campaigning, they succeeded in getting the government to legislate to uphold the rights of care home residents to see their loved ones except in the most extreme circumstances.

In the first wave of the pandemic, more than 1,300 elderly people were discharged from hospitals to care homes in Scotland before a testing regime was in place. By April 2021 Scotland's Covid-19-related deaths exceeded 100,000. A third of the deaths occurred in care homes.

Neil Findlay doggedly pursued the Scottish government over the discharge of elderly people from hospital to care homes in the early stages of the pandemic. On numerous occasions he asked them to accept that the care home discharge policy was a mistake, but they refused to do so. Then, after parliament had been dissolved for the 2021 election, the Health Minister, Jeane Freeman, who was standing down at the election, went on Nick Robinson's podcast and admitted that the care home discharge policy was a

---

[14] https://www.holyrood.com/comment/view,id-owed-it-to-my-constituents-and-my-mum-to-ask-tough-questions-during-the-pandemic; https://podcasts.apple.com/zw/podcast/scotlands-covid-reckoning-1-neil-findlay/id1477893155?i=1000643951483

mistake. Nicola Sturgeon said that with 'hindsight' she agreed. I find Neil Findlay's anger that these admissions were only made once the government was free from the threat of parliamentary scrutiny completely understandable. It is an anger shared by many Covid-bereaved families.

During the pandemic Scottish public opinion was in the main very positive about Nicola Sturgeon's stewardship of the nation. I lost count of the number of times constituents and other members of the public stopped me in the street to tell me that they weren't nationalists but admired Nicola Sturgeon for her handling of the crisis.

That view is not as widely held now as it was during the pandemic. Evidence to the Covid Inquiry has revealed that the Scottish government's decision making was perhaps not as evidence based and reliable as the public assumed at the time. In so far as my areas of expertise are concerned, that was certainly what I saw.

I didn't make myself popular with Scottish government colleagues given my stance on the jury trials issue. I wrote about this and other contemporary issues in my new weekly column in the *National* newspaper, which I had recently procured after announced my intention to seek selection as the SNP candidate for the Edinburgh Central constituency at the Scottish Parliament elections in May 2021.

Angus Robertson was being lined up for the nomination and it was known that he was the leadership's favoured candidate. He had recently moved back to Edinburgh from Moray, where he had been the local MP, from 2001 to 2017. However, many in the local branch, of which I was a member, were not happy about having him imposed upon them and approached me as a potential candidate. They wanted someone who would keep pressure on the leadership to advance the cause of independence, rather than just toe the party line. It was also felt at that time that many talented SNP MPs – for example, Philippa Whitford and Alison Thewliss – were somewhat becalmed at Westminster, where Boris Johnson had a huge majority, and would be much better off in the Scottish Parliament where they could contribute to government and furthering the cause of independence. Some of us were also seen as potential future leaders of the party, and to do that we needed to be at Holyrood.

There was no rule against double jobbing, and in fact several MPs, including SNP MPs and many MSPs, have held double mandates.[15] In February 2020, I announced that I would be seeking the nomination and that if I got elected to Holyrood I would stand down as an MP to focus on Scotland. I wrote an article for the *National* explaining my reasons,[16] and persuaded them that, as Angus had a weekly column, they should give me one too.

There was a degree of consternation when I made my announcement, as clearly Angus had been promised the seat and assumed he was a shoe-in. Mike Russell contacted me to try to persuade me to seek the nomination for the Argyll and Bute constituency instead, as he was intending to stand down at the election. I explained that I would rather represent somewhere I lived and knew well, and that I was standing at the request of local members who would rather have me than Angus Robertson as their candidate. I suggested to him that, as Angus was looking for a seat and was more peripatetic than me, he should stand for Argyll and Bute.

However, for some reason, Angus Robertson had been promised Edinburgh Central, and it quickly became clear the SNP NEC might be prepared to take steps to ensure that I would not impede his progress. It was rumoured that a new rule would be introduced against dual mandates, stipulating that if an MP wanted to seek selection as a Holyrood candidate, he or she would have to stand down from Westminster first and put up £10,000 towards the expenses of the by-election that would be necessitated. In the event the financial penalty idea was dropped, but the NEC decided at the end of July 2020 that if an MP was selected as a candidate for Holyrood, they would have to stand down in time to allow a by-election for their

---

[15] https://www.bbc.co.uk/news/articles/crmnj33dwkdo#:~:text=Dual%20mandates%20have%20not%20always,of%20MPs%20like%20Stephen%20Flynn.

[16] https://joannacherry.scot/newspaper-columns/2020/why-i-am-standing-for-edinburgh-south-west

Westminster seat to take place on the same day as the Scottish Parliament elections.

If they had hoped that floating the financial penalty and then deciding against it would detract from the impact of their announcement, they were wrong. The new rule became known as the 'Joanna Cherry rule', as it was thought to have been designed purely to keep me out of Holyrood. There was uproar in the party and some party members resigned over the issue, both in the Edinburgh Central branch and in the wider party.

In 2024, when newly elected SNP MPs including Stephen Flynn and Stephen Gethins announced their intention to stand for Holyrood in 2026, it was assumed that the party would do away with the rule, which it has, but in the meantime Holyrood has voted to ban double jobbing, so they will have no choice but to stand down from Westminster but only if they are elected to Holyrood. [17]

The 'Joanna Cherry rule' meant that if I was selected as a candidate for the Edinburgh Central constituency I would then have to quit as an MP in February of the year of the election, close my constituency office and make my staff redundant. I put out a statement saying I wasn't willing to do that, particularly in the middle of a pandemic, and that the rule change had made a fair and open contest impossible.[18]

Many of my colleagues in the SNP Westminster group were livid at the NEC's ruling, as at least some of them had been contemplating a similar move. There was an extremely heated meeting at which we attempted to discover which way the group's representative on the NEC, Chris Law, had voted. Quite extraordinarily, he refused to tell us, citing the confidentiality of NEC deliberations. We suspected this meant he had voted in favour of the new rule, and this was confirmed to me by another NEC member.

---

[17] https://www.bbc.co.uk/news/articles/c3e3zzz7lkvo.amp

[18] https://www.bbc.co.uk/news/uk-scotland-scotland-politics-53607198#:~:text=Joanna%20Cherry%20has%20ruled%20out,of%20SNP%20'infighting'%20true?

Subsequently, Marco Biagi, who had been the SNP MP for Edinburgh Central between 2011 and 2016, threw his hat into the Edinburgh Central race, but ultimately he was defeated by Angus Robertson in January 2021. Angus went on to win the seat at the May 2021 election and become a Cabinet Secretary. Many assumed that he would be the obvious successor to Sturgeon, but when she resigned his candidacy did not materialise.

One of the reasons grassroots members of Edinburgh Central SNP would rather have had me as their candidate than Angus Robertson was their feeling that the party was doing little or nothing to advance the cause of independence. This was a view widely held in the party.

As I explained back in Chapter 4, there had been a great degree of unhappiness about Nicola Sturgeon's three-point plan announced on Brexit day, and now, with the arrival of the pandemic, her plans for a constitutional convention and independence papers had been shelved. Having floated the idea of testing whether the Scottish Parliament could legally hold a second independence referendum, this issue had slipped from her agenda.

By the summer of 2020 opinion polls were showing increased support for independence, and I used my *National* column to argue that the time for avoiding discussion of a Plan B was over. A campaign group had obtained an opinion from Aidan O'Neill QC setting out the argument that Holyrood could legally hold an independence referendum.

Martin James Keatings, convenor of the group known as Forward as One, brought a case before the Court of Session seeking a ruling 'that the Scottish Parliament has power under the provisions of the Scotland Act to legislate for the holding of a referendum on whether Scotland should be an independent country without requiring the consent of the UK government or any further amendment by the UK parliament to the Scotland Act 1998'.

The Advocate General (the British government's law officer for devolved matters), the Lord Advocate and the Scottish ministers were called as defenders. It was assumed that this meant that both governments would have to set out their position in writing to the court, thereby revealing their respective positions.

Unfortunately, it did not turn out that way. The Advocate General argued that the action was hypothetical, and both the judge at first instance and the appeal court agreed. The Lord Advocate argued that the court did not have jurisdiction to consider the application because the Scotland Act made it clear that the only method by which a court could scrutinise a measure for legislative competency prior to royal assent was by reference to the UK Supreme Court. Neither court actually answered the question, because it was a hypothetical, but heavily hinted that they would have done so in the negative.

It was not a happy episode, as independence campaigners found themselves pitted against not just the British unionist government's law officer, but also the Scottish nationalist government's law officer. It was felt that the Scottish government had deliberately scuppered an attempt to get some clarity on the issue of whether Holyrood could legislate for an independence referendum. I had been asked to be part of the group bringing the action and was vindicated in my decision that it would not have been wise for me take part.

SNP rebels get elected to NEC

General unhappiness about the lack of a plan to deliver independence combined with concerns over the party's internal governance and antipathy towards Nicola Sturgeon's growing enthusiasm for identity politics prompted something of a rebellion at the SNP online conference in November 2020.

The left-wing Common Weal group and the Women's Pledge group organised a slate of candidates for internal party elections to the NEC. I stood for the role of parliamentary group representative. In the SNP only party members registered for conference can vote in these elections, but several thousand had registered and there was a great deal of interest in the contest.

Despite a campaign of vilification in the press and the circulation of a defamatory letter by members of the party, including members of the NEC, I got more votes than all the other parliamentarians put together. I was elected along with several other new members, including Chris Hanlon, Roger Mullin, Lynne Anderson, Caroline McAllister, Dot Jamieson, Allison Graham, Robert De Bold and Catriona MacDonald.

We were dubbed "the good guys.' Because we were people who wanted change in the strategic direction of the party, particularly on independence. We also wanted more transparency and accountability about the party's internal governance and a halt to the obsession with the policy of self-identification of sex. I was the ringleader and this undoubtedly contributed to the decision to punish me for my rebellious ways by sacking me from my frontbench position at Westminster in February 2021 in the circumstances I describe in the next chapter.

There had also been attempts to get the issue of the party's independence plan properly debated at the conference, which failed due to the conference committee's domination by leadership stooges.

The push to discuss our independence strategy continued into the new year of 2021. I was due to convene a discussion on the topic at an online 'National Assembly' organised by the party to be held at the end of January. The day before I was due to do so, Mike Russell, who had been elected Party President at the November 2020 conference, pulled a new plan out of his hat with his 'eleven-point strategy'.[19]

In truth, the plan was only a three-point strategy. It promised that if there was a pro-independence majority after the next Holyrood election, the government would introduce and pass a bill allowing a referendum to take place after the pandemic. It said that would leave the UK government with three options: first, to agree that the Scottish Parliament already had the power to legislate for a referendum; second, to agree a Section 30 order, as happened ahead of the 2014 vote; or third, to take action to dispute the legal basis of the referendum. There was a lot of criticism that it was a

---

[19] https://news.stv.tv/politics/snp-reveals-11-point-roadmap-to-independence-referendum

back-of-a-fag-packet last-minute ploy to prevent a rebellion at the National Assembly. In the event the plan was never adhered to.

Marco Biagi, who had lost out to Angus in the Edinburgh Central nomination battle, was given a job at SNP HQ heading up a new independence task force. He resigned four months later, saying that 'the most promising job offer he'd ever received' turned out to be the 'most disappointing'. He took the opportunity to have a swipe at Angus Robertson, adding that he was also disappointed that SNP members in Edinburgh Central had decided that they would 'rather have a pompous impressionable idiot than me'.[20]

Thereafter, it was understood that he had set his sights on challenging me for the selection for Edinburgh South West at the next Westminster election when he moved across the city to the Colinton area and was successfully elected as a councillor there on 5 May 2022. On one memorable occasion I encountered him at a constituency event, where he refused to be photographed beside me because of my views on self-identification of sex. His challenge for my seat never materialised, perhaps because he realised he would lose, and he resigned from his position as a councillor in November 2024. He is now a special adviser to the Scottish government.

In June 2021, Mike Russell was named as the new director of the SNP's independence unit. Later that summer he was widely ridiculed when he unveiled an independence campaign battle bus, which turned out to be a mobile horse box. In fairness, it was a well-meaning gesture from the Islay branch of the SNP.

Mike resigned from his position as Party President in December 2023 to take up the position of Chairman of the Scottish Land Commission. He is no longer active in the party.

While the leadership of the SNP and the Scottish government were coming under pressure from the party membership to do more to advance the cause of independence, they were also being

---

[20] heraldscotland.com/politics/19339046.snp-turmoil-indy-task-force-chief-quits-worst-job-ever-malcontent-treasurer-resigns/#:~:-text=He%20also%20said%20he%20was,idea%20what%20he%20was%20doing'.

put under the microscope by the Holyrood committee appointed to investigate the Alex Salmond affair.

During Covid, I kept in regular contact with Alex. It was our habit to have a long chat on a Sunday afternoon, often when I was making dinner for my parents. My mum's dementia was advancing, and my GP had designated me a carer for her so I could support my dad, despite Covid restrictions. Alex's wife Moira often joined in these calls. She was distraught at how Alex had been treated by his erstwhile comrades and friends.

The Committee on the Scottish Government Handling of Harassment Complaints was set up to investigate the Scottish government's botched handling of the investigation into allegations against Alex and the circumstances in which they had very expensively lost the judicial review action. Its remit included the development of the new complaints policy, the way in which the complaints were handled, the conduct of the judicial review and the question of whether Nicola Sturgeon had breached the Ministerial Code. The criminal proceedings were not within its remit, although it did consider the circumstances in which the police had first become involved.

Alex was determined to use the Holyrood Inquiry to expose the plot to remove him from public life, but he was hampered from doing so by the limited remit of the committee, the evasiveness of many of the witnesses, the determination of the Scottish government to withhold evidence and interventions by the Crown barring the publication of evidence supposedly to protect the identity of complainers at his criminal trial.

It did not help that the committee had a majority of pro-government MSPs, four SNP and one Green and an SNP convener. While, to be fair to the convener, Linda Fabiani, she sometimes exerted herself to criticise the government's behaviour, the quality of questioning from many of her colleagues was decidedly below par. Fortunately, incisive questioning by the Labour MSP Jackie Baillie and the Conservative MSP Murdo Fraser went some way to saving the Scottish Parliament's blushes.

Witnesses provided written evidence and some, but not all, were called to give oral evidence. The witnesses included civil servants involved in the development of the new complaints procedure, its application to Alex and the handling of the judicial review, including Leslie Evans, Liz Lloyd, Geoff Aberdein, Peter Murrell, the Lord Advocate and, of course, Nicola Sturgeon and Alex Salmond. Most of them, except for Liz Lloyd, were called upon to give oral evidence.

Perhaps the most disgraceful episode was the committee's initial refusal to publish Alex Salmond's evidence as submitted, which they knew would mean he would not appear in front of them. The pretext of this was protecting the identity of the complainers at the criminal trial. This was disingenuous. The *Spectator* magazine had already published his evidence in full online.

The trial judge, Lady Dorrian, had made an order preventing the publication of the identities of the complainers. The Crown Office wrote to the *Spectator* suggesting that their publication of Alex's evidence could constitute contempt of court. They argued that, if read alongside other material published by the committee, the full evidence created a risk of 'jigsaw identification' of the complainers. Initially, the *Spectator* redacted the article in the manner requested by the Crown, but then it decided to go to court to seek a variation of the order made by the judge. Like Alex and others, including myself, the *Spectator* felt that Lady Dorrian's order was being very widely interpreted as an excuse to redact information that might be an embarrassment to those in government or close to the government.[21] Lady Dorrian accepted that her order could be tightened up.[22]

Notwithstanding that outcome, the Crown Office still insisted on parliament redacting some of Alex's accusations against Sturgeon, even though they could be read in their entirety online.

---

[21] https://www.theguardian.com/politics/2021/feb/11/spectator-wins-challenge-to-court-order-in-alex-salmond-case#:~:text=Alex%20Salmond%20case-,This%20article%20is%20more%20than%204%20years%20old,that%20she%20would%20change%20it.

[22] https://www.scottishlegal.com/articles/order-preventing-publication-of-identities-of-complainers-in-salmond-case-varied-by-high-court

The Crown refused to give reasons for doing so, but nonetheless parliament complied. It was a sad day for Scottish democracy.

I am not alone in thinking the Crown went too far. Lord Hope of Craighead, a former deputy president of the UK Supreme Court and former Lord President of Scotland's Supreme Courts, said, 'I am, to say the least, very surprised that the Crown Office can tell the Scottish Parliament what it can and cannot do. That could not happen at Westminster.' Robert Black KC, Emeritus Professor of Scots law at Edinburgh University, said, 'It appears on the face of it that a faction within the Crown Office is out of control and engaged in a personal campaign or vendetta.' The Faculty of Advocates said, 'When the public discourse fails to respect the basic tenets of the independence of the system it is in danger of leading to irreparable harm. Such harm is something which might be to the detriment of Scotland as a whole or in the long term.'[23]

Citing jigsaw identification, the Crown Office also intervened to bar the publication of the evidence of Geoff Aberdein, Alex's former chief of staff. They also tried to prevent the committee from seeing the messages exchanged by participants in the infamous Whats app group which I described in the previous chapter, but relented when, for the first time in the history of the Scottish Parliament, the committee used its powers under section 23 of the Scotland Act to require the Crown to produce all the messages.

Notwithstanding the terms of those messages, the committee came to the extraordinary conclusion that they were 'in the main personal messages showing individuals supporting each other' and agreed not to publish them.

When the inquiry questioned Murrell about his messages that said it would be a good time to be pressurising the police after charges had been brought against Alex, he claimed that the messages were 'quite out of character'. Murrell also told the inquiry that there were no more messages of the type already in the public

---

[23] Alex Salmond inquiry: Nicola Sturgeon reported for comments on verdict https://www.thetimes.com/article/596068f0-77a6-11eb-9d58-b0b1ea096ce7?shareToken=83b0385b15ba3418a83bac06b733d640

domain from January 2019. As David Davis, who raised this matter in the Westminster Parliament, said, 'That statement, delivered under oath, is hard to reconcile with the dozens of messages stretching over a period of months from September 2018.'[24]

At the first of two appearances Murrell denied even using WhatsApp, only for it later to emerge that he did have WhatsApp and had used it within weeks of the evidence session.[25] Four of the civil servants who gave evidence had similar difficulties of recollection and subsequently had to correct or clarify evidence. Even Nicola, normally so on top of her brief, found herself unable to answer many questions because of a lack of recollection.

Judith Mackinnon, the civil servant who was appointed as the investigating officer, initially said that she hadn't told either of the complainants, Ms A or Ms B, that she would be the investigating officer before her appointment had been confirmed. Later, she wrote to the inquiry to say that she had in fact indicated to Ms B that she was likely to be in that role.[26]

Leslie Evans, the Permanent Secretary, initially told the inquiry that special advisers had not been involved in meetings about Alex's judicial review. However, a Freedom of Information request revealed that a special adviser had indeed been present at a number of meetings on the subject in October and November 2018, and she had to correct her evidence.[27]

Barbara Allison, the civil servant who was the recipient of Leslie Evans's text which said 'battle maybe lost but not the war' after

---

[24] https://hansard.parliament.uk/Commons/2024-07-18/debates/4DC08467-BEE4-414B-B9F5-D99EB190B0AA/AdequacyOfTheScotlandAct1998?highlight=murrell#contribution-AFB8C127-26C0-4301-BA0C-0EE57F1CDCE1

[25] See fv112

[26] https://www.pressandjournal.co.uk/fp/politics/scottish-politics/2607253/remember-remember-senior-civil-servants-who-corrected-or-clarified-evidence-to-salmond-inquiry/

[27] Report of the Committee on the Scottish Government Handling of Harassment Complaints. Para 80

Alex won his judicial review, initially denied having received the text. Shortly before she was due to appear before the inquiry for a second time, she corrected the record, admitting that she had received the message and that she wanted to 'correct the unintended inaccuracy in my previous statement'.[28]

Finally, James Hynd, who was head of cabinet, parliament and governance at the time, initially told the inquiry that he had heard 'rumours' in relation to Alex's conduct, but later he wrote to the inquiry to say that he was 'not aware of any rumours about "sexually inappropriate behaviour" on the part of Mr Salmond or other ministers'.[29] He was the person responsible for drawing up the policy on the handling of complaints in 2017. He is now under investigation by the police for making a false statement on oath.[30] I understand that the inquiry relates to whether he was telling the truth when he told the inquiry that he knew nothing of the allegations of sexual harassment against Alex Salmond while he was drawing up the procedure.

Prior to his death, in his action for misfeasance against the Scottish government, Alex was offering to prove that both James Hynd and Nicola Sturgeon knew from the outset in November 2017 that the new procedure was intended to be used against him.

While that was not the position of Nicola Sturgeon, she did admit to being aware of some concerns about Alex's behaviour back

---

[28] https://www.dailyrecord.co.uk/news/politics/scottish-government-director-corrects-evidence-22912229

[29] https://www.pressandjournal.co.uk/fp/politics/scottish-politics/2607253/remember-remember-senior-civil-servants-who-corrected-or-clarified-evidence-to-salmond-inquiry/

[30] https://www.bbc.co.uk/news/articles/c23lz2z38j9o; heraldscotland.com/news/25264407.police-probe-evidence-salmond-inquiry-ongoing/#:~:text=Already%20got%20an%20account?,Sign%20in.&text=Police%20Scotland%20has%20revealed%20detectives,in%20its%20inquiry%20Operation%20Broadcroft.&text=Get%20full%20access%20to%20The,in%20Scotland%20with%20one%20subscription.&text=He%20said%20the%20investigation%20was,after%20independent%20MSP%20election%20bid

in November 2017. However, her position was that she did not find out about the complaints against him until the spring of 2018. The date of her knowledge at that time proved very controversial.

Alex Salmond believed that Nicola knew about the complaints against him from the outset, based on changes made to briefing notes for FMQs in November 2017 referring to knowledge of two complaints against former ministers. As a former First Minister, he knew that it would not have been proper for civil servants to put such words into the mouth of the First Minister for repetition in the Scottish Parliament unless she had been briefed about what they meant.

He had also become aware that in the early drafts of the new procedure the plan was for the First Minister to be the arbiter of complaints in the same way that she was the arbiter of complaints against current ministers under the Ministerial Code. She was to be informed when complaints were made, and it was her role to decide how they were to be investigated. Thus, it would have made sense for her to have been informed of the existence of the complaints.

After 5 December 2017, the plan changed. It was decided that for the new procedure the Permanent Secretary should be the arbiter of complaints against former ministers, and the First Minister disappeared from the procedure completely. Alex believed that this was done to insulate Nicola from the not inconsiderable political damage that might result if she was to be the person who upheld complaints of sexual harassment against him. It is at that stage that Alex believed all those involved decided to pretend that the development of the procedure had been wholly independent of the allegations against him.

Naturally, Nicola says otherwise. But just what her position was on her date of knowledge was to put her in peril. On 8 January 2019, after the Scottish government had conceded the judicial review, she had made a statement to the Scottish Parliament in which she said she did not know of the complaints against Alex Salmond until her meeting with him in her home on 2 April 2018, when Alex himself advised her of them. This remained her position in her written submission to the inquiry. However, when she gave evidence on affirmation to the inquiry on 3 March 2021, she conceded that she had participated in a meeting between Liz Lloyd and Geoff Aberdein in her office on 29 March 2018, when she was advised about the complaints. Her position was that she had forgotten about that meeting until recently reminded of it.[31]

Perhaps what jogged her memory was the fact that Geoff Aberdein had given evidence under oath about that meeting at Alex's criminal trial. By the time of the inquiry, he was being backed up by the evidence of two other witnesses, Duncan Hamilton and Kevin Pringle.

Whether Nicola had knowingly misled parliament about this crucial meeting became a major issue before the inquiry. Had she done so, in terms of the Ministerial Code she would have been expected to offer her resignation. The issue was not just her date of knowledge, but also the capacity in which meetings had been held – whether they were government meetings, in which case they should have been minuted (which they weren't), or SNP meetings – and about what exactly had been said.

The committee concluded, with regards to the evidence of Geoff and Duncan, who was also present at the meeting on 2 April, that Nicola's written evidence had been an inaccurate account of what had happened, and that she had misled the committee. This, they said, was a potential breach of the Ministerial Code. However, they said that the appropriate place to address the question of whether or not she had breached the Ministerial Code was in a concurrent report being prepared by James Hamilton, a senior Irish barrister who had been appointed to prepare an independent report on whether Nicola had misled MSPs about when she first met Alex Salmond's chief of staff.

His report, issued on 22 March 2021, cleared Nicola of breaching the Ministerial Code, but it too was heavily redacted. The reason given was Lady Dorrian's court order. However, in a covering letter, Mr Hamilton said he was 'deeply frustrated that applicable court orders will have the effect of preventing the full publication of a report which fulfils my remit and which I believe it would be in

---

[31] https://www.bbc.co.uk/news/live/uk-scotland-56251990

the public interest to publish'. He said that the redactions, made at the insistence of the Scottish government, meant that his report could not 'be properly understood by those reading it, and presents an incomplete and even at times misleading version of what happened'.[32]

To this date the Scottish government is still embroiled in a series of court actions, resisting attempts on behalf of a member of the public and the Information Commissioner to put the unredacted report into the public domain, and to publish all the evidence gathered by Mr Hamilton and the legal advice they were given about it.[33]

Using parliamentary privilege, David Davis has alleged that the redactions to the Hamilton report were carried out not by government lawyers, but by SPADs. The implication being that they were done not to protect the complainers' identities, but to save the blushes of the Scottish government.[34] He says that Nicola's successors in government have continued to suppress the truth about what was done to Alex Salmond, and I agree.

As the book goes to press the Scottish government has again refused to publish a large amount of the redacted material and now faces contempt of court proceedings at the instigation of the Information Commissioner.[35]

---

32 https://www.thetimes.com/uk/scotland/article/alex-salmond-affair-what-does-the-scottish-government-have-to-hide-c2tk9qhf3#:~:text=%E2%80%9CA%20redacted%20report%20that%20effectively%20erases%20the,of%20events%2C%E2%80%9D%20he%20(%20Hamilton%20)%20complained.

33 https://www.foi.scot/foi-appeals-summary-james-hamilton-report-and-investigationhttps://www.scottishdailyexpress.co.uk/news/politics/secretive-snp-government-waste-nearly-36223047

34 https://hansard.parliament.uk/Commons/2024-07-18/debates/4DC08467-BEE4-414B-B9F5-D99EB190B0AA/AdequacyOfTheScotlandAct1998?highlight=redactions#contribution-AFB8C127-26C0-4301-BA0C-0EE57F1CDCE1

35 https://www.thetimes.com/article/a73e3c9c-0036-4718-bd1f-99d88dd21a08?shareToken=2d5c677bb8dc5df59ff14177f613cbf3

Another aspect in which the Scottish government sought to frustrate the inquiry in the fulfilment of their remit was their consistent refusal to publish the legal advice received in relation to its conduct of the judicial review proceedings. Despite the Scottish Parliament voting by a margin of 63 to 54 to demand the release of the advice on 4 November 2020, the Scottish government dug their heels in until they were faced with a vote of no confidence in the Deputy First Minister, which all four opposition parties threatened to support. It was only then, with his back against the wall, that the then Deputy First Minister John Swinney agreed to release the Scottish government's legal advice on 2 March 2021.[36]

In the committee's own words, 'Because the waiving of legal professional privilege took place at such a late stage' there was no time for the Scottish government to review the redactions in other documents already provided to the committee to assess whether some or all of them could have been lifted, nor would there have been time for the committee to have considered such a review. In this way the Scottish government was able to ensure that vital information was withheld from the committee or provided in such a way that it was not fully intelligible.[37]

What is so ironic about much of this is that while SNP MPs at Westminster were mocking the Conservative government for its heavy redactions to published advice given to the government over Brexit, the Scottish government was doing the same thing at Holyrood.

Both the Holyrood Inquiry and the Hamilton report left more questions unanswered than answered, but what cannot be denied is that few of the government witnesses came out of it well. Leslie Evans was roundly criticised for the conduct of the investigation and the judicial review. Nicola Sturgeon was found to have misled committee, and the findings of the final report were leaked, many think by SNP members to make the leak rather than the findings critical of Sturgeon the story.

---

[36] https://www.bbc.co.uk/news/uk-scotland-scotland-politics-56231222.amp

[37] Committee report at para 60

Nicola came very close to being forced to resign because of the Holyrood and Hamilton inquiries. At the same time, she was also under pressure from her supporters within the party to stop kicking the can down the road on her plans for self ID, and to rid the party of gender rebels like me.

The March 2021 NEC took place the Saturday before James Hamilton's report was due to be published on the Monday, and after the Holyrood report had been leaked. Nicola was very stressed and so the atmosphere of these already tense meetings was even worse than usual.

And then, just as Scottish politics was reeling from the fallout of the Holyrood and Hamilton inquiries, Alex Salmond made his next move with the launch of the Alba Party, on 26 March 2021.

On a Saturday night late in March 2021, I received a phone call from Alex Salmond advising me of his intention to set up the Alba Party. He explained that the party would soon be launching with some high-profile names and promised me the top position on the Lothian list for the new party at the forthcoming elections for the Scottish Parliament. He said I would be a shoe-in to be elected as an MSP for the new party.

Alex gave me 24 hours to decide whether I would join. I said that was far too short a time for me to make such a major decision and queried why he hadn't involved me in his plans sooner. His explanation was that they had wanted to keep it as tight as possible. I said I would need at least 48 hours to think about my position, and he agreed to that.

It was an incredibly difficult decision for me. I had been treated appallingly by the SNP culminating in my sacking from the frontbench in February 2021 (see next chapter), but nevertheless I had been elected by my constituents as an SNP MP, and I did not think they would appreciate my defecting to another party. Plus, I did not want to defect; I wanted to stay and fix the SNP. And I also felt that defecting would give those who had tried to bully me out of the party exactly what they wanted and would also feed the conspiracy theory that I had, as Mike Russell told me he believed, been involved in a deliberate attempt to take down the party.

Furthermore, my constituents and the wider public and most of the SNP were not privy to the information I had about what had been going on behind the scenes in the party. Many of them thought Alex Salmond was a sex pest and therefore were not likely to look kindly on my decision to throw my lot in with his new party.

Finally, I was not in the best of health mentally or physically and was planning to take some time off. The thought of having to forgo that to face the inevitable press onslaught that would follow my decision to defect filled me with dread.

Quite apart from the social media abuse, I had become worn down by the constant briefing against me and attempts to smear my character from within my own party. I had been through months of Saturday nights filled with dread about what new attack the Sunday papers might reveal, and I really needed a break from it all.

I consulted with close friends, family and advisers. One felt that I had nothing left to lose and that I should jump ship, but the majority urged caution. One friend feared that Alex wanted to use me as a human shield so that whenever he was confronted with allegations about his alleged past sexual misdemeanours, he could point to the support of a well-respected feminist. I felt there was some truth in this, but given what he had been through and the refusal of so many to accept the jury's verdict of acquittal I couldn't really blame him.

For all these reasons I decided to stay put. Alex and those who were, unlike me, in on the plans were not best pleased. Kenny MacAskill tried to persuade me by appealing to my admiration for an Irish republican heroine, telling me that this was my Countess Markievicz moment. I disagreed. I said Scotland's situation was very different from the situation in which Ireland had found itself in 1916 and thereafter. I did not think Scotland was ready for a Sinn Fein-style political insurgency. What was needed was a more middle of the road but effective constitutional nationalist party like the SNP had been under Alex's leadership.

I told Alex the answer was no and announced my decision to take some time off for health reasons. I made it clear that while I would be off work, my constituency office would continue to deal with all enquiries. I wanted it to be known that I was off the scene for the time being.

Instead of participating in the launch of Alba or the Scottish parliamentary election campaign of the party that had treated me so poorly, I rented a cottage in Northumberland and watched events unfold from the relative safety of English soil. I needed time to decide what to do, and while I kept an eye on constituency casework and contributed to my role on the JCHR, I went for long walks on the beach and thought about my position.

I had become deeply disillusioned with the SNP and the independence movement, and very focused on the fight for women's rights and lesbian rights. However, I decided that if I threw in the towel as an SNP MP, I would be handing victory to those who had tried so hard to hound me out of the party. So, I decided to stay and fight.

Like me, the late George Reid, former Presiding Officer of the Scottish Parliament and SNP MP in the 1970s, was a great fan of Northumberland. We used to joke that we planned to move the border south after independence. On a visit in 2020 and again with my parents and sister's family in June 2021, I bumped into George and his wife at the Lindisfarne Inn. He expressed sympathy for the way I had been treated by the party, and we discussed what might be done to facilitate a rapprochement between the warring factions. In his capacity as elder statesman he offered to act as a facilitator. I wrote to Mike Russell, suggesting we take him up on his offer, but nothing came of it.

Alba did not do well enough in the Holyrood elections to win any seats. I could not help but feel that all Alba had done was to remove some of my most vocal allies from the SNP, which would be even harder to reform now.

Sturgeon again failed to replicate Salmond's 2011 feat of obtaining an outright majority in Holyrood and began manoeuvres to ensure she would have one by entering a coalition with the Greens. I was glad I had not ended up in Holyrood.

In May 2021, I returned to work. I wrote to the Chief Whip and the SNP national secretary renewing my complaints against Ian Blackford and for the first time putting in a complaint about the harassment I felt I had endured at Kirsty Blackman's hands.

I referred to my previous complaints, going back to 2017, and said that I believed my sacking from the frontbench in February 2021 (covered in the next chapter) was the culmination of a campaign of bullying and harassment orchestrated by Ian Blackford and Kirsty Blackman, designed to marginalise me within the Westminster group and to blacken my name. I said that Kirsty's conduct towards me on social media, including her participation in a twitter pile on where I was wrongly accused of condoning transphobia and antisemitism,[38] combined with Nicola Sturgeon's allegations about transphobia in the party had put a target on my back. I said that the party had a duty of care towards its elected parliamentarians and that this had been repeatedly breached to my detriment, causing damage to my health and the jeopardising of my personal safety. I also accused them of discriminating against me on the basis of my sexuality and my gender-critical beliefs

My complaints were briefly acknowledged and then I heard nothing more. It seemed that the new procedure introduced for complaints against SNP MPs in 2017–18 was to continue to gather dust, having failed in its design to take me out of the picture.

In March 2021 an SNP staffer's complaints of sexual harassment dating back to 2016 against my colleague Patrick Grady had finally come to light, and he'd had to resign as Chief Whip. Despite the staffer having complained to Ian Blackford and the party, his complaint was never subjected to the procedure used against me. Ultimately, it was the Parliamentary Standards Commissioner that found Patrick guilty of one of the complaints levelled against him.[39]

The new Chief Whip, Owen Thompson, MP for Midlothian, assured me he would speak to Ian and Kirsty about their conduct towards me at group meetings. However, nothing came of my complaints, and for a long time I chose not to attend the group

---

[38] https://www.scotsman.com/news/politics/joanna-cherry-blocks-snp-colleague-kirsty-blackman-on-twitter-amid-lgbt-row-3116605#

[39] https://www.bbc.co.uk/news/uk-scotland-scotland-politics-61909112#:~:text=An%20apology%20by%20the%20SNP's,a%20social%20event%20in%202016.

meetings. I also had Fraser accompany me to Westminster whenever he could. Working in such a vile atmosphere was hard and it felt good to have a strong ally by my side.

Notwithstanding my complaints, Ian Blackford went on to be the SNP's appointee to the Committee on Standards in Public Life in June 2003 and to its successor, the Ethics and Integrity Commission in August 2025.[40] In the acknowledgements to her memoir, Nicola describes him as a 'great friend' and a 'tower of strength'. Kirsty Blackman passed vetting as a parliamentary candidate for the 2024 General Election and has gone on to become the SNP Chief Whip at Westminster. As outlined above, others with outstanding complaints against them regarding bullying have not had such an easy ride through the party's candidate vetting procedures.

Later in May 2021, Douglas Chapman, the party's new Treasurer – elected at the Nov 2020 conference having defeating the incumbent of several years, Colin Beattie – resigned.[41]

I also resigned from the NEC. I set out my reasons in a letter to Kirsten Oswald, explaining that the manner in which business was conducted on the NEC had made it impossible for me to do the job I was elected for. I added that, having sat on a number of management boards, I had never seen business conducted in such an inadequate way and in such a menacing atmosphere, except perhaps within the SNP Westminster group.

I had decided to give up on trying to reform the SNP. The good guys had failed in our attempts to do so, but we had succeeded in bringing matters to a head. We had also forced the leadership to look again at their independence plans.

I had reached the view that there would be no space to do anything more to reform the SNP until such time as Nicola Sturgeon and Peter Murrell lost their grip on the party. It seemed to me that they were now facing enough problems to mean that was only a matter of time.

---

[40] https://www.gov.uk/government/people/ian-blackford

[41] https://www.bbc.co.uk/news/uk-scotland-scotland-politics-57299030

In the meantime, I decided to devote my energies to my work on the Joint Committee on Human Rights, to defend the rights of women and LGB people, and to my constituency.

I did not have long to wait before the various crises facing the party came to a head and led first to Nicola's resignation, then Peter's. One of those factors was the spectacular crash and burn of her policy on self-identification of sex.

WOMAN – ADULT HUMAN FEMALE 6

On 21 October 2021, I attended the first conference of the LGB Alliance, the only organisation or charity in the United Kingdom that advocates purely for the rights of same-sex attracted people. I arrived late and missed the opening sessions of the conference in order to avoid having to cross a picket line that consisted of trans activists from Pride in Surrey (an organisation that has since been caught up in a very serious paedophile scandal) and my colleague Kirsty Blackman.[1] Given her past behaviour towards me, I was keen to avoid a confrontation with her. To this day, regardless of our history, I am astonished that a married heterosexual MP should have thought it acceptable to protest against lesbians, gay men and bisexual people attending a conference organised by other LGB people to discuss their rights.

That said, her presence on the picket line did not surprise me at the time. Earlier that week, when it had been announced that I was speaking at the conference, I had endured a barrage of abuse at the SNP Westminster group meeting. I was denounced as a bigot, and faced demands not to attend the conference. While the ringleaders were Kirsty and the usual Vichy gays, too young or too closeted in the past to understand the struggle for LGB equality,

---

1 https://www.telegraph.co.uk/news/2025/07/20/council-finally-cuts-ties-pride-group-founded-paedophile/

I was particularly horrified when heterosexual, married male colleagues, including Blackford, Chris Law and Pete Wishart, joined in the berating of me. The only people who dared to speak up for me were Carol Monaghan and Marion Fellows, whose courage and support I shall always be grateful for. I appealed to the chair of the meeting, Kirsten Oswald, to do something about the behaviour of our colleagues, but she declined to do so, and I left the meeting early saying I was not prepared to sit there and be shouted at for being a lesbian who wanted to speak at a conference about lesbian rights. Even as I left, Kirsten was ordering me to stay in the room. It is harder to think of a more obvious example of institutionally sanctioned harassment, victimisation and bullying.

After I left the meeting, some of my detractors demanded that I have the whip removed if I attended the conference. They were told that it couldn't be done because 'she may be a bitch but she knows about the law.' No doubt this was a reference to correspondence I had sent to the party leadership earlier that year, threatening legal action against the party if the harassment of me on account of my support for the rights of women and the same-sex attracted did not stop.

I hope the conduct I have described, in particular that of some of the SNP Westminster group, will shock. It should do. Later, at the LGB Alliance conference, the keynote speaker, campaigning black lesbian barrister Allison Bailey declared (correctly), 'Our rights as lesbians, gay and bisexual are not conditional on accepting gender-identity theory.' The same could be said of the rights of women, and indeed of any of the other protected characteristics under the Equality Act. Yet in the SNP, under Nicola Sturgeon, rights were conditional on accepting gender-identity ideology, and it was an approach that spread out across Scottish civil society.

I could devote a whole book to the institutional capture in Scotland by gender-identity zealots, but fortunately that has already been done by Susan Dalgety and Lucy Hunter Blackburn in *The Women Who Wouldn't Wheesht*. I would recommend that book to anyone who wants to understand the broader context. The title of the book refers to the exhortation 'Wheesht for Indy', which was current in the SNP when divisions began to appear and members were encouraged to keep quiet about any misgivings about the direction of the party for the sake of the independence cause. The word 'Wheesht' is Scots for 'keep your mouth shut'.

What I want to do here is to locate what happened in the history of the SNP and the nationalist movement over the last ten years, to set out what I observed and experienced as a lesbian feminist MP who would not bow the knee to Nicola Sturgeon's diktat, and to explain why Sturgeon embraced gender-identity ideology quite so enthusiastically.

I struggle now to remember exactly when I first realised that the movement for LGB equality had been appropriated by activists who wished to subordinate the rights of LGB people, women and indeed everyone to the notion that feelings about identity should trump material reality.

When I was elected in 2015, I didn't anticipate being involved in LGB rights activism. To my mind, the battle for equality had been won. It had been very different when I came out as a lesbian while at university in Edinburgh in the mid-1980s. At that time gay men were dying often at home and alone without proper medical care during the AIDS crisis. If an LGB person came out at work or was outed they faced losing their job with no recourse to discrimination law. Lesbians were losing their children in custody battles because they were seen as unfit mothers. On top of that we faced a Tory government intent on introducing legislation to make sure children growing up could not learn anything positive about homosexuality.

Stonewall, set up in the wake of the campaign against Section 28, changed all that. By 2003 lesbians and gay men had won the same right not to be discriminated against that had been afforded to trans people some years earlier (1999). Civil partnerships were introduced in England in 2004 and in Scotland in 2005, and then equal marriage followed in England in 2013 and in Scotland in 2014.

In 2015 the SNP Westminster group was dubbed 'the gayest parliamentary party in the world'. At that time 8 of the 56 – 14 per cent of our group – were out as lesbian or gay: Mhairi Black, Angela Crawley, Stewart McDonald, Stuart McDonald, Alyn Smith, John Nicolson, Martin Docherty-Hughes and me. Stonewall and other

LGBT campaigning groups were keen to laud and recruit us through a plethora of newspaper articles and photo opportunities.

I was a little puzzled by the huge interest in the number of lesbian and gay MPs in the SNP, and the amount of posturing that went on around it. In my naivete, I thought that with equal marriage, the fight for equality for LGB people was over. I couldn't understand why some of my colleagues were so keen to virtue signal around this issue. I decided that it must have been that for the younger members of the group, like Mhairi Black, who hadn't been around at the time, and for the older members of the group, like John Nicolson and Alyn Smith, who hadn't been out until more recently, this was their opportunity for a moment in the limelight.

I had not yet cottoned on to the fact that because the battle for LGB equality had indeed been won, a lot of professional, well-paid activists were going to be out of a job if they did not find something new to campaign for under the rainbow umbrella. Some argued that the natural way forward was to campaign for LGB equality in other countries, but it turned out there was more money in joining the campaign to put self-identification of sex at the heart of public policy, even if that meant undermining the rights of same-sex attracted people across the world.

This is exactly what the new CEO of Stonewall, Ruth Hunt, proceeded to do, despite having promised lesbian activists that she would not, before she was elected. In doing so she was following the lead of Scotland's Equality Network, which had embraced gender-identity ideology from its inception in 1997. From the moment the Scottish Parliament was founded in 1999 the Equality Network were campaigning for the inclusion of the concept of 'gender identity' in all areas of public policy.[2]

Groups like Stonewall and the Equality Network operated by stealth to replace the concept of sex with gender identity. This 'under the radar' approach explains why so many of us took so

---

[2] see *The Women Who Wouldn't Wheesht*, chapter one.

long to understand the depth and penetration of this dogma.[3] Much of what was done bypassed the Scottish Parliament and was implemented by way of policy and guidance. Even when the lobbyists persuaded government or parliamentarians to further their cause with amendments to bills going through parliament, they attempted to hide what they were doing or to minimise its effect. By the time the controversy over the Gender Recognition Reform Bill hit the headlines, self-ID was already the policy of many major organisations both public and private in Scotland.

It was only gradually, and not until 2018–19, that I became aware of the magnitude of what was happening.

Back in 2015, when lesbian and gay SNP MPs were being courted by groups like Stonewall, my attitude was that I hadn't come into politics to be a professional lesbian, and while I was happy to be open about my sexuality, I didn't really see it as an issue. At that time, I could not possibly have foreseen how much of an issue my sexuality was going to become, and that I would find myself in a vicious fight to defend the right to be same-sex attracted in which I would be pitted against members of my own party.

It is hard to convey the deep pain that this has caused me. To find my own political party turning on me because of my defence of the rights of lesbians and my refusal to sign up to an ideology that threatened to excise the very existence of lesbians was deeply traumatic. I never imagined that in my fifties in a so-called left wing progressive party I would find myself being harassed, bullied and discriminated against in my workplace on account of my sexuality and beliefs.

To those who say there were other lesbians in the SNP group who weren't harassed, such as Mhairi Black, I would say yes, because she embraced gender-identity ideology and was happy to attack women who did not. To my mind she was compliant with the erasure of lesbian life while I fought it.

---

[3] https://www.spectator.co.uk/article/the-document-that-reveals-the-remarkable-tactics-of-trans-lobbyists/

In 2015 colleagues who were enthusiastically taking part in the love in with the gay SNP seemed a little irritated by my lack of enthusiasm. However, at the time it seemed to me that there were more important issues, and I had a lot on my plate as a frontbench spokesperson with a double brief. Looking back on those events, I suspect I was marked out at an early stage as the wrong sort of lesbian who might cause trouble to the project. This perhaps explains a very unpleasant incident that occurred a year later and came to be known in my office as 'dykegate'.

In September 2016, I attended an event in Glasgow to mark the second anniversary of the independence referendum. There were speeches and a cabaret, including a performance from a women's comedy group called Witsherface. Their act included a skit on the number of lesbians in Scottish politics, which referred to Ruth Davidson as 'dykey Davidson'. I was live tweeting the event and indicated that I had found their performance amusing. Thereafter I was widely criticised for approving of the use of the word 'dyke'. Both I and Witsherface were accused of homophobia, but as the elected politician I became the focus of self-righteous wrath on social media. It didn't make any sense to me, because, like many of the members of Witsherface, I am a lesbian of the generation who reclaimed the word 'dyke' and used it as a proud badge of identity. But most of those joining in the social-media pile-on didn't know or understand that.

Some of those who attacked me on social media included self-styled progressives like the political commentator Gerry Hassan. He was at the event, we had been chatting shortly before my offending tweet, and it seemed not to bother him in the slightest that he was finishing off the drink I had bought for him as he joined in the kicking I was getting on social media.

It was my first experience of men mansplaining to me how to be a lesbian. It would not be my last. It was also the first time I found myself openly criticised by fellow SNP MPs including Angela Crawley and Mhairi Black, who saw fit to join in the social-media pile-on without speaking to me first to see what had actually happened. Their action was, of course, in breach of the party rule against public criticism of other members, but like most rules in the SNP it was enforced on an arbitrary basis and only against those who had displeased the leadership.

The social-media storm moved into the mainstream press, fuelled by a comment from the rent-a-quote Conservative MSP Annie Wells, herself a lesbian, who accused me of homophobia. Interestingly, when the gender wars properly commenced Annie Wells was nowhere to be seen in the defence of lesbian rights.

I was very surprised by the level of the outrage. The story literally dominated the airwaves for days, culminating in a question from Annie Wells at First Minister's Questions the following Thursday. I was driving at the time, listening on the radio when I heard her invite Nicola Sturgeon to condemn me as a homophobe. I felt so sick I had to pull over to the side of the road. To Nicola's credit she declined to do so, saying that it's difficult to describe a lesbian who's been out for 30 years as homophobic.

By this time, I had put a letter in the public domain outing myself fully and setting out my history of gay rights activism.[4] I had been under intense pressure from the SNP media operation not to do this and simply to apologise. Alex Salmond advised me not to apologise, saying that when you apologise in politics it simply feeds the mob. As so often he was right, and despite putting out the letter explaining my position, I heard the head of the Equality Network, Tim Hopkins, somebody I had campaigned alongside in the late eighties, join a Radio Scotland chat show and repeatedly put the boot into me. I contacted him asking why he felt it necessary to be quite so brutal and did not get a satisfactory response.

In the end I was very glad that I put my letter in the public domain fully setting out that I was a lesbian and had been out for years and campaigned against Section 28. It made it a lot easier for Nicola to defend me, plus I think it's fair to say that in September 2016 she did not see me as a potential rival. Despite losing her outright majority at the 2016 Scottish election, she was still in her

---

[4] https://www.heraldscotland.com/news/14752147.snp-mp-regrets-offence-caused-homophobic-slur-independence-event/

pomp. I have no doubt that if 'dykegate', as we came to refer to in my office, had occurred after I became a target for team Sturgeon then I would have been thrown to the wolves as a homophobe, notwithstanding my history as a lesbian rights activist.

Nevertheless, the heat and the fury from others, including my SNP colleagues, was just a small foretaste of what was to come if a lesbian stepped out of line with the new zeitgeist. As ever, there was no room for rationality. While it was alright for the LGBT movement to reclaim the word 'queer', it was not alright for lesbians to reclaim the word 'dyke'.

Ruth Hunt, the new chief executive of Stonewall whom I had met socially, joined in the public opprobrium being heaped upon me. I wrote to her demanding an apology and got an extraordinary diatribe back, telling me all about how she had been bullied at school. From that moment on I was a target for Stonewall as well as the Equality Network, and for some of my colleagues in the Westminster group. I confronted them at the next group meeting, asking them why they had seen fit to join in the social-media pile-on without first picking up the phone to me to find out what had happened, but I never got a satisfactory response.

In 2017, I attended Pride in London. It was the first time I'd been since the 1990s and I was horrified by how commercialised it had become. Over the next couple of years, when I was invited to speak at Pride events in Edinburgh, I noticed how dominated the movement had become by men who identified as women and by demands for 'trans rights now'.

I was puzzled by these demands, given that trans people already had the same rights as everyone else under the Equality Act, but of course the demand was not for trans rights. Rather it was for the right for anyone to identify as a member of the opposite sex to be enshrined in law.

After 'dykegate', I felt less inclined to march or campaign alongside those who had been prepared to so roundly condemn me. Gradually, I became aware that I was not alone in my sense of unease about the way in which the demand for self-identification had taken over the LGBT rights movement. I was also aware that many feminist campaigners were concerned about the impact of self-identification on the rights of women to privacy, dignity and safety.

In September 2017 a group of women from a range of backgrounds, including trade unions, women's organisations, academia and the NHS, started Woman's Place UK to ensure that women's voices would be heard in the consultation on proposals to change the Gender Recognition Act at UK level. They were London-based and in 2018 some of them visited parliament to lobby female labour MPs. Labour staffers found out, labelled them a transphobic group and threatened to ensure that Labour MPs who met with them were deselected. I asked for a meeting with them, which was carried out under conditions of secrecy in order to protect me from similar attacks by SNP MPs and staffers. I met with Kiri Tunks and Karen Ingala Smith. We discussed their manifesto and their concerns about gender-identity ideology's impact on the rights of women, and I found everything that they said absolutely reasonable.

Women were also organising in Scotland, and like Woman's Place UK found their public meetings harassed and disrupted by male masked protestors. In June 2018, For Women Scotland (FWS) was formed, and the policy collective Murray Blackburn MacKenzie (MBM) came together in October that year.

On International Women's Day in March 2019, I was visited at my constituency surgery by my constituent Sally Wainwright (who would go on to form Scottish Lesbians and Lesbian Persistence) and Marion Calder of FWS. They sensed I would be on side, and they were right. We embraced and I promised to speak up publicly.

It was clear to me that gender-identity ideology was taking a firm hold in the SNP. Joan McAlpine, my MSP colleague, was the first elected SNP parliamentarian to stick her head above the parapet when she tweeted about the implications of confusing sex with gender in the legislation paving the way for the Scottish census. In February 2019 she put out a now famous Twitter thread that brought condemnation on her head from fellow SNP politicians and activists, and which ultimately led to the gerrymandering of her effective deselection in 2021.[5]

In April 2019, I was asked to be one of a group of SNP MPs, MSPs and councillors who wrote a letter to the *Scotsman* urging caution in the rush to legislate for self-identification.[6] At this stage I was looking for a good moment or an opportunity to make what I hoped would be an effective political intervention. The moment arrived when a senior Twitter executive appeared before the Joint Committee on Human Rights in connection with an inquiry into the social abuse of MPs, and I got to quiz her on Twitter's mediation policies. At that time Twitter routinely shut down the accounts of gender-critical women who tweeted such hitherto uncontroversial statements as 'women don't have penises', while at the same time failing to do anything about extremely abusive and threatening tweets posted by trans activists. In a portion of the evidence session that later went viral on social media I spent ten minutes cross examining their executive about their practices and why sex was not a protected characteristic in their hateful conduct policy. I elicited a promise from her that she would look to remedy things.[7]

Hundreds of women contacted me to thank me for my intervention, but at the same time I received a high level of abuse from trans activists. There were also death threats, one of which the police took seriously enough to arrange a police escort to my constituency surgery the following Friday.

I had planned my intervention carefully, including prefacing my questions with a statement of support for equal rights for trans people, but that of course didn't matter. Activists on the other side of the argument were furious that a Member of Parliament had dared to break the silence and call into question their dubious tactics.

---

5 https://www.dailymail.co.uk/news/article-14628115/amp/JOAN-MCALPINE-called-trash-standing-women-SNP-led-Nicola-Sturgeon-tried-shut-Ive-got-absolutely-NO-regrets.html

6 https://www.scotsman.com/news/politics/letters-snp-politicians-spell-out-concerns-over-gender-change-bill-1419211

7 https://www.bbc.co.uk/news/technology-48118566

Fraser, my chief of staff, had warned me in advance of my intervention that I needed to be prepared for a huge backlash and that it would destroy any hopes I might ever have of leading the SNP. At the time I thought he was exaggerating. He turned out to be correct. Some of the most vicious attacks upon me that followed came from members of the SNP, including people who held office within the party.

In the meantime, a constituent who identified as a trans woman came to see me at my surgery, and we wrote jointly to Shirley-Anne Somerville, who was then the Cabinet Secretary for Social Justice, suggesting a citizens' assembly to facilitate a respectful evidence-based debate about self-identification.[8] Our suggestion was declined. I was reminded of this when, on the publication of her memoirs, Sturgeon gave interviews saying she should have 'paused' her plans for self-identification because of the controversy surrounding them. This would have been the perfect opportunity to do so, after a joint request from people on either side of the debate.

Several constituents came to see me with concerns about their workplace culture and the treatment of their lesbian daughters in schools, where they were being encouraged to view themselves as trans rather than lesbian. Eventually, we organised a group that met regularly for coffee at my office or at one of the constituent's houses to support each other.

In June 2019, I was invited by the SNP Club in Edinburgh to give an update on my parliamentary activity along with the other Edinburgh SNP MPs. I was determined to tackle the issue and was delighted when a group of like-minded SNP women had turned up to support me. Among them was the writer Dr Victoria Whitworth. We started dating and she was to become a stalwart support to me over the years that followed.

Around this time Bev Jackson and Kate Harris met in London and began their plans to set up a new organisation that would

---

[8] https://www.holyrood.com/news/view,joanna-cherry-calls-for-gra-reform-citizens-assembly#:~:text=The%20planned%20legislation%20was%20further,run%2Dup%20to%20May's%20election.

campaign solely for the rights of LGB people. They contacted me and encouraged me to get involved, but at this stage LGB Alliance were already being vilified as a 'hate group' and I knew that if I did, I would lose my frontbench seat and my SNP membership. All this was taking place at the height of my activism in the campaign against Brexit and I did not want to undermine my effectiveness in that fight.

Over the summer of 2019, I met Julie Bindel when she attended Edinburgh for the funeral of Magdalen Berns, one of the founders of FWS who had died tragically young from a brain tumour. I also met Lucy Hunter Blackburn of MBM, Victoria's best friend from her Oxford days, and together we met their old friend and one of the original founders of Stonewall, Simon Fanshawe, who was in Edinburgh for the festival and shared our concerns.

All the while, in the background, I was facing a steady stream of abuse on Twitter, much of it from SNP activists. One of my most vocal critics was Jordon Henderson, the then boyfriend of SNP MEP Alyn Smith, tweeting under the name @Montague90.

That summer, I received an apology and an out of court settlement from the *Pink News* after they had wrongly accused me of homophobia.[9] After the settlement Jordon continued to repeat their defamatory allegations about me on Twitter. I contacted Alyn, asking him to intervene, but he declined. Later, Jordon shared my private correspondence with Alyn on social media. The complaints I made to the party about what was going on were ignored.

In July 2019, Mhairi Black made a video with the online political lads' mag Political Joe in which she was filmed reading out letters from concerned gender-critical women, ridiculing them and calling them 'Jeremy Hunts'. To my horror the official SNP Twitter account retweeted it.[10] I appealed to several people in leadership positions in the party to have the tweet taken down, but they refused.

The fact that a major political party thought it was appropriate to retweet a video of one of their parliamentarians calling concerned

---

[9] https://www.thepinknews.com/pagicle/correction/

[10] https://www.joe.co.uk/news/mhairi-black-self-id-transphobia-236380;

feminists rhyming slang for cunts reveals the degree of institutional capture and the extent to which any sense of rationality or proportionality had been thrown out of the window.

Later that year, when I raised the number of undealt-with complaints about this incident at NEC, Nicola Sturgeon replied by threatening me in front of all those present that if I wanted complaints against Mhairi Black dealt with, she was sure she could find some complaints about me that would also have to be dealt with. I doubt she would have carried through this threat, given what I'd said to her back in May, but the fact that she made it in front of the assembled NEC is indicative of the atmosphere in which we operated within the SNP at that time.

In October 2019 the SNP women who had started organising at the Spring Conference launched the SNP Women's Pledge. A packed meeting was held with security at an off-conference venue in Aberdeen, as we were not allowed to be part of the conference fringe. The meeting was addressed by me, Joan McAlpine, Margaret Lynch, Rhona Hotchkiss and Caroline McAllister.[11] None of us are now active members of the SNP. Many SNP women attended, and we were all photographed standing behind a banner.

One of those in the photograph was Catriona MacDonald, a very able young lawyer who had been selected as the SNP candidate for Edinburgh South at the forthcoming General Election. Alyn Smith's boyfriend Jordon then tweeted the photo with a red circle around Catriona's head, saying that he didn't fancy Edinburgh South's choice much. There was an outcry, but no disciplinary action was taken, even though he was known to be the partner of a prominent SNP MEP. This inaction meant that many other misogynistic young men in the SNP were emboldened to attack other SNP gender-critical feminists on Twitter. They added a red circle or target to the Twitter profiles, proudly proclaiming their targeting of their fellow female party members, and became known as 'the

---

11 https://www.theguardian.com/uk-news/2019/oct/14/snp-women-close-to-quitting-gender-recognition-proposals-trans-rights-scotland

red circle gang'. Despite many complaints, no action was taken by the party.[12]

As the General Election of December 2019 got underway, the Labour Party showed a little bit more gumption when the candidate selected to fight my seat tweeted that I should be squirted with bleach because of my opposition to self ID. She was promptly replaced with another candidate. As matters progressed, I had to contend with more attacks from within my own party than without. However, that was as nothing to what was done to Neale Hanvey, the SNP candidate for Kirkcaldy and Cowdenbeath. I suspect he was singled out for a particularly vicious treatment as it was very damaging to the gender-identity ideology cultists to have a gay man who was a former Nurse Director questioning their theory, particularly from a child safeguarding viewpoint. A trawl through Neale's social media posts was carried out and the thumbnail for an article he had shared was found that could have been interpreted as an antisemitic slur on George Soros, which was sent to the media. The party also alleged a tweet of his was antisemitic, but they weren't able to produce that tweet at his later disciplinary hearing. .In the storm that followed Neale was immediately suspended from party for antisemitism.

The spiteful action taken against Neale had severe personal consequences for him and his husband, who were fostering two vulnerable young boys. They faced losing custody of the boys because of the resultant social work investigation into his suitability as a parent. Thankfully this didn't happen and now their adopted sons are thriving. He went on to be elected as an independent MP, notwithstanding the campaign of vilification against him, and most of his local SNP comrades continued to campaign for him. To Neale's credit he apologised for the Soros social-media slur and underwent antisemitism training.[13]

---

[12] https://www.thescottishsun.co.uk/news/5355127/snp-holyrood-abuse-trans-rights-activist-election/

[13] https://antisemitism.org/snp-readmits-neale-hanvey-mp-following-sanction-training-and-apology-to-community/

It has been pointed out that other SNP candidates could equally have been open to accusations of antisemitism for historic social media posts.[14] However, these individuals were on the right side of the gender debate so far as the party was concerned, and thus their behaviour did not seem to be problematic .

At the first meeting of the SNP Westminster group after the election I raised the friendly fire that had been directed at me and Neale, and was subjected to a haranguing from the usual suspects, including Blackford. New MPs Stephen Flynn and Dave Doogan both approached me privately afterwards to express their concern about how I was spoken to and to ask if that's what the meetings were always like. I said yes. Welcome to our world.

As the year progressed the atmosphere at the group didn't get any better. In February 2020 a scandal blew up when Mhairi Black attended an event at a local primary school with a drag queen, Flow Job. Pornographic content was later found on his social media feed which children had accessed.[15] I was not the only MP to raise concerns, but even after John Swinney had condemned the decision to invite the performer into the school[16], Mhairi was allowed to deliver a standing tirade against me at the group meeting with the approval of Blackford. To his credit, Martin Docherty-Hughes intervened to say we should not be conducting meetings in this way, but Mhairi had a sense of entitlement that was always indulged.

I was never a fan. Although she was lauded for her oratory in the rare contributions she made in parliament, it is hard to identify any concrete achievements during her parliamentary career. I also felt many of the points she made in her speeches were cliched and

---

[14] https://wingsoverscotland.com/two-woke-princes/

[15] https://www.dailyrecord.co.uk/news/politics/scots-drag-queen-flow-jobs-22997878; https://www.pressandjournal.co.uk/fp/politics/scottish-politics/2037892/john-swinney-condemns-drag-queens-visit-to-school-and-distances-himself-from-snp-mp-mhairi-blacks-views/

[16] https://www.thetimes.com/article/79ebda0e-5881-11ea-ae40-36d0719ad0bc?shareToken=bae71cf54a5d2e8c354dc74c5c4f9783

jejune. Like many of my colleagues I didn't think much of her work ethic and I found her at times rude. I don't think a subsequent diagnosis of ADHD excuses this.

Although I was well disposed to Stephen Flynn's later Westminster leadership bid from the outset, I found myself unable to support him when he presented the group with the fait accompli that, if he became leader, Mhairi would be his deputy. When I asked him why he had done this, he said it was because she was attractive to working-class voters. I queried this assumption and pointed out that, having gone straight from university to a salary of £90,000 per annum in her early twenties, it was hard to imagine anyone further removed from the typical Scottish working-class experience. Indeed, most middle-class Scots cannot hope to achieve such a salary in their lifetime.

In early 2020, LGB Alliance launched in Glasgow at an event at Oranmore. It was made very clear to me that if I attended the event I would be expelled from the SNP. Victoria went and came back full of enthusiasm. The next month we attended a huge event organised by Woman's Place UK at University College London.

And then came lockdown. Trans activists in the SNP continued to rage against gender-critical women on social media. Meanwhile, gender-critical feminists continued to organise in the SNP, and for the NEC elections held during the party's online conference in November 2020, the SNP Women's Pledge group, together with the left-wing Common Weal group, organised a slate of candidates. There was a big crossover between those with the gumption to call out Sturgeon's embrace of gender-identity politics and those prepared to question her independence strategy and the way in which she and her husband ran the party. Despite a campaign of vilification against us, we were elected in large numbers, deposing some of Sturgeon's most ardent acolytes.

By this time opposition to gender-identity ideology had taken a firm hold in the SNP and was becoming more of a mainstream issue across the United Kingdom. J.K. Rowling had tweeted her support for Maya Forstater in December 2019. When she was monstered, I spoke up in her defence.

In May 2020, she contacted me to thank me, and we became friends, despite having been on opposite sides of the independence referendum. Our friendship is just one of many I have made with women and some men who were on the unionist side of the referendum but with whom I have joined forces in the fight to protects women's rights, including lesbian rights. By this time I had become thoroughly disillusioned with the SNP leadership and I had lost all confidence in their ability to advance the cause of independence. Making alliances across the constitutional divide to defend women's rights seemed a better use of my time. It was not something I could ever have foreseen when I first entered parliament in 2015.

In time I became one of many women and men across the UK who were able to take advantage of J.K. Rowling and her husband's generosity to defend ourselves when trans activists came after us.

In December 2020, Baroness Kishwer Falkner was appointed Chair of the Equality and Human Rights Commission. This followed a confirmation hearing before a joint meeting of the JCHR and the Women and Equalities Committee, at which I questioned her closely on the need for the EHRC to speak out on behalf of women's and LGB rights, as well as trans rights. She indicated her intention to do so. She kept her word and had to face down determined attempts to undermine both her and the EHRC.[17]

I continued to be regularly attacked by SNP members on social media and in the press for my activism against gender-identity ideology throughout 2020. As the SNP's online conference started at the end of November, I publicly called on Nicola to do something about the abuse and named and shamed some of those who had signed a defamatory letter organised by SNP activists but signed by people from other parties accusing me of transphobia

[17] https://www.personneltoday.com/hr/ehrc-closes-probe-into-allegations-against-chairwoman/; https://www.theguardian.com/society/2024/nov/13/equality-human-rights-commission-chair-kishwer-falkner-staff-complaints-new-term; https://www.equalityhumanrights.com/human-rights-regulator-retains-status-0

and seeking to prevent my election to the SNP NEC.[18] One of the signatories was SNP councillor Mhairi Hunter, who worked in the First Minister's constituency office. The letter also purported to be signed by my colleague Stewart McDonald MP and the leader of the Scottish Liberal Democrats, Alex Cole-Hamilton MSP, although they later said that this had happened without their permission and had their names removed. I instructed solicitors and the letter was toned down, but no steps were taken by the SNP to address what had occurred. The letter did not damage my election chances, and I received more votes than all the other candidates put together for the post of parliamentary representative on the NEC.

In a *Times* newspaper interview with Magnus Linklater,[19] I warned my party against a cult-like approach to the leadership and accused the party of having an unhealthy tendency to shut down debate. Interviewed on the radio later, Sturgeon claimed not to know what I was talking about but condemned abuse in general terms, particularly the abuse which she said she received.

Attacks on me from within the party continued unabated. In January 2021 a discussion I had been asked to convene at an online national assembly on the issue of our independence strategy was disrupted by an SNP Westminster staffer, on account of my views. Complaints from irate SNP members were ignored.

Things were really starting to come to a head in the party. It felt like trench warfare at the NEC as the group of newly elected rebels tried to assert their mandate while party loyalists who had been removed from their NEC positions by the membership were co-opted back onto the committee by their pals who remained.

The official SNP line was that preparations for an independence referendum were halted to focus on the Covid pandemic, but plans to advance the agenda of identity politics were not so halted.

It is well documented that trans activists have a suite of legislative measures they push governments to introduce in order to

---

[18] https://wingsoverscotland.com/the-poison-within/

[19] https://www.thetimes.com/article/6fcca3f2-30fb-11eb-8bd6-64d3c9126a9b?shareToken=c0e0ff0132e2f8ae443590b5e4e6c480

embed gender-identity ideology. Kate Harris has referred to these as a triptych: hate-crime legislation that makes it very difficult to criticise gender-identity ideology; so-called anti-conversion therapy legislation, which makes it difficult for counsellors to suggest to a child with gender dysphoria that they might not be trans but gay or just going through a phase; and, of course, legislation paving the way for self-identification of sex.

In Scotland the lobbyists were pushing for all three, and in early 2021 a new bill codifying and updating hate-crime legislation was going through the Scottish Parliament. Like many other gender-critical feminists, I was very concerned that a new crime of stirring up hatred on the grounds of transgender identity would be used to silence critics of the identity politics agenda.

Humza Yousaf was in charge of piloting the bill through parliament and, as always, he was open to discussion. He and I held a couple of online meetings with his SPAD present, during which I explained my concerns. He took them on board and introduced an amendment to the Hate Crime Bill to address the concerns raised not just by me, but by a wide range of civic society bodies, MSPs and others. The amendment was designed to ensure that women who wished to discuss women's sex-based rights would be protected from charges of transphobic hate crime. This seemed reasonable in a democracy bound by the duty to protect free speech under Article 10 of the European Convention on Human Rights.

On the morning that Humza' SPAD emailed me with details of the amendment, I checked with him that it was in the public domain before tweeting approvingly.[20]

Almost immediately both Humza and I were accused of transphobia for our support for this government amendment. Separately, I was already being attacked by SNP activists, parliamentarians and staffers, including the ubiquitous Kirsty Blackman, for my support for an English barrister, Sarah Phillimore, whose Twitter account

---

20 https://x.com/joannaccherry/status/1354378624095432705?s=51&t=_s_WNsml10-qFdtTr9lYMQ

had been suspended because of confected allegations of transphobia and antisemitism. [21]

Elected SNP members and internal groups like 'Out for Indy' were demanding that action be taken against me. Humza came under huge pressure to withdraw the amendment, which he did the following week.[22]

On 28 January, Nicola Sturgeon posted a video message on Twitter saying that she had heard reports of 'mainly young people in significant numbers leaving the SNP because they do not consider the party to be a safe tolerant place for trans people'. She pledged to do everything she could to change that impression and to persuade them that the SNP was where they belonged. This became known as her broom-cupboard broadcast, because of the amateurish way in which it had been produced.[23]

I had become increasingly concerned about the way I was being treated by the party. A whistleblower who worked for the Westminster group had disclosed correspondence which Kirsty Blackman and a staffer had sent to the Chief Whip suggesting how I might .be expelled from the group and the party based on my sex realist views. I took legal advice from experts north and south of the border who thought I would probably have a claim for discrimination or harassment on account of my gender-critical beliefs. In accordance with the traditions of the Scottish Bar, the Dean of the Faculty of Advocates offered to represent me for free if I wanted to take legal action against the SNP.

---

[21] https://www.scotsman.com/news/politics/joanna-cherry-blocks-snp-colleague-kirsty-blackman-on-twitter-amid-lgbt-row-3116605

[22] https://www.scotsman.com/news/politics/humza-yousaf-accused-of-ignoring-concerns-over-protections-for-free-speech-in-hate-crime-bill-3151019

[23] https://www.scotsman.com/news/opinion/columnists/euan-mccolm-hate-crime-act-damaged-from-the-start-by-influence-of-campaigners-and-weakness-of-nicola-sturgeon-4581976#:~:text=In%20the%20clip%20–%20filmed%20on,welcoming%20place%20for%20trans%20people."

On 30 January, I wrote to the party's National Secretary Stewart Stevenson and Business Convener Kirsten Oswald, pointing out that I would have legal remedies if the party proceeded to take disciplinary action against me by characterising my support for women's rights, lesbian rights and free speech as 'transphobic'. I copied the letter to the SNP Chief Whip (then Patrick Grady), Ian Blackford, Nicola Sturgeon and Keith Brown.

Later that weekend, a well-wisher tipped me off that I was going to be sacked from the SNP frontbench. I was grateful to them because, on the Monday afternoon, Ian Blackford gave me 30 minutes' notice before he announced his changes. The press release that went out made no reference to me or gave any thanks for the work I had done in the role of Justice and Home Affairs spokesperson over the last five years. It seemed I too was to be airbrushed from the party's history, just as Alex Salmond had been.[24]

However, thanks to the tip off, I was able to get ahead of the story and tweeted: 'Despite hard work, results and a strong reputation I've been sacked today from the SNP frontbench. My constituents and fellow party members who gave me a resounding mandate in recent NEC elections should rest assured that I will continue to work hard for them.'

My well-wisher told me that they understood the decision to sack me was taken because it was thought I was likely to be on strong ground with a legal challenge if disciplinary action was taken against me by the party. Punishing me with a political decision could not be the subject of legal challenge.

However, if they had hoped to humiliate me, they must have been taken aback by the size of the adverse reaction. There was a public outcry, with commentators on the left and the right questioning the wisdom of the decision. I also received an avalanche of supportive messages from constituents and from party members who were outraged about the decision, and over the next few days

---

24 https://www.edinburghnews.scotsman.com/news/politics/alex-salmond-airbrushed-out-of-snp-online-history-1422781?r=2863

it was reported that hundreds of party members had cancelled their membership in protest. [25]

I was inundated with flowers, champagne, wine and chocolates from across the UK, Ireland and the world. I was particularly touched that the first bouquet of flowers to arrive came from Harriet Harman, who knew what it was like to be sacked in publicly humiliating circumstances.

However, my sacking did have one very unpleasant consequence. On the evening of the day I was sacked I received a series of threatening messages, including threats of rape from a man who turned out to be a member of the SNP. I reported the matter to the police, who took it very seriously. A young man called Grant Karte, who was a member of the Bannockburn branch of the SNP, was subsequently arrested and charged. Peter Murrell told the press that the young man was no longer a member of the party, but I was shown documentation by an official from his branch confirming that he was. I was not surprised. At the time he was part of a coterie of young men collected around Stirling University who were very vocal in their support for trans activism. Many of them had been members of the 'red circle gang'. They regularly attacked feminist and lesbian members of the SNP who disagreed with them online, and it was no surprise to me that a troubled and impressionable young man who already had a criminal record for carrying a knife[26] would have felt that threatening me in this way was acceptable.

What he did has never been publicly condemned by anybody in a leadership position in the SNP, notwithstanding his conviction after he pled guilty to sending me abusive and threatening tweets.

---

[25] https://www.thenational.scot/news/19071631.scottish-independence-joanna-cherrys-sacking-not-right-credible/; https://www.theguardian.com/politics/2021/feb/05/joanna-cherry-sacking-brings-snp-trans-rights-row-off-twitter-and-into-the-light#:~:text=As%20one%20MP%20said:%20%E2%80%9CThe,other%20issues%20fall%20into%20them.%E2%80%9D; https://www.bbc.co.uk/news/uk-scotland-scotland-politics-55905895

[26] https://www.dailyrecord.co.uk/news/scottish-news/sheriff-calls-psychiatric-report-snp-23926011

After the reshuffle, one of Scotland's leading newspaper columnists, Iain Macwhirter, posed the question: 'Was Joanna Cherry sacked for thinking women are female?'[27]. Ian Blackford let it be known that I had been sacked for 'unacceptable behaviour', but he never actually spelt out what he meant by that.

In February 2021 the NEC went on to pass a definition of 'transphobia' that was worded in such a way as to make it possible for the party to discipline members for using forms of address or pronouns that didn't correctly reflect the gender with which somebody identified. I advised them that their definition would not survive a human rights challenge and asked why they didn't have a similar definition of lesbophobia and why their equalities policy hadn't been updated in relation to any of the other protected characteristics since 2012. A young woman who had been co-opted onto the committee told me that the law was a tool of imperialist racist oppression. No one in authority including Sturgeon herself a lawyer challenged this nonsense. I was vindicated in my advice when a couple of years later the Liberal Democrats received the same advice from the distinguished equality law expert Karon Monaghan KC.[28]

At this time the NEC also gerrymandered the party's selection rules to punish Joan McAlpine for her feminist activism by ensuring that she was unlikely to win at the upcoming Scottish elections. The Scottish Parliament is elected by a mixture of first past the post and proportional representation, with a top-up list of MSPs taken from regional party lists. Candidates for the list are selected by local party members and Joan always topped the poll in Dumfries and Galloway. The NEC decided, against independent legal advice from a very senior Scottish QC based on the relevant provisions of the Equality Act, to have a policy of positive discrimination on the grounds of disability and race, and Joan was displaced from her top position on the list by Emma Harper, a local MSP who suffered

---

[27] https://www.heraldscotland.com/politics/19059050.iain-macwhirter-joanna-cherry-sacked-thinking-women-female/

[28] https://sex-matters.org/posts/updates/lib-dems-revise-transphobia-definition/

from diabetes. It was hard to see how this could be classed as a disability justifying preferential treatment when at the time she was working as a nurse as well as an MSP. When the election came round this manoeuvre ensured that Joan lost her seat.

The legal advice in question was discussed in detail at the NEC. It was quite clear that the mechanism would not withstand a legal challenge and yet the Business Convenor used her casting vote to ensure that the legal advice was ignored.

The frenetic activity around the confected problem of 'transphobia' in the party provided a useful distraction from what was going on in the Salmond inquiry. The heat continued throughout February and reached a crescendo in March as Sturgeon awaited the outcome of an independent inquiry into whether she had misled parliament over the date of her knowledge about the allegations against Alex Salmond. . It was an extremely tense time for me because of the repeated attacks I was facing and because of the appalling atmosphere within the party that played out with unpleasant scenes at Westminster group meetings and at NEC meetings, most of which were conducted online.

Later that summer *Holyrood* magazine gave me their award for Best Scot at Westminster. I was a bit tired and emotional when I went up to receive the award at the ceremony, and indicated that I thought 'my time in politics might be coming to an end'.[29]

I had already started to make plans for what I might do if life in the party became unbearable for me. In May I had been approached to represent Marion Millar, a gender-critical woman who had been charged with threatening and abusive behaviour for posting messages on Twitter that were allegedly homophobic and transphobic. Now that I had more time on my hands, I decided to return to my practice at the bar on a part-time basis to represent her.

---

[29] https://www.thetimes.com/uk/politics/article/snp-will-try-to-oust-me-says-joanna-cherry-grh6v500j?gaa_at=eafs&gaa_n=AWEtsqeRJPQ-sUyM7WcJoCK3CEnrPeYzcaewgwN5B_qqnMyJO1g0fjCHpA3K4&gaa_ts=694290f1&gaa_sig=WDm4LRXJf3ff4DwkcoZCqeHFfdMNJi9NF-bO9Oc1wN1uE_SS33a9krOW95Rt1nDXe71arq-jespq63EDMopt5lA%3D%3D

The Dean of Faculty of Advocates granted me a dispensation to reflect the fact that my availability to be instructed would necessarily be limited by the requirement to be at Westminster regularly and to fulfil my duties to my constituents. I was following in the tradition of fellow members of the Faculty of Advocates, including the late John Smith and Menzies Campbell, who had also combined the occasional practice of law with their duties as MPs.

The complainers in the case against Marion Millar included a police officer and two others whose identities were not disclosed to the press.[30] This was baffling as there was no anonymity order from the court. This sort of protection is usually afforded only to complainers in sex offence cases or witnesses who are vulnerable.

I also learned that an officer involved in the police investigation was an LGBT rights activist who was active in the LGBT police group. Then I was passed information from a police whistleblower alleging that the complainers had been put in touch with the activist police officer by a senior SNP activist and councillor who was close to Nicola Sturgeon. I was unable to verify this information before the case came to court but it was my intention to investigate what I had been told. The politicisation of police forces across the UK in relation to issues of gender ideology is now well documented. [31]

---

[30] https://www.theguardian.com/uk-news/2021/oct/28/scottish-prosecutors-drop-transphobia-case-against-marion-millar#:~:text=against%20Marion%20Millar-,This%20article%20is%20more%20than%204%20years%20old,sexual%20orientation%20and%20transgender%20identity.

[31] https://ministryofinjustice.co.uk/police-impartiality/#:~:text=A%20High%20Court%20ruling%20by,flag%20associated%20with%20transgender%20ideology.; https://www.localgovernmentlawyer.co.uk/litigation-and-enforcement/400-litigation-news/61679-judge-upholds-legal-challenge-to-decision-to-allow-police-officers-to-take-part-in-pride-event; https://policyexchange.org.uk/publication/transgenderism-and-policy-capture-in-the-criminal-justice-system/#:~:text=The%20Gender%20Recognition%20Act%202004,rather%20than%20their%20biological%20sex.; https://murrayblackburnmackenzie.org/2025/01/16/police-scotland-review-of-sex-and-gender-whats-the-story/

There is no doubt that the activities of Marion Millar, something of a maverick, were becoming an embarrassment to Nicola Sturgeon. A video was circulating on Twitter of Ms. Millar driving by an event attended by Sturgeon in Glasgow and leaning out of the car to shout, 'Hey, Nicola,' upon which Nicola looked round smiling, clearly expecting to see a fan, and then Ms. Millar shouted, 'Women Won't Wheesht.'

It was apparent from social media that some trans activists had also got Marion Millar confused with Marion Calder, one of the directors of For Women Scotland, who were starting to have quite a high public profile. Many suspected that this was why Marion Millar was targeted for a police complaint. Perhaps it was a case of, 'Who will rid me of this troublesome priest?'

Her case became a *cause célèbre*. The complaint against her was verging on ridiculous. It included reference to her having tweeted a photograph of a purple, white and green suffragette ribbon tied to a wire fence, which was interpreted as being a noose for one of the complainers on the most flimsy pretext. I lodged a defence based on breach of her rights to freedom of belief and expression. Her first appearance at Glasgow Sheriff Court was attended by a big demonstration, with some women dressed as Margaret Atwood-style handmaidens, and followed by a rally addressed by gender-critical activists from across the UK.

Towards the end of October 2021, I received confirmation that the Crown had dropped all charges against Ms Millar and celebrated with a bottle of champagne on the House of Commons terrace. As so often in the gender wars, the brave stand of one woman had seen off an attempt by bullies to silence her. But I remain shocked and concerned by the information I had received that suggested political influence had been brought to bear on the police and the Crown when Ms Millar was charged.

Although the Crown ought to be commended for dropping the charges, I know that the decision was taken at the highest level because, thanks to crowdfunding, Ms Millar was able to instruct senior and junior counsel. I do wonder what would have happened if she had not been able to afford such representation.

Together with civil litigation, the mounting of successful defences to spurious criminal charges has played a very important role in the fight back against gender-identity ideology to ensure that both women and men can speak up without losing their liberty or their livelihoods. Perhaps the most significant victory so far has been that of Maya Forstater, who established at the Employment Appeal Tribunal that gender-critical beliefs are 'worthy of respect in a democratic society'.

During the last few years, I have travelled around the UK to support women who have found themselves having to take their employers or trade associations to court. Allison Bailey, the black lesbian barrister who successfully sued her chambers for unlawful discrimination against her when she spoke up in support of LGB Alliance. Denise Fahmy, in Leeds, who successfully sued her employers the Arts Council when she was harassed and bullied for defending the award of a grant to LGB Alliance, LGB Alliance's successful defence of its right to exist as a charity and Sandie Peggie's employment tribunal against NHS Fife which was held in Dundee.

I was able to use Maya's case to resist attempts to have me expelled or deselected from the Scottish National Party. I was also able to call upon it when I found myself cancelled by the Stand Comedy Club in Edinburgh in 2023.

Over the years many good people in the Scottish National Party at grassroots level defended me, and some of them suffered for it. I met one woman who had been suspended from the party for retweeting one of my newspaper columns that was critical of the party on the identity politics issue. She was not alone. This sort of draconian approach to gender-critical women stood in strong contrast to the SNP's lackadaisical approach to the complaints against Mhairi Black for calling gender-critical women 'Jeremy Hunts' and the complaints of sexual harassment and bullying against several men in the party.

In early 2021 an SNP government minister phoned me to tip me off that my MP colleague Anne McLaughlin and her SNP councillor boyfriend, Graham Campbell, were attempting to organise a petition in one of the Glasgow constituency associations to have me expelled from the party. I was not surprised. Campbell, a member of the NEC, was one of the most assiduous critics of gender critical women and those who wanted to see reform in party governance. The petition did not materialise.

In early 2022, grassroots members of the Edinburgh Central branch led by party stalwarts Dave Williamson and Isobel Knox rallied round to resist an attempt to have me censored by the branch for my gender-critical views. The campaign against me was led by two relative newcomers to the branch: Michael Sturrock, an aide to Angus Robertson, and an American woman, Kat Cary, who became a member of the branch shortly after the independence referendum, caused a lot of trouble and unpleasantness over identity politics, and then mysteriously returned to America not long after Sturgeon's resignation.

I also benefited from wider support networks across the UK. In April 2022, J.K. Rowling brought together some of the stalwarts of the gender-critical movement at a lunch in London. The guest list included Maya Forstater, Helen Joyce, Kathleen Stock, Julie Bindel, Allison Bailey, Suzanne Moore, Bev Jackson and Kate Harris. Photos got into the press, and we caused something of a stir, becoming known as 'the ladies who lunch'.

Later in 2022 two pivotal events occurred, the tribunal hearing of the attempt to have LGB Alliance struck off the charitable register and the passing of the Gender Recognition Reform Bill. In 2021 the Charity Commission had accepted LGB Alliance's application to register as a charity, but only after a lengthy inquiry into their suitability for registration as a charity, after trans activists objected. A vicious campaign to overturn that decision followed, culminating in legal action to have them struck off the register. The case was brought by Mermaids, a charity set up to support children and young people questioning their gender identity.

The LGB Alliance tribunal took place in the week after the Queen's death on 8 September 2022, when there was a lull in normal life. Parliament wasn't sitting, so I was able to stay in London and observe most of the case. It was a quite extraordinary experience to watch lesbian women on trial for their beliefs while they were attacked by men who thought they knew better than them what a lesbian was.

There were also some considerable personal tensions in the small tribunal room. Jolyon Maugham, my erstwhile comrade from the prorogation case was supporting Mermaids challenge through his organisation, the Good Law Project. He had become an enthusiastic proponent of gender-identity ideology after a family member transitioned and had told me he could no longer remain my friend. He said he valued what we had done together and that he would never attack me publicly. I think he has kept his word there; however, he has become increasingly radicalised, and it has been difficult for me to return the compliment, particularly given his pursuit of many women who have become my friends.

It was hard to cope with his presence in the small tribunal room. But even harder to sit through the extraordinarily bombastic performance of my SNP colleague John Nicolson MP in the witness box, a man who has spent much of the twilight of his political career policing the lives and language of lesbians. I have never seen a witness put on a more arrogant and ridiculous display. He even presumed to tell the court and counsel that they were not approaching the case properly and were taking up too much of his valuable time. In most Scottish courts he would have been firmly put in his place, but the tribunal chairs in London displayed extraordinary forbearance. I have no doubt he helped LGB Alliance win their case.

Another memorable moment in the hearing was when my friend Kate Harris, co-founder of LGB Alliance, broke down in tears in the witness box when she was being cross examined by Mermaids counsel to try to get her to agree that a lesbian can have a penis, i.e. that a lesbian can be a man. After she composed herself she made the following memorable speech: 'I'm going to speak for millions of lesbians around the world who are lesbians because we love other women ... We will not be erased, and we will not have any man with a penis tell us he's a lesbian because he feels he is. A lesbian is attracted to another biological women, full stop.'

Ultimately, Mermaids lost on the issue of standing, meaning that the court did not consider they were sufficiently affected by the decision to register LGB Alliance as a charity to be entitled to object. But the tribunal also said: 'Charitable status does not come with any guarantees of funding nor any freedom from criticism or debate. It is no part of the Commission's function (nor of this Tribunal) to tell people what to think, or to regulate public debate in a context where there are deeply held, sincere beliefs on all sides of the discussion.'[32]

However, LGB Alliance's victory came at a considerable cost. Mermaids was then a wealthy charity. LGB Alliance was not, and they were left with a bill for over £250,000. Not for the first time I was left to wonder at the wisdom of the rules that costs cannot usually be awarded in tribunal proceedings.

As 2022 came to end, Holyrood sat late into the night to pass the Gender Recognition Reform Bill. The committee scrutiny of the bill had been a joke. A partisan committee heard mainly from witnesses who were in favour of the legislation. Women were ejected from the public gallery for wearing suffragette colours, while MSPs on the committee sat resplendent in rainbow lanyards. The parliament as a whole did not do much better.

Various amendments proposing safeguards to the bill were voted down, including an amendment to prevent known sex offenders from obtaining a gender recognition certificate; an amendment to prevent those awaiting trial on sex offences from applying for a gender recognition certificate (designed to protect rape victims from the humiliation of having to use female pronouns to refer to their attacker in court); amendments to protect vulnerable women in prison; amendments to ensure those receiving intimate care could elect to receive it only from members of their same sex; and amendments to allow the continuation of single-sex wards in healthcare settings.

However, for the first time in the history of the devolved parliament a minister resigned on a point of principle, when Ash Regan stood down to vote against the bill. In all, nine SNP MSPs voted

32 https://www.judiciary.uk/wp-content/uploads/2023/07/Mermaids-v-Charity-Commission-judgment-060723.pdf

against the bill, the most significant rebellion the SNP has faced in nearly two decades of government.

As the bill passed, MSPs stood to applaud trans activists in the gallery, some of whom had issued violent threats against women on social media.[33] However, their triumphalism was short lived. Not long into the new year, Alister Jack, the Scottish Secretary, announced that enactment of the legislation would be blocked using Section 35 of the Scotland Act because it would have an adverse effect on reserved matters. He was particularly concerned about the impact of the bill on equal opportunities under the Equality Act and the protected characteristic of 'sex'.

It was a vindication of the argument of gender-critical campaigners, but there was a predictable outcry from the Scottish government and trans activists. The SNP Westminster group called an emergency debate portraying the block as an attack on the devolved parliament. Stephen Flynn, the newly elected group leader, asked me if I would vote with the Tories. I said no but I wanted to abstain, and he said that I should go ahead, as for me it was a matter of conscience. The contrast with Blackford could not have been more pronounced.

From a constitutional viewpoint I also thought the attack on Scottish democracy line was hyperbole. To describe the use of the Section 35 power to block the bill as an attack on devolution doesn't really make sense. It is of the essence of devolution that the devolved parliament is subservient to the UK parliament – that's why nationalists want independence. Power devolved is power retained.

Furthermore, in an independent Scotland the passing of the bill by a parliamentary majority would not necessarily have guaranteed that it would become law without further challenge. If we were an independent country with a written constitution, the bill could have faced a legal challenge based on the concerns about its impact on equality law and human rights. In the summer of

---

33 https://www.thescottishsun.co.uk/news/10201373/trans-activist-suspended-scottish-greens/

2014, the SNP had published plans for a transitional constitution in a white paper with a foreword by Nicola Sturgeon. It proposed to enshrine the protected characteristics of the Equality Act in Scotland's new constitution, as well as the rights protected by the European Convention on Human Rights. [34]Accordingly, the impact of the Gender Recognition Reform Bill on the protected characteristic of 'sex' would still have been in issue.

In my *National* column I argued that those who wish to see independence shouldn't waste their time kicking against the inevitable constraints of devolution and picking legal fights they cannot hope to win. When the Scottish government sought a judicial review of Alister Jack's decision they lost at first instance when Lady Haldane found for the UK government in the Court of Session. By then Humza Yousaf was leader, and he did not take the appeal further.

While the Section 35 furore was at its height, along came 'Isla Bryson', a trans-identifying male rapist called Adam Graham who was sent to a women's prison following his conviction for two rapes. The photograph of Graham standing outside the court in a blond wig and tight pink leggings that accentuated his male genitalia peaked most of Scotland.

Nicola Sturgeon was humiliated under skilled questioning by ITV News reporter Peter Smith, which exposed a fundamental incoherence in her position when she suggested that perhaps not all trans women were women,[35] and that perhaps there was a third sex of 'rapists'.

Shortly thereafter she resigned. Identity politics played an important part in the leadership election that followed. Sturgeon loyalists and trans activists coalesced around Humza Yousaf as the continuity candidate. The other two candidates were Kate Forbes and Ash Regan. I thought carefully about which of them to support.

---

[34] https://webarchive.nrscotland.gov.uk/20190118174515/http://www2.gov.scot/Publications/2014/06/8135/downloads

[35] https://www.itv.com/news/2023-01-30/trans-prisoner-pause-was-to-give-clarity-says-nicola-sturgeon; https://spectator.com/article/watch-sturgeon-ties-herself-in-knots/

In the end I chose Ash because of her courage in resigning her ministerial post to vote against self-identification. In fairness, Kate, who was also understood to oppose self-identification, had been on maternity leave at the time, but there was another factor which made me hesitate to support Kate, and that was her conservative views on issues like equal marriage and abortion. My advisers felt that if this became an issue in the election I would be portrayed by my political enemies as socially conservative on wider issues than the self-identification issue, and that this would drive me and all of them mad.

In the event Kate Forbes' views proved to be far more high profile than my advisers could ever have imagined. She gave a somewhat ill-advised interview in which she said that she wouldn't have voted for equal marriage, and was thereafter monstered by her opponents in and outwith the party. The situation got completely out of control, and some of the things that were said about Kate and her religious faith were unforgivable. A constituent stopped me in the street to tell me how disgusted she was by the behaviour of the SNP towards Kate, and I could not disagree. Things got so bad that I asked Mike Russell as president of the party to intervene and call the dogs off Kate, but he refused to do so. It proved to be the end of our friendship when I expressed my disgust at his refusal and asked him what he thought previous party presidents such as the late Neil MacCormick would have done in the circumstances.

Alex Salmond was instrumental in persuading Kate not to throw in the towel, and I understand he may have reached an agreement with her that if she became party leader the Alba rebels would be welcomed back into the fold. In the event she lost out to Humza by a very small margin. Ash came a distant third and later defected to Alba. However, as I travelled round Scotland with Ash campaigning, I was left in no doubt that many party members were deeply unhappy with what was happening to the SNP.

The leadership battle exposed the huge divisions in the party. On a visit to Dublin later that spring to talk about nationalism and unionism, an Irish wag quipped, 'Sure, Joanna, won't you tell your colleagues they're supposed to have their civil war after the war of independence, not before it.'

Cancel culture

In January 2023 my colleague and friend Tommy Sheppard MP, co-founder and promoter of the Stand Comedy Club in Edinburgh, approached me to see if I would like to appear as one of their guests in a series of 'in conversation' events at that year's Edinburgh Festival Fringe. What was envisaged was a wide-ranging chat about my political career. I had done a similar event with Matt Forde on the Festival Fringe in August 2022, and it had been a sellout. There was no financial gain in it for me, but I thought it might be fun. A contract was signed. Then, shortly after my appearance was advertised, I became aware that some trans activists were making a fuss about it. Tommy came to see me at my constituency office and took me for a drink, and it became clear to me during the conversation that he was asking me to cancel myself. I refused to do so, whereupon the Stand themselves cancelled the event, making a public statement that their staff did not feel 'comfortable' working with me.

They said that their staff felt unsafe working with me because of my gender-critical views, and that their duties to their staff overrode their free speech and non-discrimination obligations. As a matter of law this is completely wrong, The providers of goods and services cannot hide behind the discriminatory views of their staff in order to avoid a claim of unlawful discrimination. Otherwise, someone who owns a bar could say, for example, that they would love to welcome black customers into their pub but they cannot do so because their staff would not serve them.

With the financial backing of J.K. Rowling and her husband, I instructed solicitors and senior counsel to challenge their decision, and I'm pleased to say that the venue backed down. I then published the detailed opinion of Senior Counsel on my website, and other feminists have been able to use it to resist attempts to bully venues into no platforming or cancellation. This included FiLiA, the international feminist organisation whose conference in Glasgow was threatened with cancellation after pressure was put on the venue by trans activists later that year in October 2023.[36]

There were signs that the tide might really be turning when Humza Yousaf condemned the trans activists who stood outside the venue shouting, 'Fuck you,' at feminist activists from across the world. He had invited me in to see him earlier that month, and we had a long heart to heart in which I think he really did listen to my concerns about the impact of gender-identity ideology on the rights of women and LGB people. However, Humza did not last long.

When John Swinney succeeded Humza, we spoke on the phone, but I did not detect the same openness to my viewpoint as I had seen in Humza. I told him he must meet with gender-critical campaigners. Two years on he has yet to do so. John got a taste of what women like me have had to put up with when he came on a campaign visit with me during the 2024 election and saw a trans-identified male following me around shouting 'transphobic bitch' at me.

Losing my seat in July 2024 did not come as a shock; rather more something of a relief. When I was down in London clearing out my Westminster office, I got the opportunity to meet one of the women I most admire, Martina Navratilova, who had become a strong advocate for the rights of women and lesbians. She invited me and a friend to be her guests at Wimbledon and to have dinner with her. Martina is a lovely, warm woman with a particular interest in politics. The selfie I took with her went viral. Somebody asked me how it felt to meet one of my heroes and I said it had been considerably easier than the last time I met one of my heroes, after which I ended up becoming an SNP MP.

Some people have suggested that my gender-critical activism contributed to my losing my seat in the 2024 General Election, but there's no evidence of that and my experience talking to constituents about this issue was overwhelmingly positive. Most people

---

[36] https://news.stv.tv/west-central/feminist-conference-supported-by-joanna-cherry-to-go-ahead-as-lawyers-overturn-decision-to-cancel-in-glasgow

who approached me to talk about it supported my stand, and even some of those who didn't said they respected me for my courage in taking it. On election day a woman came into my campaign office to say that, following a conversation we'd had during the campaign, she had changed her mind about my views and was going to vote for me.

However, my stance on this subject has affected my decision making about my post-political employment and activities. I am pretty sure that I would find it very difficult to be appointed to any public board in Scotland. When I accepted a place as a trustee on the board of LGB Alliance, another major human rights charity withdrew their offer to make me a trustee. I was approached by several headhunters but decided that I would return full time to the bar, where I am now gainfully employed and considerably happier than I was in my later years as an SNP MP.

My fight to assert freedom of speech and the rights of women and LGB people in the face of gender-identity ideology has led to the creation of strong bonds with women in other parties, particularly the Labour Party, and some unexpected cross-party friendships, including with my parliamentary predecessor, the late Alistair Darling and his wife, Maggie Vaughan, also close friends of J.K. Rowling. In the years before the 2024 General Election, I was wooed by senior Labour Party figures who wanted me to defect, but I resisted their offers. Watching their slow-motion car crash since the General Election I am very glad I did, but I was never really tempted because of their opposition to Scottish independence.

In truth, I am relieved to be out of Westminster. I look at the current House of Commons and despair because it is so packed full of professional virtue-signalling career politicians who are out of touch with their constituents' views on many issues. I also would have found it impossible to support much of Keir Starmer's policy programme, particularly his attack on the rights of pensioners and disabled people living in poverty.

Nevertheless, I continue to work with Labour and Conservative women who oppose gender-identity ideology, and indeed women of all parties and those of none. Our greatest legal victory to date came in 2025, when For Women Scotland won their long-running battle with the Scottish government over the meaning of 'woman' in the Equality Act. Now we know beyond doubt that it is a reference to biological sex. For years the Scottish government persisted with the disingenuous position of telling parliament that self-identification was simply an administrative change with no effect on the rights of women, while arguing in court that self-identification changes the meaning of the word 'woman' in the Equality Act to anyone who says they are a woman. When they lost that argument, they tried to argue that the word woman includes any man with a Gender Recognition Certificate. Now they have lost that argument as well.

When FWS first told me they were going to try to win the latter argument I thought they would fail. However, when I sat through the arguments in the Supreme Court in November 2024, I watched the Scottish government's arguments wither and die in the face of careful questioning from the Supreme Court justices. In my opinion the Scottish courts did not cover themselves in glory with their rather superficial treatment of the arguments. In particular, when they opined that there was 'no such thing as being legally lesbian'. [37] It was this statement that prompted lesbian groups including LGB Alliance, Scottish Lesbians and the Lesbian Project to get together and make written submission on the impact on lesbian rights of expanding the definition of 'woman' in the Equality Act to include some men. In the event our intervention proved very helpful, as did that of Sex Matters. We became known as 'the lesbian interveners', which does sound rather like an awful girl band from the nineties.

On the day the judgment was to be announced, 16 April 2025, the atmosphere at the Supreme Court was electric. I had been in Argyll working on this book, but I travelled down to London. The feeling of jubilation and vindication when we won is hard to describe. Outside the Supreme Court, as we celebrated with champagne and media interviews, I was reminded of how I felt on the

---

[37] https://www.scotcourts.gov.uk/media/11imtxvx/court-of-session-judgement-reclaiming-motion-by-for-women-scotland-limited-against-the-scottish-ministers-01-november-2023.pdf at [57]

day of my victory against Boris Johnson when his prorogation of parliament was ruled unlawful. Denise Findlay, a former SNP and Alba activist who was there with me, told me she felt the same way, and it made her feel sad. She was treated appallingly by the SNP on account of her gender-critical views, yet campaigned for me in the 2024 election when SNP activists were thin on the ground. She said being with me at the Supreme Court as a second major victory was announced in a significant case in which I had been instrumental made her think of what might have been if Sturgeon had involved me in her legal strategy to get a second indyref. I was touched and also saddened.

Outside the court I demanded an apology from Sturgeon and a U-turn from the Scottish government as a result of the win. Both have yet to materialise.

The Scottish government's intransigence and denialism in the face of defeat have been hard to thole but not unexpected. The reality for John Swinney is that the SNP has become so hollowed out in recent years as a result of the divisions caused by espousing this ideology, failing to advance the cause of independence and purging all opposition, that the people he might have relied upon to support him in doing what is necessary to close this chapter simply are not there anymore. Instead, he is surrounded by activist MSPs and staffers, and others who are merely acquiescent cowards or fools.

NICOLA STURGEON – MY PART IN HER DOWNFALL

7

Around five o'clock in the morning of 5 July 2024, after I had lost my Westminster seat at the 2024 General Election, I was interviewed on live TV from the Edinburgh count, on a split screen with Nicola Sturgeon who was sitting in a studio in London as a paid commentator.

It was suggested to me that the reason for the huge SNP losses that night was that we had put independence at the front and centre of our campaign. I argued that it could never be a mistake for the party of independence to put independence at the heart of their message. Rather the problem was that over the last decade not enough effort had been put into making the case for independence, winning over sceptics and devising a strategy to get a second vote. I also pointed out that the SNP does best and the cause of independence rides high when the party governs with competence and integrity, and that had not been the case lately.

ITV's Tom Bradby asked me whom I held responsible for the failure to pursue independence in the way I would have wanted. I put the blame squarely on the leadership style espoused by both Nicola Sturgeon and her faithful lieutenant Ian Blackford. I said their leadership did not brook discussion, debate or argument on policy or strategy. I also argued that the party had missed big opportunities to advance the cause of independence when we were close to holding the balance of power during Theresa May's Brexit trials and tribulations, and after my defeat of Boris Johnson in the UK Supreme Court.

At the time I didn't realise I was on a split screen so everyone could see Nicola's tight-lipped reaction to my criticisms. I was tired after being up all night and I had to go straight to the airport to travel to Oxford for my friend Nina's memorial service later that day. So when the reporter at the count asked me if I wanted to keep my earpiece in to listen to Nicola's response, to his amusement I replied no, took the earpiece out and walked away. I had heard more than enough from her over the years, and I was disgusted with her behaviour that night.

Later, I found out that Nicola had not answered any of the points I'd made, instead employing her favoured strategy of playing the man and not the ball; she said that I was a critic who had not posited alternative strategies.

History and, I hope, this book will demonstrate that that is simply not true. In fact, I repeatedly made suggestions about how things might be done differently, particularly in respect of her independence strategy and gender issues, but I was not just ignored but also demonised and marginalised for my efforts.

It was galling to lose my seat on the back of so many failures of which she was the author and against which I had counselled and offered alternative ways forward, but in truth I also felt a huge sense of relief. I'd had enough of the SNP Westminster group, and being a member of it in its diminished state with Kirsty Blackman as Chief Whip would have been unbearable for me. I had very much enjoyed being a committee chair, but as the SNP were no longer the third party that would not have been an option for me any longer and I would have been trapped on the opposition backbenches for five years in a parliament where the SNP voice was diminished to the point of irrelevance.

Unlike the SNP MPs who lost their seats in the General Election rout on 4 July 2024, Nicola Sturgeon will never have to face the wrath of the electorate for SNP failings in the years she led the party and governed the country. She resigned as First Minister on 13 February 2023 and announced that she would not stand again as an MSP on 12 March 2025, well before that verdict could be delivered at the 2026 Holyrood election. She has left behind a litany of policy failings, internal party difficulties and a financial scandal, all problems that developed on her watch.

And yet as I and 37 of my colleagues found ourselves very publicly sacked in the early hours of the morning of 5 July 2024, Sturgeon was on television talking about the party in the third person, as if what was happening had nothing to do with her. I was not alone in being incensed by her brass neck. As the night progressed at counts across Scotland, loyal candidates and staffers who had to deal with the fallout of her legacy were hurt and bewildered by her behaviour.

At the time I was determined that Nicola Sturgeon should not be allowed to rewrite history and wash her hands of responsibility for that defeat, and I remain so. When Nicola Sturgeon resigned on 13 February 2023 it took many people by surprise, but for those who had been playing close attention and had insight into at least some of what was going on behind the scenes, it wasn't so surprising.

At the end of November 2022, Nicola's independence strategy had hit the brick wall of the UK Supreme Court ruling that the Scottish Parliament could not hold another independence referendum without the permission of Westminster. I was not convinced by her road to Damascus conversion to using the next General Election as a de facto referendum on the issue of independence. I felt it was something that she had done because her back was against the wall and she had no other option. She must have known that it was doomed to fail, and I suspected she didn't want to be in the driving seat when that failure happened.

She was also losing her grip on the party. In December 2022, against her wishes. the leader of the Westminster group and one of her strongest allies, Ian Blackford, had been forced to resign to make way for a new leader, Stephen Flynn, who was prepared to stand up to her.

Stephen's Westminster leadership challenge annoyed her and she did her best to frustrate it, but he had worked assiduously to recruit support from those in the Westminster group who'd had enough of Blackford. Eventually, Ian had no choice but to resign to avoid the humiliation of defeat in a leadership election.

By early 2023, Nicola was floundering in the media in a way she never had before, over the crash and burn of her self-ID policy. The problems that gender-critical feminists had warned about were personified in the rapist 'Isla Bryson', who hit the headlines in January 2023 just as the UK government announced they would block the self-ID legislation.

Finally, rumours were rife that the police were close to interviewing both her and her husband over concerns about the SNP finances. If this had happened while she was in office she would have had to resign in ignominy.

Nicola said she was going because she was worn out and had become a divisive figure, but within weeks of her resignation her husband had been arrested, her home was being searched, and a forensic police tent had been erected on her lawn.

I believe that watching the resignation of her hero, New Zealand PM Jacinda Ardern, on 19 January 2023, in which she said she no longer had 'enough in the tank', made Nicola realise that if she got out at the right time she could go gracefully and control the narrative.

It wasn't just her independence and self-ID policies that had hit the buffers. She was faced with a host of other problems in education and the NHS, with record drug deaths, problems in delivering the National Care Service she had promised, and multiple issues with ferries to the islands.

Her popularity had slumped since the end of the Covid pandemic, and the public inquiry into that period was looming with the consequent threat to her image as 'chief mammy'. It was all a long way from the heady days of 'I'm with Nicola', the catchphrase that encapsulated the euphoria of the first two years of her leadership. Despite my better judgement I was initially a little caught up in that euphoria, but as I have described in previous chapters I quickly began to be disillusioned.

I was not a particular fan of Nicola Sturgeon when she became SNP leader at the end of 2014, but I felt she had earned the right to lead based on the skills she had shown as a communicator and debater during the independence referendum. As far as I was concerned, if Alex Salmond wanted her as his successor that was enough for me.

I imagine that the plan of Nicola's chief of staff Liz Lloyd and those advising Nicola after she became party leader and First Minister in November 2014 was to park independence and get on with running the devolved administration, keeping Nicola in office for as long as possible. This was a reasonable strategy, given that we had just lost the referendum.

However, Brexit derailed this plan and put Independence firmly back on the agenda. But it was not just Brexit that derailed Sturgeon's initial plans, it was also her inability to deliver on her policy promises, her desire to stifle debate or dissent completely, and her immediate circle's focus on taking down Alex Salmond and then covering up their botched plan. The latter also undermined her focus on dealing with Brexit and advancing the cause of independence.

Her missteps in the aftermath of the Brexit vote and the significant loss of MPs at the 2017 Westminster General Election badly dented Nicola's confidence and made her and those around her who were dependent on her patronage for their well-remunerated roles paranoid about a leadership challenge, whether from Alex Salmond or me.

The other aspect of the plan to save her leadership was to shore up her popularity and to find her a power base within the party. When she became leader, she must have been aware of her relative unpopularity – both within the party and with the public – and that must have made her feel a little insecure. On her own admission she suffered from 'imposter syndrome'.[1]

Many saw her as cold and lacking in charisma. She was known as a 'nippy sweetie', the Scots term for a sharp-tongued or peevish women. She knew the SNP well, having joined at the age of sixteen, but after the independence referendum the party grew from

---

1 https://www.dailyrecord.co.uk/news/politics/nicola-sturgeon-admits-suffering-imposter-15844677

a membership of around 25,000 to over 100,000. She and Peter knew the existing membership, but the new members were an unknown quantity.

This could only have exacerbated her insecurity, and I am sure it influenced the decision that Murrell should stay on as chief executive of the party, notwithstanding advice from Alex Salmond and what he had understood to be an agreement to the effect that Murrell would stand down from this post when Nicola became leader. It was a fateful decision that, while ensuring she would ride high for many years, also laid at least some of the seeds of her downfall.

Peter Murrell had been chief executive of the party since 2001. Prior to that he had worked as an SNP parliamentary staffer for various MPs and MEPs, including Alex Salmond. He and Nicola got married in 2010, but they had been together for a number of years before that. He was generally regarded as being an effective administrator and campaigner. So far as I could see he had a firm grip on everything that happened at SNP HQ. My impression was that Alex Salmond pretty much left him to his own devices, although it was well known that there had been tensions between the two during the independence referendum campaign.

As leader Nicola ruled the government and the party with a rod of iron and micromanaged everything. With Peter as Chief Executive they made a formidable team

Peter created a new persona for Nicola, built her reputation as a strong leader and found her a power base within the party. After she became leader, he set about creating a new image for her. Like many feminists it infuriates me that women in politics are judged by how they look in a way that men are not. To be fair, Jeremy Corbyn got a hard time for looking like he dressed himself after an absent-minded trip to the Oxfam shop, but compared to the stick women come in for this is as nothing. Nicola had always been seen as a little dowdy or frumpy. During the indyref her image had sharpened, but as leader, with her Totty Rocks-commissioned designer outfits, hairstyle change, improbably high heels and *Vogue* photo shoots, her image changed beyond all recognition.

Around this new image Peter encouraged the development of the cult-like adoration of this relatively young and stylish leader, which I had first seen at the Hydro rally in Glasgow. It became central to everything the party did. Every leaflet was about her. Every announcement was made by her. Every press line parliamentarians were given to utter was about what she had said or what she thought about the issue of the day. We were not encouraged to have our own thoughts or lines; indeed, this was very much frowned upon.

As SNP leader she faced another potential problem. Past SNP leaders had found a power base within the party with either the independence gradualists or the fundamentalists, or in Alex's case geographically, in the Northeast of Scotland. When Nicola became leader in 2014, she did not have an obvious power base. Other than perhaps the Glasgow parliamentarians, councillors and those on the payroll, whose support she certainly had in the years to come, she was lacking a natural constituency of support within the party. Having become leader on the back of Alex Salmond's recommendation, she had not had the opportunity a leadership campaign would have afforded to cement her position. I believe that concern about her lack of a natural power base in the existing party membership, never mind the vastly expanded membership, prompted her and Peter Murrell to cast around for a way to build one. They alighted on the idea of cultivating young people in the party.

Nicola had already scored a great success with young people during the independence referendum campaign. That she saw the benefits of building on this can be seen in the way her premiership progressed, with her emotional promise to overhaul Scotland's care systems and to listen to care experienced young people at the October 2016 conference.[2]

---

[2] https://www.thenational.scot/news/14896524.every-young-person-deserves-love-sturgeon-announces-overhaul-of-care-system-and-puts-inclusion-at-the-heart-of-speech/#:~:text=At%20conference%2C%20a%20clearly%20emotional,review%20will%20be%20published%20soon.

In the past the youth wing of the party had often been marginalised and had little influence. Under Nicola that was to change. Indeed, in the years that were to come, the noisy and often nasty activities of some of the youth wing on Twitter led to them being nicknamed the 'Twitler youth'. But back in 2017, after the initial hysteria and adulation of her new leadership had worn off, and after the bruising experience of the 2017 General Election losses, Nicola was badly in need of a Praetorian Guard, and she and Peter decided to capitalise on her appeal to young people.

She and her advisers were also looking to do something that could be characterised as 'progressive'. Perhaps her nose was a bit pushed out of shape by the fact that it was Alex, not her who had introduced equal marriage in Scotland, although she was Deputy First Minister at the time and First Minister when the change came into force. Certainly, later in 2024, on the tenth anniversary of the Marriage and Civil Partnership (Scotland) Act 2014 coming into force, she tried to steal the thunder for its introduction.[3] And in her memoir, she wrongly claimed that Alex had opposed it.[4] There is no evidence to suggest this beyond what she has said. Alex's chief of staff has thoroughly debunked this slur[5] and Alex Neil, the minister who was ultimately in charge of the bill, says Alex Salmond handed him the brief because Nicola was sick of it. [6]

---

[3] https://www.independent.co.uk/news/uk/nicola-sturgeon-scottish-parliament-patrick-harvie-national-records-of-scotland-holyrood-b2664798.html

[4] Frankly page 189

[5] https://www.heraldscotland.com/news/25404850.salmond-aide-fury-sturgeon-falsehoods-late-fm/

[6] https://www.thetimes.com/uk/scotland/article/scottish-child-payment-plan-turned-down-nicola-sturgeon-mtghw6zpx?gaa_at=eafs&gaa_n=AWEtsqcqnXdGypYjO5pq8wmboySm5-KeLOkQzGH-VGZnwZG0gtTLqVG71wRq&gaa_ts=6935b32b&gaa_sig=k5xr954Z_vCx1r0Ma8hZtj85EUWzFeLh_EaOUqWvNLnT_ujU6mWeRxSwJHtp8oFhG6Idebn1T1xp4T5e5YPKjg%3D%3D

Gender-identity ideology is widely supported by young people who are politically active, particularly those who consider themselves 'progressive', if not young people in general. Nicola and those around her perceived that 'trans rights', or rather the right to self-identification (because trans people already have equal rights under the Equality Act), was the next great frontier for progressive politicians. Once equal marriage was won, that was the message being pushed by lobby groups like Stonewall and, in Scotland, the Equality Network, and they had some very active allies within the Westminster and Holyrood parliamentary groups. Being a 'trans ally' looked like an easy win and a route to popularity with young people and self-styled 'progressives'.

Wrapping herself in the progressive flag became even more important after the disaster of the 2017 election, when she had to distance herself from the prospect of an immediate second independence referendum following the Brexit vote. Now that she was running scared of the cause of independence as a vote loser and a threat to maintaining her power as head of the devolved parliament, she was in search of a legacy and a springboard to a career after politics. I have no doubt that the plan was for the introduction of self ID in Scotland to be her legacy and her route to a high profile and lucrative international position when her time as First Minister came to an end.

However, over time it became clear that the issue was more complicated than she had appreciated and risked dividing the party. That's when Nicola began the game she had followed in her independence strategy of kicking the can down the road on delivering a self ID bill.

But, on the surface at least, she remained 100 per cent committed and implacable in the face of demands to rethink the policy. When my colleague and friend Joan McAlpine, then an MSP and Chair of Holyrood's Culture, Tourism, Europe and External Affairs Committee, remonstrated with Nicola about the unintended consequences of the policy, Nicola told her it had to be done 'because young people are very upset'.

Despite her appalling treatment of other women who disagreed with her, including Joan McAlpine and me, Nicola styled herself as Scotland's 'first feminist'. Yet she had no discernible history of feminist activism. Prior to becoming FM feminist causes were not to the fore of her political activity. Likewise, despite her attendance at Pride marches as First Minister, unlike myself and others she was not part of or a supporter of the LGB rights movement in the eighties or nineties, and indeed when recall of the equivalent of Section 28 in Scotland was first mooted by the then Scottish Labour government in 2000, she had sat on the fence.[7]

A charitable explanation of her behaviour towards dissenters on self-identification would be that her lack of a hinterland in the feminist and gay rights movements meant she was not in the best position to understand the concerns raised by seasoned activists from these movements about her policies. A less charitable explanation is that, as with other dissenting voices, she simply was not prepared to listen. Instead, she took the assurances of the handsomely paid self-appointed spokespersons for LGBT people and feminism in third-sector organisations and lobby groups at face value and was happy to decry the concerns of women and LGB people, many with a long history of human rights activism, who were working for free in grassroots groups. Embracing the 'no debate' mantra espoused by Stonewall and others came easy to someone whose natural urge as leader was to suppress debate and marginalise those who questioned her views.

There was a significant overlap between those who questioned Nicola on her self-ID policies and those who questioned her on her independence strategy and the way in which she ran the party. The result of the NEC elections in November 2020, when rebels including me did so well, rattled her and Murrell badly. This is where her Praetorian Guard came in handy, as the Twitler youth handed out what Robin McAlpine has described as 'punishment beatings' on social media to anyone who dared question her.[8] The activists who booed those who advocated a plan B on

---

7 http://news.bbc.co.uk/1/hi/scotland/769639.stm

8 https://robinmcalpine.org/this-is-the-one-tall-tale-that-matters/

independence off the stage at the November 2019 conference were the same activists who attacked me and others as transphobes in the months and years that followed.[9]

Nicola had to keep them on side by being vocal about the introduction of self-identification legislation, while delaying actually doing so for fear of splitting the party. The onset of the pandemic gave her cover for a time, but by the end of 2020 her power base was getting restive. This is why, as Robin McAlpine describes, her 'rhetoric escalated' to the point of the broom-cupboard broadcast in January 2021, when it looked like some of her strongest allies might be about to leave the party unless she found a sacrificial lamb to prove her intolerance of 'transphobia'. Hence my sacking a few days after that broadcast.[10]

However, just as she had placated her supporters for the time being, another problem became acute as the fallout from the Salmond inquiry escalated to the point where parliament voted by 63 to 54 votes to demand the release of the Scottish government's legal advice during Salmond's judicial review. When she tried to ignore this vote she faced a vote of no confidence, and so had to release the damning information that her government had wasted public money continuing to defend Alex's judicial review for months after their lawyers told them they would lose. Without a majority in the Scottish Parliament, Nicola knew she faced further trouble unless she could win an outright majority at the 2021 Scottish Parliament election.

Her failure to do so is why she made a pact with the Greens after the election. As Robin McAlpine has argued, the Bute House Agreement afforded vital protection against further damning parliamentary scrutiny. It gave her a majority and bound the Greens into collective responsibility, but it also 'tied her to a party that prioritised ... self ID over almost every other policy'.[11] The time

---

9 https://www.newstatesman.com/politics/2019/10/snp-leadership-crush-conference-rebellion-plan-b-independence; 3

10 https://robinmcalpine.org/this-is-the-one-tall-tale-that-matters/

11 https://robinmcalpine.org/this-is-the-one-tall-tale-that-matters/

for kicking the can down the road on self ID was over. Hence the rush to get the Hate Crime legislation through in 2021 and the Gender Recognition Reform Bill in 2022.

Ultimately, what went wrong with the Gender Recognition Reform Bill is a microcosm of everything that was wrong with the SNP approach to policy under Nicola's leadership. It was an ill-thought-through policy that was never debated on the floor of conference; she refused to listen to those with legitimate concerns, dissenters were demonised, but above all, as opinion polls have repeatedly shown, she failed to take the public with her.

Nicola's prioritisation of gender politics over the SNP's primary goal of independence also alienated large sections of the party membership and independence supporters. By the time of her resignation, it was clear that despite all her electoral victories, despite Brexit, the unlawful prorogation of parliament, the chaos of Boris Johnson's administration, the plaudits she had received for her handling of the Covid Crisis, and the madness of Liz Truss, she was not going to be able to deliver independence.

Opportunities to do so were missed because of an approach that favoured grandstanding over statecraft. A leader of the strategic calibre of Alex Salmond would have been able to capitalise on these amazing opportunities. But Nicola had seen him off and instead she slowly reversed the SNP's independence strategy up a blind alley.

She repeatedly promised a second independence referendum, which she knew she could not deliver, issuing a never-ending list of dates and targets that were missed, and marched her troops up and down the hill until many of them deserted in disgust. When some party members and parliamentarians suggested she might need a plan B rather than repeatedly banging her head on the brick wall of the British government's refusal to grant permission for a second independence referendum, she, and those around her, demonised us and encouraged her lackeys to attack us.

For years she refused to countenance or discuss a legal strategy that might have delivered competent Scottish Parliament legislation on a referendum. Then, when she ran out of road to kick the can down, she went cap in hand to the UK Supreme Court in a manner and at a time when anyone with an inch of legal nous could have advised her that she was going to lose.

By 2022 the Covis crisis was over, another request for a Section 30 order had been refused, and the strategy of delay and prevarication was wearing very thin. Nicola had to do something. The promise of legislation to hold a referendum had turned out to be a smoke and mirrors exercise. The last time such legislation had been brought before the Scottish Parliament, a Section 30 order had first been secured from the UK government so that there was no question over the competence of the Scottish Parliament to legislate. Whether the parliament had the competence to do so without such permission was not clear as a matter of law. However, unlike myself and other leading lawyers, neither of the Lord Advocates whom Nicola Sturgeon appointed during her premiership were persuaded by the argument that it could. When legislation was finally introduced in 2019 it was merely to facilitate the holding of referenda in general.[12]

The problem Nicola faced in 2022 was that she couldn't follow the much-promised plan to introduce a bill to hold another referendum in the Scottish Parliament because the Lord Advocate did not think that such a bill would be competent under the Scotland Act. She was in a bind. However, it wasn't a bind she needed to be in. There were senior lawyers, including me, who held the view that a competent bill could be crafted. She could have appointed one of us to the role of Lord Advocate. Indeed, one might have expected her to do so if she was intent on adopting the strategy to which she was ostensibly committed.

I know for a fact that she met with a number of potential appointees before replacing the outgoing Lord Advocate James Wolffe in May 2021. Either she did not inquire of them what their position was on the competency of a Scottish Parliament independence referendum bill, or she did and equivocation was acceptable to her. In 2022 she approached the United Kingdom Supreme Court seeking an answer to the question of whether the Scottish Parliament

---

[12] Referendums (Scotland) Act 2020

could legislate for a second independence referendum without the permission of Westminster. The strategy was doomed from the start – from both a legal and political perspective. Legally, because of the timing. The Supreme Court had previously shown a rather narrow and conservative approach to construing the legislation underpinning the Scottish Parliament in *Miller I*. However, after their judgment in the prorogation case it was hoped that the court might be prepared to take a more creative approach to interpreting the devolved settlement. That was in 2019. By 2022, the Supreme Court had changed in its character and composition, and lawyers on both the left and on the right agreed that it was more conservative in its approach.

The strategy was doomed from a political perspective because had we been defending a bill passed by the Scottish Parliament, as I had advocated, it would have had the weight of Scotland's democratically elected representatives behind it, and we could have presented a loss in court as a setback for Scottish democracy and an underlining of the limited powers of the Scottish Parliament. A campaign using the much-promised Constitutional Convention could have been built on the back of that.

Yet, despite my extensive writings and interventions on these subjects, Nicola never consulted me on the strategy to be followed. The only communication I received was a phone call to inform me that she had decided to pursue the strategy of seeking permission after she had done so. I was exasperated but kept quiet in the interests of party unity, hoping against hope that there might be a victory.

I visited the Supreme Court on the morning the hearing started and made some supportive comments to journalists, but I took the decision not to sit in the court throughout because I did not want to be too closely associated with a strategic move I feared was doomed to failure and on which my advice had not been sought.

In the event, not only did Nicola lose, but an unintentional result of the separate submissions lodged on behalf of the Scottish National Party on the issue of self-determination was that the Supreme Court made some rather unfortunate comments suggesting that Scotland does not enjoy that right. Thankfully, that aspect of the judgment is not binding and has been debunked by experts on international law,[13] but it was not helpful.

It seemed that Nicola had reached the end of the road on her independence strategy when, to most people's astonishment, she announced that the only step open to her was to make the next UK General Election a de facto referendum. It was an extraordinary volte face on her previous refusal to even countenance a discussion about doing such a thing and an extraordinary misstep, as it should have been clear to anyone that the SNP were not going to do as well at the 2024 General Election as they had in 2019. Even at the peak of our popularity, when we won 56 out of the 59 seats in 2015, we achieved just short of 50 per cent of the vote.

MPs including loyalists like Stewart McDonald were up in arms.[14] They were right to be. Over the next eighteen months her successors struggled with the policy and confusion over whether victory would constitute winning a majority of the seats or a majority of the votes. That debate turned out to be academic when we won neither.

While all this was going on, concerns about party finances, which had been bubbling under since the election of the SNP rebels to the NEC in November 2020, had come to a head with a criminal investigation. Kicking off in the summer of 2021 under the name Operation Branchform, this investigation initially concerned allegations that approximately £660,000 raised by the SNP since 2017 specifically to campaign for independence in a second independence had been spent, at least in part, on other things. The scope of Operation Branchform became wider when the police announced in July 2023 that the investigation had gone beyond the initial allegation of fraud and was now looking at potential embezzlement and the misuse of funds.

I had had longstanding concerns about the manner in which the party's internal affairs were being run. That is why I stood for election to the NEC in November 2018. I did not stand again

---

13 https://www.albaparty.org/international_legal_opinion

14 https://www.bbc.co.uk/news/uk-scotland-scotland-politics-64566957

in November 2019, as I was sickened by my treatment after I had raised concerns about the way in which the party was conducting the investigation into Alex Salmond. But in November 2020, I was persuaded to do so again. Despite a campaign of vilification in the press and the circulation of a defamatory letter by members of the party, including members of the NEC, I got more votes than all other parliamentarians put together. I was elected along with several other new members who were keen to improve transparency and accountability. Over the months that followed, most of us resigned because of the impossibility of getting any answers to our perfectly reasonable questions about the party's internal governance. We were vilified for trying to do our job as representatives of the membership on the party's governing body, and hounded by Sturgeon's supporters at meetings, in the press and on social media.

It is hard to convey the menacing atmosphere in which NEC meetings were conducted. I was made to feel very uncomfortable for taking a note of proceedings.

At a meeting in November 2019, the First Minister threatened me in front of everyone present that if I wanted complaints from party members against Mhairi Black (for calling women cunts on social media) to be addressed, she was sure complaints against me could be found and pursued. This is indicative of the level of intimidation employed against those who challenged her leadership of the party. The fact that this threat was delivered in a room full of people and no one, apart from Chris McEleny, demurred is indicative of the confidence she had that her behaviour would go unchallenged.

Peter Murrell was arrested on 5 April 2023 while police carried out an extensive search of his and Nicola's marital home, including the garden. When photos of the forensic tent erected in their garden emerged, one wag on social media inquired "Has anyone seen Joanna Cherry recently?" Police also searched and removed documentation from SNP HQ in Edinburgh. A motorhome was subsequently seized from Peter Murrell's mother's driveway. Colin Beattie, who had been the party's treasurer throughout the material time, was arrested in April 2023, and finally Nicola herself was arrested on 11 June 2023. Unlike Michelle Thomson, none of the arrestees were suspended from the party pending the outcome of the investigation.

Peter Murrell is currently awaiting trial on charges of embezzlement, having appeared on petition in March 2025. At the same time as he appeared on petition it was announced that there would be no further proceedings against Nicola Sturgeon or Colin Beattie. Nicola has spoken of her relief on being 'exonerated'. She has also spoken of the incredible stress of being under suspicion for so long. I hope that this might give her some insight into what Alex Salmond went through. However, it is noteworthy that she gives more weight to the Crown's decision not to press charges against her than to the jury's decision to acquit Alex.

In the immediate aftermath of Nicola's resignation, it became clear that she had done little or no succession planning. The much-expected leadership bid from Angus Robertson did not materialise. Keith Brown, the deputy leader, ruled himself out, as did former and now current leader John Swinney. Nicola's favourite, Màiri McAllan MSP, also ruled herself out. In the end the candidate favoured by those close to Nicola was Humza Yousaf, more by default than by design. He became known as the continuity candidate.

MPs couldn't fill the shoes of First Minister because we were members of the UK Parliament, not the Scottish Parliament. The candidates had to be MSPs. The gerrymandering of the rules for Holyrood selection before the last Scottish election had made it a practical impossibility for me to run for the leadership. I wasn't too pushed, as by that time I had become extremely disillusioned with the party and didn't fancy having to sort out the mess that Sturgeon had left it in. The party was also deeply divided and I was not sure I was the person to bring it back together.

The leadership race turned out to be something of a farce. It was the first leadership election in the SNP for almost twenty years, yet it was held on an expedited timetable. This meant that candidates were bounced overnight into a very short campaign with no resources, no preparation, no backup team and no facility or time to develop a policy programme.

The initial plan was to hold hustings in private, and it was only after protests that this idea was changed. The feeling was that the party machine wanted to keep a lid on any disputes and to avoid discussion of controversial topics like gender reform, the party's independence strategy and its internal affairs. They also didn't want people to see Humza going up against Kate Forbes, who was a much more skilled debater.

There was widespread concern in the Forbes and Regan camps that there might not be an honest and open contest. Questions were raised about the secondment of employees of the party to the Humza's campaign and the use of party resources to assist him.[15] An MSP was censured but not disciplined for breaking the leadership election rules by sending an email to party members using the special access she had to them as a member of the Scottish Parliament.[16] There were calls for the election to be independently moderated, as it is with other parties.[17] I accused the party machine of supporting Humza.[18]

The press had reported that the party's membership had dropped by around 30,000. Murray Foote, the SNP's media chief, described these reports as 'inaccurate' and 'drivel'. They turned out to be true. Initially, SNP HQ refused to publish the party membership numbers, but under pressure from the candidates and several parliamentarians, including me, the NEC eventually agreed to do so. It was duly reported that as of 15 February the membership was

---

15 https://www.thenational.scot/politics/23359697.joanna-cherry-snp-members-optimistic-future/

16 https://www.thenational.scot/news/23365022.emma-harper-email-privileges-suspended-breaking-snp-rules/

17 https://www.scotsman.com/news/politics/snp-leadership-candidates-call-for-independent-auditor-amid-concerns-over-vote-4066587

18 https://www.heraldscotland.com/politics/23365020.joanna-cherry-claims-snp-party-machine-backing-humza-yousaf/

72,186, which was indeed down approximately 32,000 from the last published membership figures of 104,000 in 2021.

Murray Foote resigned, saying that he had been acting in good faith.[19] Clearly, he had been misled. On 18 March Peter Murrell also resigned as Chief Executive of the party with immediate effect in the face of a threatened no-confidence vote.[20]

The party was in turmoil. Deep divisions had been exposed. Despite everything thrown at Kate, she lost to Humza by only a narrow margin. He did not appoint her to his cabinet, and she was left on the backbenches. I felt this was a cowardly move prompted by his fear that if he appointed her, those who had attacked her religious views would be up in arms. There was a shocking level of hypocrisy to all of this, particularly when, shortly after assuming office as First Minister, Humza posted a photograph on social media of him and his male relatives praying in Bute House. I have no objection to him practising his faith, but I couldn't help but imagine the furore that would have followed if Kate had shown herself at prayer in the same situation.[21]

In June 2023, Humza held the independence strategy summit promised by Nicola, which had been delayed due to her resignation and the leadership campaign. As I had suspected it turned out to be nothing but a talking shop where no decisions were taken. The party was stuck with the strategy of using the General Election as a de facto referendum, which had already been announced by Nicola.

I was vindicated in my decision not to attend. My dear friend Nina, to whom this book is dedicated, had been diagnosed with terminal cancer in April the previous year, and she was nearing the end of the road. She wanted to die at home. Sitting at her bedside during the last few days of her life, in the dark silent nights as

---

[19] https://www.theguardian.com/politics/2023/mar/17/snp-head-of-communications-resigns-amid-row-over-membership-figures

[20] https://www.bbc.co.uk/news/uk-scotland-65000606

[21] https://www.telegraph.co.uk/politics/2023/03/29/scotlands-first-minister-leads-ramadan-prayers-first-night-bute/

I held her hand and listened to her breathing, I reflected on the fragility and uncertainty of our lives and wondered what on earth I was doing staying in the SNP. Nina died on 28 June 2023.

Around the same time, Winnie Ewing, whose Hamilton by-election win in 1967 had heralded the breakthrough of the SNP, had died. I travelled to Inverness for her memorial service on 15 July 2023, the day after Nina's funeral. I was accompanied by Fraser and my nephew Jamie, who did the driving. As I listened to Winnie's eulogies delivered by Alex Salmond and Alex Neil, I was reminded of the importance of the cause and what my party had once been, and I decided not to make any precipitate decisions.

Unlike Alex Salmond, Alex Neil, myself and other senior nationalist politicians who were invited by Fergus and Annabel Ewing to sit at the front of the Cathedral, Nicola arrived flanked on either side by Susan Stewart and Jeane Freeman and sat in the body of the kirk. She was not invited to speak.

Later that summer, Humza extended an olive branch to me and invited me in person for an hour-long chat at Bute House without any advisers present. During that conversation I explained to him the toll that the party's espousal of gender-identity ideology had taken on me and other women, and urged him to change the party's direction. He listened sympathetically but did nothing, at least not until the Cass Report was published in April 2024.

In the meantime, Nicola's reputation took another blow when the UK Covid Inquiry came to Edinburgh to hear evidence in January 2024. It heard from witnesses including Nicola, John Swinney, Liz Lloyd and civil servants and advisers who had worked closely with the First Minister during the pandemic. The picture that emerged was not flattering. It became clear that there had been a mass deletion of WhatsApp messages by senior figures as well as unminuted 'gold command' meetings held between Sturgeon, Lloyd and Swinney that seemed designed to bypass cabinet decision-making. There were also accusations that she had politicised the pandemic to further the cause of independence.

A well-respected journalist who was formerly a Nicola fangirl said that the evidence to the inquiry had revealed 'shocking levels of secrecy', 'control freakery' and 'serious problems' with Nicola's leadership'.[22] The families of Covid victims and survivors, particularly the elderly in care homes, were very angry, and Nicola famously wept under cross examination as she made her apologies to the bereaved.

A month later, Alex Salmond gave a bravura performance when he appeared before the Commons Scottish Affairs Committee to give evidence to their inquiry on relations between the Scottish and UK government over 25 years of devolution. He was asked whether the Scottish government had a policy for deleting WhatsApp messages while he was First Minister, and he said that there was no such policy. He also commented on Liz Lloyd's evidence to the Covid Inquiry and drew attention to the fact that it was 'miraculous' that amid all the missing WhatsApp messages, the one message that had survived was the one that referred to Boris Johnson as a 'fucking clown'.

There was much comment on his eloquence and recall of events, in contrast to Sturgeon's performance at both the Covid and Holyrood inquiries.[23] Meanwhile, the continuity candidate was having a hard time. On 25 April 2024, Humza invited the joint leaders of the Scottish Green Party, Patrick Harvie and Lorna Slater, into Bute House and very publicly sacked them from their cabinet positions, thus ending the Bute House Agreement. Harvie's response to the Cass Review is understood to have been a factor in Humza's decision. The independent review of NHS gender-identity services in England vindicated many of the concerns of gender-critical organisations like LGB Alliance. But in a major interview on BBC Scotland's flagship politics programme, Harvie dismissed it as

---

[22] https://www.theguardian.com/politics/commentisfree/2024/feb/01/nicola-sturgeon-covid-inquiry-pandemic

[23] https://www.heraldscotland.com/news/24132038.salmond-rounds-sturgeon-mps-raise-deleted-whatsapps/

transphobic and questioned its validity as a scientific document. This had caused a significant backlash and much criticism from within the SNP.[24]

Whatever the reasons, Humza very quickly faced a no confidence vote in the Scottish Parliament, where he no longer had the numbers. It looked like the Alba Party might save him, but then he resigned.[25]

Nicola might have been gone but I have no doubt she played a big role here. There were rumours that her operatives within government had brought Humza down when it looked like he was serious about relying on Ash Regan of the Alba Party to survive the vote. For obvious reasons Nicola could not let the party of her arch enemy Alex Salmond have such influence in her successor's government.[26]

In the turmoil that followed, John Swinney stepped into the breach. In truth, I don't think anyone else fancied the leadership much after what had happened to Humza, and John is a solid party man with a strong sense of duty. Kate Forbes toyed with the idea of standing against him. I said I would support her and was part of the discussions that ultimately led to her decision not to stand. John duly appointed her as his deputy first minister, but then shamefully failed to defend her when the Greens attacked her in parliament.[27]

John and I had known each other as teenagers. He telephoned me after he became leader to try to bring me back into the tent, but I explained to him that my support was conditional on him listening to the voices of gender-critical women and addressing the party's internal problems. He has yet to do either. Although he is credited with having steadied the ship, he has largely done so by

---

[24] https://www.heraldscotland.com/news/24291755.yousaf-harvie-comments-cass-review-strained-bute-house-agreement/

[25] https://www.albaparty.org/statement_resignation_humza_yousaf

[26] https://www.spectator.co.uk/article/did-nicola-sturgeon-kill-humza-yousafs-alba-deal/

[27] https://www.heraldscotland.com/politics/viewpoint/24696725.harvies-hounding-forbes-religion-really-makes-cross/

keeping the lid on the problems of the Sturgeon years rather than addressing them.

His first sip from the poison chalice he inherited from Nicola Sturgeon was leading the party through the doomed General Election campaign, which was announced days after he took office.

For me, the General Election campaign was an ordeal. The anger on the doorsteps towards the SNP's record in government and the scandals dogging the party was palpable. At least it was not personal, and many of my former constituents told me that if I was standing as an independent, they would have been happy to vote for me, but on this occasion they simply could not vote SNP. At one canvassing session a man who was fixing his roof came down off the ladder and ran up the street to shout and swear at us, but he stopped when he saw me and said, 'So you're out doing this yourself. You're brave. I've got no problem with you – it's just your bloody party. Why have you stayed in it when they treated you so badly?' This was a difficult question for me to answer.

Alistair Darling told me that he knew I was going to win his old seat in 2015 because when he was out on the campaign trail people would not look him in the eye. I experienced the same phenomenon in 2024, but at least I was resigned to my fate.

After I lost my seat, I was approached by headhunters in London. However, I was not overly tempted by the idea of running some big organisation. The thought of corporate life filled me with dread after years of dealing with the SNP bureaucracy. I was also worried that in any organisation my gender-critical views would be weaponised against me. I decided that I would rather return to my previous career at the Scottish bar, where I could be self-employed and my own person, and where effort and reward are more closely linked.

Alex Salmond asked me to go on his Youtube channel programme to raise the morale of independence supporters, but I told him that I couldn't because I had lost heart. At the end of July, I announced my plan to step back from frontline politics to take some time to reflect on what had happened to the SNP and the independence movement in the ten years since the referendum.

I announced my return to the bar in October 2024, shortly before Alex died on 12 October. One of his last acts was to champion the Scottish petition for judicial review of the UK and Scottish government's decision to cut the winter fuel payment. I was instructed as senior counsel.

When I heard that Alex had died of a heart attack, I was shocked but not surprised. The last time I saw him was at an anniversary event in Glasgow marking ten years since the independence referendum. I was worried by his appearance and thought he looked very unwell. I believe that the stress he suffered and his anger at the way he had been treated by the SNP contributed to his untimely death. This is also the view of his widow Moira, who knew him best. Like many at his funeral I wept bitter tears, disgusted by the way the SNP had treated their greatest leader and heartbroken at what they did to him.

In the aftermath of his death, there were some disgraceful attacks on his reputation. But by and large, obituaries to him were favourable and conferred upon him the status of a great political leader that he deserves. His legacy is already seen as being stronger than that of Nicola's.

Unlike her, he has concrete achievements to his name, including taking the SNP from obscurity as the fourth party of Scottish politics to the main party of opposition and then the party of government. He achieved an outright majority in a system designed to prevent such a thing happening and took Scotland to the brink of independence. Many of the policies the SNP trumpet most loudly on the doorsteps were delivered on his watch, such as free tuition fees and free prescriptions.

Nicola's memoir *Frankly* seeks to downplay his role in all these matters and also contains some disgraceful slurs about him, which have since been debunked by those who worked closely with him.[28] It is telling that she finds it necessary to continue to attack him even when he is dead and cannot defend himself.

[28] https://www.heraldscotland.com/news/25404850.salmond-aide-fury-sturgeon-falsehoods-late-fm/

I believe that history will judge his contribution to Scottish politics as transformative in a positive way; I don't believe it will be so kind to hers.

Nicola's leadership has set back the cause of independence. It may also have irretrievably damaged the SNP. It has certainly damaged Scottish society, which feels more fractured and divided than it has at any time in my life. Many lack hope.

Yes, Nicola won a lot of elections, but the conditions were such that the SNP probably would have won those elections anyway. The hugely successful electoral machine that she inherited was created on Alex Salmond's watch. Moreover, politics isn't just about winning elections; it's what you do with the power you get when you win, and that matters not just for the success of the country, but also for the welfare of your political party.

Nicola could not or would not construct a strategy to exploit the opportunities afforded by Brexit and the Boris years to advance the cause of independence, and she alienated those who tried to help. Much of the energy that should have gone into this instead went into clearing up the mess created by the botched attempt to smear Alex in 2017–18 and the efforts to make sure there was no question of him making a political comeback. Such energies as were left were devoted to creating a personal legacy for her by making Scotland the first part of the UK to deliver self-identification. In this too she failed.

As well as setting back the cause of independence, she also undermined the SNP's reputation for competence in government and left a litany of broken promises in the area of public policy; her promises to close the attainment gap, to cut NHS waiting lists, to deliver a publicly owned not-for-profit energy company, to dual the A9 and make it 'our first electric-enabled highway', to reduce greenhouse gas emissions and the promise to deliver a National Care Service.

It is hard to identify a positive legacy of her leadership from Scotland's point of view, except the Scottish Child Payment, a weekly credit paid to households with children in receipt of certain benefits or tax credits. When she introduced it in 2021 she heralded it as a 'game-changer', and it is certainly making a significant difference, although the extent of that difference is contested.[29] However, it was a policy she initially dismissed as unaffordable when it was brought to her by Alex Neil in 2016. [30] She may have introduced it, but she has left her successors with the headache of working out how to pay for it as charities and third-sector organisations demand ever-higher increases.

Nicola and her supporters often list the baby box – a box of essential items given to every parent with a newborn baby in Scotland since 2017 – as one of her proudest achievements. When it was introduced Nicola promised it would improve child health and mortality, but whether that is the case is disputed.[31] Others have explained that the idea came from Finland, where the baby box was part of a wider package of measures for supporting parents and training them to provide good childcare, with the baby box merely a perk at the end. The Scottish government took the perk and ignored the rest of the wraparound package.[32]

Nicola's much-trumpeted leadership during the Covid crisis has since taken a knock because of what emerged at the UK inquiry hearings in January 2024 and in the final report of the module concerning "decision making and political governance" published in November 2025.[33] That report paints a rather different picture from the Scottish exceptionalism encouraged by Sturgeon and her

---

[29] https://www.gov.scot/publications/child-poverty-evidence-in-policy-making/

[30] https://www.thetimes.com/uk/scotland/article/scottish-child-payment-plan-turned-down-nicola-sturgeon-mtghw6zpx?gaa_at=eafs&gaa_n=AWEtsqcqnXdGypYjO5pq8wmboySm5-KeLOkQzGH-VGZnwZG0gt-TLqVG71wRq&gaa_ts=6935b32b&gaa_sig=k5xr954Z_vCx1r0Ma8hZ-tj85EUWzFeLh_EaOUqWvNLnT_ujU6mWeRxSwJHtp8oFhG6Ideb-n1T1xp4T5e5YPKjg%3D%3D

[31] https://www.thelancet.com/journals/lanpub/article/PIIS2468-2667(23)00121-4/fulltext#:~:text=The%20analysis%20comprised%20182%20122,and%20National%20Records%20of%20Scotland.

[32] https://robinmcalpine.org/the-sturgeon-era-control-paranoia-and-vanity/

[33] https://covid19.public-inquiry.uk/documents/module-2-full-report/

supporters. It concludes that Scotland like the other nations of the UK failed to take immediate emergency steps in early 2020 when Covid was starting to spread across the world; that Scotland like the rest of the UK had no strategy for exiting lockdown and that the Scottish public were misled by her zero covid strategy. She was also heavily criticised for excluding her cabinet ministers from decision making. The report found that instead crucial decisions were taken in unminuted meetings of a 'Gold Command' group made up of Sturgeon, Swinney and Lloyd. This, the report said "diminished the role of the Scottish cabinet and reduced the transparency of decision making.".

The report highlights one particular decision on which the cabinet "should not have been sidelined" which merits closer scrutiny. This was the decision to close Scottish schools taken by Sturgeon and Swinney just before the lockdown in march 2020. I was not alone in being taken by surprise by this decision as the day before the shutdown was first announced the National Clinical Director, Jason Leitch, had been adamant that such blanket closures were neither contemplated nor necessary. [34] Then the next day at 3pm on 18th March the Scottish Government briefed the press that Swinney would announce the closure of all schools and nurseries to parliament the next day. It was a huge story at the time. I do wonder whether this volte face had anything to do with the fact that the defence case in Alex Salmond's trial was its height at that time and less than 3 hours earlier Geoff Aberdein had given his bombshell evidence suggesting that Nicola Sturgeon had known about the complaints against Alex at an earlier date from the version of events she had given the Scottish parliament.[35] The unexpected school closure story certainly knocked the story that Sturgeon might have misled parliament off the headlines.

What cannot be denied about Sturgeon's legacy is that when she resigned, she left her country and her party in the lurch.

---

[34] https://www.tes.com/magazine/archive/coronavirus-no-plan-close-schools-next-week

[35] https://www.theguardian.com/uk-news/2020/mar/18/alex-salmond-trial-told-sturgeon-took-part-in-meeting-with-complainant

She inherited a healthy party with huge numbers and enthusiastic activists. Now the party has a vastly reduced membership and very few activists who are prepared to put boots on the ground. Apart from a few party stalwarts, those who assisted with my election campaign in 2024 were largely former members, non-aligned nationalists and gender-critical feminists.

From the country's point of view, none of the policies that over the years she described as her 'defining missions' have been delivered. Initially, she staked her reputation on closing the educational attainment gap. She failed to do so and latterly she rarely talked about it.[36] She also promised to lead the world on climate change, yet her government and its successors have missed eight out of their last twelve annual targets and failed to achieve their 2030 emissions reduction goal.[37]

Her government and its successors' energy policy is a mess, with a 'just transition' much talked about, but little action taken to implement it; a hokey-cokey on support for shutting down the North Sea; and a country scattered with wind turbines, not one of which is in Scottish ownership. Meanwhile, families and pensioners live in fuel poverty in one of the most energy-rich nations in the world, and the national energy company she promised to set up in 2017 in order to lower their bills has never materialised. The Welsh government has managed to do this, but not the Scottish.

Nicola did not deliver on this and other policies because her politics were purely performative. She governed by announcement and press release. She wasn't interested in discussing policy or strategy. This had two unfortunate results: she was unable to deliver on her promises, and she was open to policy capture of the sort that led to the disaster of her self-ID policy. These shortcomings were compounded by a mixture of insecurity and hubris which meant that she alienated most of those

---

[36] https://www.dailyrecord.co.uk/news/politics/nicola-sturgeon-legacy-in-tatters-34744635

[37] https://www.bbc.co.uk/news/articles/crgrv45ed1po

who might have made a useful contribution to policy and strategic development.

A lasting metaphor for her style of government dates from 2017 when the MV *Glen Sannox*, an unfinished ferry at the heart of an ongoing troubled government contract, was due to be launched by her. However it wasn't ready. In the end she launched it with painted-on windows and plyboard funnels. It took many more years for the vessel to be seaworthy, and it is still dogged by troubles.[38] While delays, cost overruns and mismanagement of the ferry contract have continued, this faux launch has become a symbol of the performative politics at which Nicola excelled.

Despite parroting her support for 'progressive politics' and independence, she lacked an overarching narrative about the kind of Scotland she wanted to see. In this she resembles Keir Starmer, whose Labour Party seems ideology- and vision-free, and hence has been something of a disaster in government so far.

She was not interested in ideas and for all her much-trumpeted love of reading you will struggle to find any discussion of ideas gleaned from her reading in her speeches. Likewise, Scottish cultural references are thin on the ground. And with her attitude towards freedom of expression she can hardly be described as someone who celebrated the ideas of the Scottish Enlightenment.

Many people assume that Nicola Sturgeon and I fell out over my opposition to her plans for self-identification of sex in Scotland. In truth, the roots of her antipathy towards me lie in the fact that I challenged her lack of strategic thinking in relation to independence and Brexit, and the way in which she and her husband ran the party. From 2016 onwards my growing popularity in the party also threatened her. She and her close circle were very concerned when I called out what was happening behind the scenes in relation to Alex Salmond and stood by him in public. My election to the NEC

---

[38] https://www.bbc.co.uk/news/articles/c1mrdy0p104o#:~:text=Glen%20Sannox%20was%20launched%20by,had%20led%20to%20unforeseen%20complications.

in November 2020 as part of a group dedicated to better governance of the party was also a huge threat to her. My opposition to her enthusiastic embrace of gender-identity ideology, which was not in the public domain until 2019, was simply the icing on the cake that enabled her to label me a transphobe and a bigot, to have me sacked from my position as a frontbench spokesperson and to have me branded a pariah in the party. I was also a useful scalp to keep the Greens and her Praetorian Guard of activists on side.

Nicola's reign as First Minister, while longer than any other to date, came to a premature end in February 2023 when her mishandling of the independence strategy, the very public collapse of her self-ID policy and the party's financial troubles all came to a head at the same time. The Alex Salmond affair almost brought her leadership to an even more premature end two years earlier, in March 2021. While I regret that I was unable to successfully address these issues within the party despite my best efforts, I feel vindicated in having called them out at the time and to have correctly predicted that the way in which she and her advisers approached matters was bad for the SNP, bad for the cause of independence and, most importantly, bad for the country.

Despite her attempt to rehabilitate her reputation with a very one-sided and selective account of the events of her premiership in her memoir *Frankly*, major question marks now hang over her reputation. While she still has her fanbase, she cuts something of a diminished figure. It is not at all clear what she will do when she gives up her seat as an MSP. The much talked about job at the UN has failed to materialise and is now unlikely to do so given the scandals with which she has been linked.

While the SNP under her leadership is often held up as a bastion of liberalism and progressivism, in reality the opposite was true. She was an authoritarian, as shown by her approach to party management, the Covid pandemic and the flawed hate crime legislation, which she championed. She promised much and delivered little, while demonising those who opposed her – in this she resembles many of the populists who have dominated politics across the world in recent years. The cult of personality she allowed to develop around her and which her supporters actively encouraged was also redolent of populism.

Nicola Sturgeon's leadership was all style and no substance. Public life and public discourse in Scotland have been debased by her intolerance of disagreement and debate, and by the lack of transparency and accountability with which she governed the country and the SNP. These features have spread out wider into our public life.

Looking to the future, this damage needs to be addressed, as well as finding a way forward for the independence movement.

THE WAY FORWARD

8

In the town hall of the beautiful hilltop town of Tárrega in Catalonia, the mayor's display cabinet contains a bottle of Scottish Parliament malt whisky and a quaich (a shallow silver Scots drinking cup) inscribed with the words 'Voterem', which means 'we will vote' in Catalan. It is accompanied by a letter of support I wrote to the people of that town following my experiences there on 1 October 2017 when, at the invitation of Diplocat, the Public Diplomacy Council of Catalonia, I joined an international cross-party parliamentary delegation to witness the Catalan independence referendum.

On a sunny autumnal day, Fraser and I travelled with a small group of delegates north of Barcelona, visiting polling stations in the city and in small towns and villages a few hours outside of it. We witnessed a quiet and dignified determination to vote in the face of considerable interference, both physical and electronic, and state repression on a scale not seen in Western Europe for decades.

After we left Barcelona we arrived at Sant Andreu de la Barca, near Montserrat, in the aftermath of an attack by the Spanish Civil Guard, to find smashed windows in a community centre, bruised people who had been assaulted and old ladies weeping. I have video footage of the retired mayor, a man in his seventies or eighties, who said he had not seen anything like this since he was a boy living under Franco. He told us that even *los grises* – 'the grey ones', the Francoist armed police – would never have acted like that. He was visibly shaken and astonished at the brutality he had seen meted out to people quietly queuing to vote. But the Catalans were organised. The ballot box had been spirited away before the police could get it, and after they had left the polling station had re-opened. We walked along a long corridor in a health centre, past queuing people and into the polling area to observe the steps taken to properly conduct the vote. When we walked back down the same long corridor the whole building erupted in applause for us – for taking the time to help them and bear witness. The emotion of the people was palpable as their applause hit us, and everyone in the delegation was reduced to tears.

When we arrived at Tárrega, we were taken to the town hall to meet the mayor and local councillors. There was a huge crowd outside and a young woman was filming when two strangers to the town, young men dressed in sports gear, tried to stop her. Fraser noticed that they were both wearing identical pairs of trainers and correctly identified them as Spanish secret police. He defended the young woman from their aggressive attentions and sent them packing to cheers, clapping and the Catalan version of 'Cheerio, cheerio, cheerio'.

We were taken by the mayor and local councillors for a lavish lunch in an underground restaurant in the old town. Towards the end of the meal a young man ran into the restaurant shouting 'Guardia Civile', and everyone got up, including Fraser and me, and ran through the narrow streets of the medieval town to the polling station, which was in a modern community building on the outskirts of the town. Spanish Civil Guard military vehicles were doing handbrake turns outside the polling station, and it was feared they would enter by force to remove the ballot boxes, as had happened at the previous town we visited. Together with the other international observers, Fraser and I stood outside holding up our international accreditation while the locals smuggled the ballot boxes out the back door into a Clio and drove them off across the field. Locals embraced us and gave us flowers.

Later, at Sabadell, a city north of Barcelona, we witnessed the fire service protecting the civilian population and polling stations from attack. Women were kissing them and handing them flowers while locals sang the Catalan national anthem – 'Els Segadors'.

When we congregated with other international observers in the evening, some of them had rubber bullets, which they had picked up off the ground in Barcelona. A voter lost an eye that day.

I was reminded of the ugly scenes witnessed that day when Labour MP and former leadership candidate Lisa Nandy suggested that the UK should 'look to Catalonia' for lessons on how to defeat Scottish nationalism.[1]

I hesitated to begin this chapter with a reference to Catalonia because, of course, Scotland's situation is very different from that of Catalonia. The Spanish constitution does not permit Catalonia to secede. There is no such prohibition against Scotland's secession from the union in the unwritten British constitution, which greatly relies on custom and precedent. There is a precedent for secession of one part of the union of the UK, because Ireland left its union with the United Kingdom in the early part of the twentieth century, ultimately by agreement and an international treaty after Sinn Fein won an outright majority of Irish seats in a UK-wide general election.

Prior to the advent of devolution, it was thought that a simple majority of pro-independence Scottish MPs would be sufficient to open negotiations on independence. The British constitution has already shown it is flexible enough to permit an independence referendum for Scotland, and Scotland's right to self-determination was recognised in the Edinburgh Agreement in 2014.

The Good Friday Agreement recognises the right of the people of Northern Ireland to choose their constitutional future and provides for a referendum on the reunification of Ireland. This has been enshrined in statute in the Northern Ireland Act of 1998, which provides that the UK Secretary of State should hold a poll if at any time it appears likely to him that a majority of those voting would express a wish that Northern Ireland should cease to be part of the United Kingdom and form part of a united Ireland. Such polls may be repeated at a minimum of seven-year intervals.[2]

---

[1] https://www.bbc.co.uk/news/uk-scotland-scotland-politics-51139519

[2] Northern Ireland Act 1998, section 1 and schedule 1.

Over the years I have wearied of unionists banging on about 'illegal referendums' in Scotland. There is no such thing. Yes, thanks to Nicola Sturgeon's inept approach to the UK Supreme Court it is now beyond doubt that Holyrood could not hold an independence referendum, but there is no reason why, with appropriate funding and support, a constitutional convention or other body in Scotland could not organise one.

Where parallels can be drawn with Catalonia is in the intransigence of the UK government and the failure of the leaders of the Scottish self-determination movement, by which I mean the SNP, to find a way forward.

The Catalans voted Yes on October 2017, but the result was not recognised. Some of their leaders fled to avoid prosecution, others served jail time. Many activists expected a Unilateral Declaration of Independence in the wake of the vote, but the politicians baulked at this and eight years on there is a stalemate not entirely without parallel to the situation we currently face in Scotland. The parallel lies not in the constitutional background, which is very different, but in the struggle to find a route to make the right to self-determination real and the failure of nationalist politicians to find a way out of the stalemate created by the refusal to cooperate.

Professor Clara Ponsati, the distinguished economist who formerly held the Chair of Economics at St Andrews University in Scotland, was Minister of Education in the Catalan government at the time of the referendum. After the referendum she went into exile in Scotland and successfully resisted extradition by the Spanish government with a huge campaign of support from the Scottish public. She went on to be elected as an MEP and to go home to Catalonia after an amnesty was announced. She has become a friend and someone I very much admire for her courage and insights. She has written powerfully of the failings of the Catalan nationalist leadership who, she says, in the aftermath of the 2017 referendum lacked strategy and conviction. When I heard her deliver a speech at Westminster in 2023, I was struck by the parallels with the strategic failures of the SNP leadership in the aftermath of the 2014 referendum and the failure to capitalise on the opportunities that arose after the Brexit vote shook the UK political landscape.[3]

One of the main reasons for the strategic failures in Scotland has been the refusal to listen to advice from anyone outwith a very tight circle or to allow proper debate and discussion about the options available, at least until very recently.

The result of this is that the history of the SNP since the Brexit referendum has been one of missed opportunities because of a failure in focus. If half the energy that has been put into identity politics and silencing dissent had been put into our independence strategy, then Scotland would probably be an independent country by now.

Another factor in the SNP's failure to find a way forward has been a lack of courage and a desire to protect the vested interests of professional politicians' jobs in the devolution firmament.

The mess we are in

Just as I was finishing this book, the SNP produced yet another white paper on independence and debated their independence strategy at their October 2025 conference. The white paper was thin and widely criticised as containing nothing new on key issues such as post-independence policies on currency, pension, EU accession and cross-border trade.[4]

What remains of the party's rebels were defeated once again when conference delegates embraced the leadership's 'back to the future' strategy that a mandate for a second independence referendum will be achieved only if the party wins an outright majority of the seats at the Scottish election in May 2026. The dwindling group of party rebels failed to convince the conference that simply

[3] https://www.thenational.scot/politics/24096634.big-takeaways-scotland-clara-ponsati-speech/

[4] https://www.gov.scot/publications/fresh-start-independence/documents/

re-embracing the failed strategy of going cap in hand to the UK government is doomed to fail.

The leadership of the SNP seem unable to grasp that the strategy which worked in 2014 worked because it was the first time it was used, because the SNP were popular and seen as a competent government, because Alex Salmond was such a skilful strategist and because David Cameron assumed the Yes side were doomed to fail in the referendum. The present-day situation is totally different.

The SNP's popularity has plummeted from gaining 48 per cent of the vote at the 2021 Holyrood election to opinion poll support hovering around 33 per cent. The same polls show that the majority of voters believe the Scottish government is not doing a good job.

The Scottish electorate are volatile. Like the Labour party, the SNP can no longer take them for granted. The SNP face an election where voters are much less strongly attached to a particular political party and far more likely to change their vote depending on the circumstances. Reform is the new kid on the block and is garnering significant support. There is another new party, Your Party, which could well pick up seats on the list vote. It may even support a second referendum, if not independence itself. The Scottish Green Party is unrecognisable from that of 2011. Alba have polled as much as 6 per cent and may return MSPs. Former SNP and Alba MSPs may stand as independents for independence.

There is more than a whiff of Culloden (where the Jacobites chose the wrong ground on which to fight the government forces and lost miserably) about the SNP strategy. It totally fails to take account of the ground we are fighting on now and the alliance of allies who are for independence. By going for an 'all of our yesterdays' approach the leadership have totally failed to address any of the relevant facts about what is happening today. It is a strategy that is doomed to failure – that is, if the party really wants a second independence referendum, which I am not alone in questioning.

Firstly, it is highly unlikely that the SNP in its current state is capable of replicating the feat pulled off by Alex Salmond in 2011 when he obtained an outright majority despite a voting system designed to make sure that that doesn't happen. When Alex achieved that vote his government was widely respected and seen as competent. That is not the case with the current SNP government. Besides, even when Nicola was at height of her popularity, she failed to achieve an outright majority at the 2016 election.

I saw the anger of voters on the doorsteps in June and July 2024, and while at least some of that anger is now directed towards the Labour Party, who have proved to be so hopeless in office, I believe that when the full attention of the press is on the SNP government's record, that anger will be seen again.

The enormity of what happened to the SNP vote at the 2024 General Election must not be ignored. On 18 September 2014, 1.6 million Scots voted for Scotland to become an independent country. On 4 July 2024 only 724,758 Scots voted SNP. Less than half of the Yes vote from 2014 and a drop of half a million from the 1,242,380 votes the SNP got at the 2019 General Election.

Secondly, even if they achieve an outright majority, the SNP have no plan for what to do if the British government say no to a Section 30 order. Keir Starmer has already said that he does not think there should be another independence referendum within his lifetime. Memorably, John Swinney said that no one knows what he will do if the British government say no, to which most people replied, Aye, including you.

It is an insult to the intelligence of the SNP membership and the wider electorate to pretend that John has some sort of secret plan. The gullible were convinced for years that Nicola had a secret plan until she ran out of road and resigned. It would be extraordinary if people allowed themselves to be fooled again, and I hope most will not. But the SNP leadership is counting on the optimism and wishful thinking of independence supporters to keep them in power at Holyrood, even though they have long since run out of ideas for what to do with that power, which is not good for the independence cause or for the country.

A far more likely scenario for May 2026 is that the SNP will not win an outright majority, but together with seats won by the Greens and possibly Alba or other independent nationalist candidates like Fergus Ewing, they will have an outright majority. However, the 'back to the future' policy ensures that they won't be able to rely on a pro-independence majority in the Scottish Parliament as a mandate for a second independence vote unless that majority is solely comprised of SNP MSPs.

Thus, the SNP will have devalued a result that should mean something. This is an affront to democracy and a gross dereliction of the duty of the national party of Scotland. It flies in the face of the Scottish constitutional principle of the sovereignty of the people and replaces it with the sovereignty of one party. How very Westminster.

Shamefully, both this policy and the 'Your Right to Decide' white paper also look to shut down perfectly legitimate expressions of popular sovereignty rather than open them up, by arguing that it is only at a Holyrood election that such expressions can be expressed.[5]

It is unconscionable that, having sat on their hands for the last decade as they watched Nicola Sturgeon reverse the SNP's independence strategy down a blind alley, the current leadership should now rouse themselves from the backseat of the cab and start to brick up the exit route. Thanks to Nicola's failed strategy they are operating in a restricted space, and they should be opening up opportunities rather than closing them down.

If starting with a blank piece of paper, one might think that the first thing to do would be to unite the various factions of the independence movement, but instead the SNP has devised a policy that will further alienate them. It will be remembered that having promised a constitutional convention and a number of policy papers on independence issues on Brexit day in January 2020, Nicola delayed the publication of the independence papers until after the pandemic, and so far there's been no sign of a constitutional convention being set up. When the deputy leader of the SNP, Keith Brown, stood up at the October 2025 conference to give his support to John Swinney's strategy, he said that the civic movement would start tomorrow. We're still waiting. A motion tabled by me in October 2023 and accepted by Humza Yousaf when he was leader made it clear that holding a constitutional convention was party policy. Yet nothing has been done to get it off the ground.

[5] https://www.gov.scot/publications/right-decide/ at page 11

The new SNP policy embeds the notion of Westminster parliamentary sovereignty at the heart of the SNP strategy. If Westminster says no, then Scottish independence will not happen. It's a travesty of a policy for any independence party to adopt, let alone one that is supposed to lead the independence movement in a country founded on the tradition of the sovereignty of the people.

History shows us that independence is taken, not given. For the avoidance of doubt, I don't mean by violence, but I do mean by assertiveness. Instead, the current SNP leadership are simply embedding Nicola's misguided strategy of claiming a referendum backed by a Section 30 order is 'the gold standard' method for Scotland to become independent. This incredibly short-sighted view of how Scottish independence might be achieved perils all on a section of a statute barely 25 years old, when the union between Scotland and England has been in existence for more than 300 years and prior to that Scotland was recognised as an independent nation state since 1320.

I was particularly irritated at the time of the 2025 conference to hear SNP ministers parroting the line that if an outright majority of SNP MSPs were to be obtained the British government would be legally bound by convention and precedent (because of the Edinburgh Agreement) to agree another referendum. A delegate with public law experience, and who therefore should have known better, put forward this argument at the conference and John Swinney said it was 'absolutely fantastic legal advice'. It is not. While there is a political precedent there is no legal precedent. In *Miller I* the UK Supreme Court has ruled that constitutional conventions even when enshrined in statute are not enforceable in law. I would have expected the Scottish government to have been aware of this, as they were on the losing side of the argument in that case.

It reeks of amateurism at best, and worst, opportunism, for the First Minister to have jumped upon this flawed argument to support his policy. He has law officers and a team of lawyers to hand who must know that the argument is fundamentally misconceived. It is real back-of-the-envelope stuff. However, as cynics have already noted, it's a useful strategy if the SNP want to stay in power, as it can work to maximise their vote by telling pro-independence voters that only a vote for the SNP will deliver independence.

I predict that what the SNP leadership foresee in the coming years is business as usual, with them governing as a minority government or in a coalition with the Greens and independence on the back burner.

The SNP don't deserve an overall majority, and if they gain one they could further set the cause back with their poor performance in government, lack of ideas and no sign of an effective strategy to deliver the goal of independence.

I would like to be able to vote SNP, but I am disgusted by their cynicism. I fear they won't become any more competent in government than they have been for the last few years, because they're losing some of their most experienced people and replacing them with a new generation of SNP candidates who are largely young political hacks with no life experience and certainly no experience of running a major organisation or business.

The why of Indy

Brexit and the Johnson, Truss and Sunak Tory administrations have accentuated Scotland's sense of political alienation from Westminster. Labour in government under Keir Starmer's leadership has nothing concrete to offer Scotland in either the short- or long-term.

Since Labour came to power, we have seen them sit on their hands while Scotland's only oil refinery, Grangemouth, was shut down. Their inaction here sharply contrasts with their efforts to save British steel plants in England at the same time. We have also seen them means test the winter fuel payment, thus plunging thousands of Scottish pensioners further into fuel poverty and putting the Scottish government in an impossible position. On world affairs Scots have been disgusted at Labour's equivocation in the face of the slaughter of innocents in Palestine. These are just a handful of the reasons for the huge disillusionment with the Labour Party in Scotland.

There has been no offer of more powers for the Scottish Parliament, and the federalism and reformed UK constitution, which the likes of Gordon Brown and others so often talk about, will not happen because it is not anywhere near the top of the list of priorities of politicians in England. This can be seen from the Labour Party's repeated failure to implement their promises to meaningfully reform of the House of Lords. All that we hear is repeated statements of an implacable opposition to a second independence referendum, notwithstanding the results of elections in Scotland.

The constitutional turmoil and economic damage that followed the Brexit vote suggests that an independent Scotland could fare better than it has in the UK, and that the cause of Scottish independence should not be written off. Scotland does not need to adopt an isolationist strategy. Majority opinion appears to favour accession to the European Union. Others favour participation in the European Economic Area through membership of the European Free Trade Association, like Norway. EU accession would be my choice so that Scotland would have the sort of influence in decision-making that does not come with mere EEA membership. For all its faults, the European Union behaves more like a union of equals then the United Kingdom. Had the European Union been making a decision as momentous as Brexit, the smaller nations within the union would have had the kind of say in the decision to leave that Scotland did not have.

If, as former SNP MP and Depute Leader Jim Sillars argues in his new book , The New Case for Optimism,[6] we put emotion aside and look purely at state interests, it can no longer be argued, as it was in 2014, that Scotland needs the shelter of the powerful economy of the United Kingdom. Britain is broken. It is, as the *Daily Telegraph* has said, a poor country pretending to be rich.[7]

Scotland has strategic importance for NATO because of our geography and the nuclear weapons based at Faslane. Unionist

---

6 https://www.brownsbfs.co.uk/Product/Sillars-Jim/The-New-Case-for-Optimism/9781913212421

7 https://www.telegraph.co.uk/news/2022/12/21/britain-poor-country-pretending-rich/

parties talk of shutting down the North Sea or drilling it dry, while Scotland could be looking to it as a long-term resource. Distasteful as it might seem to some, our strategic importance and assets give Scotland great economic and bargaining power.

For those who think the North Sea should be shut down, Scotland also has great potential in renewable energy, but it seems that on the watch of both the British and, sadly, the Scottish governments, there is no proper plan for a just transition and Scotland's renewable energy wealth is being squandered, just like it happened with North Sea oil and gas.[8]

With its whisky, seafood, tourist trade, world-class universities and life sciences industries Scotland could have a bright future as an independent country. There's just one problem with all of this. And that's the fact that people have lost faith in the SNP to deliver independence.

The How of Indy

Over the last ten years a huge amount of energy has been devoted to discussing the process of independence, but there is remarkably little to show for it. Conversely, very little has been done to answer the questions that troubled voters during the 2014 independence referendum in the field of economics, for example currency and pensions. To that list has been added the problems posed for cross-border trade with England as a result of Brexit and further question marks hanging over an independent Scotland's accession to the European Union.

Despite all the sound and noise and controversy, we find ourselves in a difficult place to begin the journey to independence because of past mistakes. To quote the Irishman asked for directions, if I was advising someone how to get to independence I wouldn't start from here. But we are where we are, and what is

---

[8] https://www.futureeconomy.scot/publications/135-rethinking-scot-wind-maximising-scotland-s-offshore-wind-potential?ref=ed_direct

needed is to plot a path from there to where the independence movement needs to be.

As a matter of international law, the people of Scotland have the same right to self-determination as other peoples and are not prohibited from exercising that right by way of secession from the United Kingdom after a democratic expression of the view of the Scottish electorate.[9] However, this principle needs to be restated by the SNP because the UKSC judgment has given currency to those who wish to thwart the independence movement. We are stuck with the UKSC's opinion on the limits of Holyrood's competence, but we don't have to accept their mistaken view on the right of the Scots to self-determination.

Confusion has arisen between the rights and competences of the current Scottish Parliament, which is a creature of statute and the devolution settlement and the rights of the people of Scotland. The former may not have the power to end the union between Scotland and England, but the latter certainly do, and this was the received wisdom of even Unionists until lately.

Regardless of what the Supreme Court may have said about the right to self-determination, history tells us that the political reality is that movements for self-determination can be delayed but not, ultimately, denied. The way forward now is to try to limit the delay by getting our long-term strategy in order and building support.

Scotland already has most things in place in terms of institutions and infrastructure to enable us to have quick and straightforward recognition as an independent state by the rest of the world. The easiest way for Scotland to be recognised as an independent state would be for the UK government to be the first to offer that recognition and for Scotland to withdraw from its union with England through a treaty.

To bring about such a treaty or to bypass it and receive recognition by other nations of the world, we need to establish that independence is the will of the Scottish people. That requires a

---

[9] https://www.scottishlegal.com/articles/alba-legal-opinion-claims-supreme-court-justices-were-mistaken-in-law

democratic vote. To achieve that we need independence to be the settled will of people living in Scotland. Then that sentiment needs to be translated into a democratic event that gives clear expression to the desire to withdraw from the Union of the UK. That can happen at a scheduled Scottish Parliament election, at a Westminster election, at an agreed referendum or at some other vote. If there was a will at large in the country, a pro-independence majority of the Scottish Parliament could collapse the parliament and hold fresh elections with a coalition for Yes being put forward.

Alternatively, a Yes alliance could stand at the next Westminster election in 2029. That would have the advantage of distancing support for independence from support for the SNP's record in government. Every Yes alliance candidate would stand on a mandate which stated that if the Yes alliance gains more than 50 per cent of the vote, they will consider that a mandate to withdraw from the Treaty of Union, re-establish Scotland's independence and seek recognition from the international community on the basis of Chapter 1, Article 1 of the UN Charter. That platform could be supported by a statement that should the UK government wish, the Yes alliance would be willing to confirm that mandate via a referendum to be held on the same terms as the Edinburgh Agreement and within a defined period of the election, say six months. If no such referendum is requested or conducted the Declaration of Independence based on the election result would automatically be considered to stand.

The Yes alliance MPs would not take their seats at Westminster. Instead, they would devote their energies to negotiating the independence treaty, rather than putting that in the hands of a lame duck SNP government in Edinburgh. Once independence was secured and an interim constitution put in place, a general election would be held. This is very close to what Wings over Scotland has suggested, except he suggested it be done on the constituency vote for the Scottish Parliament.[10]

---

[10] https://wingsoverscotland.com/the-snp-manifesto-2021/

There are several reasons why I favour a Westminster election, including the weakness of the SNP government at Holyrood, the low esteem in which Holyrood is held, and the fact that we get higher turnouts at Westminster elections. Furthermore, it has previously been thought that the Holyrood franchise was preferable because sixteen- to eighteen-year-olds are allowed to vote at Scottish elections and they tend to be more pro-independence than older people. However, the UK Labour government plans to introduce votes for sixteen- to eighteen-year-olds at Westminster – presumably in time for the next general election.

Accordingly, a referendum is not the only means for Scotland to become independent. There are a number of ways it could be achieved. Far too much of the past decade has been spent musing over these routes rather than actually moving the argument for independence forward and extending and deepening the support for independence by the people of Scotland. The SNP have been arguing about the crescendo without actually warming up the orchestra.

The fact that the pro-independence Scottish Green Party's vote has risen and that other pro-independence parties have launched is because independence has grown from a niche point of view championed seriously only by the SNP to a mainstream perspective. That happened during the campaign leading to the 2014 referendum and then because of the way Scotland was treated in the aftermath of that vote with English votes for English laws, the failure to deliver the vow, the Brexit process and the pandemic. The current SNP strategy ignores the reality of where we are today.

What is required is a broad-based civic campaign like the grassroots campaign that sprang up in the lead up to the 2014 referendum. It needs the SNP to be one of many voices and not to try to squash other efforts or ridicule fellow travellers in a foolish attempt to retain control.

The function of that movement will be to move independence on from the mainstream to being the settled will of the Scottish people.[11]

---

[11] https://robinmcalpine.org/why-the-current-indy-strategy-wont-work-part-one/

This is what happened between the devolution referendum of 1979 and the devolution referendum of 1997. Support for devolution increased from a third of the voters to three-quarters because of the cross-party and civic movement that grew up in response to years of Tory government for which Scotland had not voted.

One of the tasks of this movement will be to answer the questions of those not yet convinced that it would be in the best interests of themselves and their country to vote for independence. It is nothing short of a disgrace that despite a decade in government since the independence referendum and after nine years as the third party at in Westminster, with all the resources that brought the SNP, they have failed to do so. There's no reason to believe that will change on the current course, particularly in the light of the latest white paper, which is simply just a rehash of what went before.

Moreover, the SNP leadership has deliberately set their face against those of us within the party who had ideas about how to answer these questions, and others from outwith the party who offered their help. I have lost count of the number of times when clever people from Dublin, Cardiff, London, Brussels, the USA and beyond told me they'd had the door shut in their face when they sought to have access to the SNP leadership to share ideas that might have helped.

One of the most vexed problems the SNP has faced is economic strategy. In 2019 the Sustainable Growth Commission, which had been set up by Nicola Sturgeon in 2016, published a report making recommendations to the Scottish government on the currency and economic policy of an independent Scotland.

The approach it advocated was conservative, neo-liberal and thus very much out of step with the vision of a new, different kind of Scotland cherished by so many in the Yes movement and in the SNP. When it came to currency the report recommended sterlingisation until six tests had been met, and many feared that these six tests would never be met and 'would effectively negate the very point of seeking independence for Scotland'.[12] The party tried to put off having it debated at conference.

---

[12] https://www.thenational.scot/news/17492223.george-kerevan-bids-change-snps-scottish-currency-policy/

I shared the concerns of many in the membership. I also felt that the report didn't properly tackle the challenges and opportunities of European Union accession for the economics of an independent Scotland, including the vexed question of the euro.

Unionists wrongly insist that an independent Scotland would have to join the euro immediately upon joining the EU. However, all that would be required is a commitment to join. Many experts think joining could in the long run benefit an independent Scotland.[13] Others disagree. The SNP needed to be seriously thinking about these issues, and I did not feel that they were.

It seemed to me that our economic strategy and our EU strategy were travelling on two parallel tracks and needed to be brought together. At the SNP spring conference in April 2019, the leadership were keen for conference to endorse the Growth Commission report. There were signs that a serious rebellion was likely, and I indicated my intention to propose remitting the motion back for further consideration. This was not just a delaying tactic; it would also have offered time for what was needed – further consideration to take the memberships concerns on board and to marry up the economic strategy with our EU strategy. The reaction of the leadership to my motion to remit back was verging on the hysterical. I think, given my popularity at that time, they knew it was very likely to succeed.

On my way to conference on the morning of the motion I was repeatedly phoned by Derek Mackay MSP, who was then the Scottish government's Finance Secretary and the party's business convener. When I arrived, I met Fraser and my sister, Alison, who was also there for moral support, and the three of us were swept by a phalanx of party suits to the inner sanctum of the party leadership, where I was harangued by Derek and Ian Blackford to drop my motion to remit back. Derek was particularly concerned that if we didn't have an economic policy in place the unionists would 'crucify us over the next six months'. I pointed out that they were likely to crucify us anyway because the report was problematic in so many

[13] https://www.heraldscotland.com/politics/19932277.kirsty-hughes-independent-scotland-may-benefit-joining-euro/

respects. In the end we reached a compromise that I would drop my motion to remit back in return for an undertaking from Nicola, which was conveyed to me via Ian, that I would be put in charge of convening a party committee to look at the issue of marrying up our economic and EU accession strategies. This undertaking has never been honoured.

In the event, the conference rebellion succeeded against the sterlingisation aspect of the Growth Commission policy and delegates voted to adopt a new currency 'as soon as practicable after independence day'. I voted with the rebels but didn't speak; however, I have no doubt that this episode contributed to the resurrection and leaking of the groundless bullying claims against me, which I addressed earlier in this book.

The Growth Commission report remained a *bête noire* for many nationalists, and by spring 2021 Nicola was distancing herself from it,[14] kicking the can down the road on replacing its recommendations with something better. The party membership has continued to vote for conference motions that support a new Scottish currency.

Other reforms

It is axiomatic that Westminster needs reform, but that's not where those of us who want Scottish independence should channel our energies. The Scottish Parliament does, however, also need reform, and that is something I'm more interested in because I hope one day that it will become an independent parliament.

Sadly, trust in the Scottish government is at its lowest ebb since devolution began.[15] The MSPs themselves seem to have fallen out of love with the parliament as a record number are standing down before the next election.

---

[14] https://www.heraldscotland.com/news/19237832.nicola-sturgeon-admits-snps-ecomomic-plan-independence-now-completely-date/

[15] https://www.holyrood.com/news/view,trust-in-scottish-government-at-lowest-level-since-devolution-began

The scandals of the Sturgeon years have illustrated the need for reform of the Scottish Parliament, including strengthening the powers of committees, granting MSPs parliamentary privilege, legislating for a duty of candour and dividing the role of the Lord Advocate into the two separate roles of Government Legal Adviser and Director of Public Prosecutions, to avoid the perception of a conflict of interest.

Some of the issues the Scottish parliament faces are due to the way it was set up by Westminster in 1999, and therefore only Westminster can tackle matters such as whether MSPs should have privilege. Other matters, such as the make up of committees, could be addressed by the Scottish Parliament itself.

The Holyrood committee investigating the Salmond affair was hobbled by not having the same powers as a Westminster committee to insist on the attendance of witnesses and the production of documents. Fears have also been expressed that MSPs and parliament officials are 'too deferential' – witness their behaviour in quickly deleting evidence in the Alex Salmond inquiry from its website in 2021 after the Crown Office made representations. Such a request of a Westminster Select Committee from the Crown Prosecution Service would have received short shrift.'[16]

As we saw during the so called 'scrutiny' of the Gender Recognition Reform Bill, it is all too easy for a Holyrood committee to be hijacked by vested interests – in this case the trans lobby – and for it to be less than impartial. Although, to be fair, the same has happened to the Women and Equalities Committee at Westminster.[17]

However, generally, Westminster committees are far more exacting in their scrutiny of government and quangos than Holyrood. When the former Scottish Conservative leader Douglas Ross carried out a very effective grilling of Sir Peter Mathieson, the University of

---

[16] https://www.thetimes.com/article/bce38a72-6421-44ea-b1fa-5dca4b780610?shareToken=08de484917c089c9d91a1425cb943ac6

[17] https://www.thetimes.com/article/a7da1f85-ced8-41cc-ba8c-928002912d32?shareToken=6304c4cd57975c5511d388da36b2e481

Edinburgh Vice Chancellor, in June 2025, pushing him about the justification for his salary of £422,000 and other perks in the light of the financial crisis gripping the university, some of his colleagues actually thought he had gone too far and accused him of bullying and hectoring the witness.[18]

The party whips have far too much control over committee membership at Holyrood. They appoint both the chairs and the members of the committee. At Westminster the chairs and the members are elected by backbench MPs and thus are more independent minded.

The Scottish government and parliament should change the things in their control now like the committee system. In respect of things that can only be changed by Westminster, successive UK governments have pledged reform, for example to give MSPs the same legal protection as MPs and to reform the role of the Lord Advocate, but done nothing.

MPs enjoy absolute privilege, which means that subject to strict sub judice rules they can say pretty much what they like in the House of Commons. Accordingly, if they want to challenge the government of the day or other powerful third parties, they can do so using parliamentary privilege.

The Labour government at Westminster have promised to impose a legally enforceable duty of candour, the so-called Hillsborough Law, on the UK government and public agencies. The Salmond affair and the Covid years show that that duty of candour needs to be imposed on the Scottish government as well in its dealings with the Scottish Parliament.

The Salmond affair also highlighted the potential conflict of interest inherent in the role of the Lord Advocate, Scotland's chief law officer who holds two roles, the role of government chief legal adviser and the head of the prosecution service. The report of the Scottish Parliament's inquiry into the Scottish government handling of harassment complaints found that events showed a

---

[18] See fn15

long-standing tension in the dual roles of the Lord Advocate, and they said that 'public perception' was important. I agree.

Furthermore, as I have argued throughout this book, from a nationalist point of view, it is most unfortunate that the SNP have not had the benefit of a political government legal adviser that the UK government has enjoyed. With the sign-off of a political law officer, Nicola Sturgeon could have taken a bill to hold a second independence referendum through parliament and defended it in the Supreme Court with legal arguments while political arguments played out in the court of public opinion. By feebly going to the UK Supreme Court without a bill passed by Scotland's parliament, divorced from any campaign and concerted move towards independence, Nicola Sturgeon simply squandered a move that should have been played differently at a different time.

When I was still an MP in January 2024, I introduced a private members' bill designed to give the Scottish Parliament the power to amend the role of Scotland's law officers, including dividing the role of the Lord Advocate into two separate jobs.[19] It didn't get anywhere, and the matter has yet to be addressed by Westminster, despite Tory and Labour support for it. Meanwhile, the Scottish government, having promised to consult on this issue back in 2021, continue to kick the matter into the long grass.

The public sector in Scotland also requires reform to rid it of nepotism and to protect it from the sort of policy capture and attacks on free speech and equal rights that we have seen because of the mission creep of identity politics. At present in Scotland, we suffer from a culture of impunity whereby high-ranking officials both in the civil service and in the NHS seem able to evade scrutiny and hang onto their jobs despite the most appalling incompetence and huge waste of public money on failed virtue-signalling projects.

[19] https://hansard.parliament.uk/Commons/2024-01-10/debates/744C82F0-559A-4EA1-B66D-DCCCFA65DDF6/ScottishLawOfficers(Devolution)?highlight=lord%20advocate#contribution-82C9BD56-8F99-4D38-B24E-38570E1888D9

It is nothing short of a disgrace that both the Scottish government and many other public institutions have taken so long to obey the ruling of the UK Supreme Court in the For Women Scotland case. This sort of behaviour threatens the rule of law. As have attacks on the UK Supreme Court from members of the Scottish Parliament such as Maggie Chapman. None of these organisations or individuals seem to be accountable for their actions.

There seems to be a widespread ignorance about the importance of constitutional checks and balances among our political class. Many of our parliamentarians don't understand the role of the judiciary or the importance of preserving their independence. MSPs, including SNP MSPs who really ought to have known better, seemed to become fixated on an English notion of the supremacy of parliament when the Gender Recognition Reform Bill was challenged. But in an independent Scotland, with a written constitution embodying human rights and the protected characteristics of the Equality Act (as Nicola Sturgeon argued for back in 2014),[20] a legal challenge could have happened even if the bill had been passed by the Scottish Parliament.

Nor, as we saw with the GRRB, do our parliamentarians seems to understand the universality of human rights and that there is no hierarchy of either rights or protected characteristics under our equality law.

Conclusion

The definition of insanity is 'doing the same thing over and over again and expecting different results'. This quote is often misattributed to Albert Einstein; in fact, it comes from a novel written by the great lesbian feminist Rita Mae Brown in 1983.[21] I don't think the

---

[20] https://www.theguardian.com/politics/2014/jun/16/scottish-constitution-first-draft-issued-nicola-sturgeon; https://joannacherry.scot/newspaper-columns/2023/gender-bill-legal-challenge

[21] Sudden Death. Rita Mae Brown.

Scottish National Party is insane, but I do think it is tired, out of ideas and cynical. Until it addresses the failures of the decade that followed the independence referendum and faces up to them it will, in my opinion, be incapable of delivering its aim of independence.

It is highly unlikely that the SNP will win an outright majority in the imminent future. If they do, they have no plan for what to do if the UK government say no to another independence referendum. With a few honourable exceptions they will not have parliamentarians with the experience or strength of character either to find a way forward through the constitutional morass or to govern well. Their continuation in government risks damaging further the self-belief Scots need that we can govern ourselves effectively. An alliance with the Greens will not deliver independence because the SNP have stupidly said that is not a mandate. What it is likely to deliver is more virtue-signalling, more unpopular flawed policies like self-identification, and more botched policy delivery.

It might be better for the SNP, the cause of independence and the country if they retreated to opposition for a term to enable a period of introspection on where they have gone wrong and to implement a major reset. That is what is needed to attract politicians of the calibre of Kate Forbes back into the fold and the many members that they have lost including me.

The reality is that, thanks to Labour's ineptitude in government at Westminster, they are unlikely to be able to form a government at Holyrood and the door has been opened to Reform, thus splitting the unionist vote. The SNP may find themselves continuing in government by default, even though they have been in government for nearly two decades, the last ten of which have been dogged by policy failure and scandals.

The only hope for taking the cause of independence forward is a civic movement. The good news is that this has been done successfully before in relation to devolution, and with considerable success during the independence referendum campaign in 2014.

Opinion polls repeatedly show that most young people who have reached eligibility to vote in the decade since the independence referendum support independence. Thanks to devolution they are a generation more in tune with who they are and where they came from and with less of the Scottish cringe than my generation and certainly the one before that.

Eighteen years passed between the devolution referendums of 1978 and 1997. During that time huge changes were wrought in Scotland and the UK. We are now nearly twelve years down the hill from 2014. Even greater change has taken place in this time. It looks like a generation may indeed pass before Scotland votes for independence, but there is every reason to think it will happen. Despite all that has happened the dream is still alive. There is hope – but there is still much work to be done.

ACKNOWLEDGEMENTS

This book is my personal memoir and analysis of events I witnessed during a tumultuous decade in Scottish and British politics. I have told the truth to the best of my ability and I'm confident in my recollections. Unfortunately, I have been hampered in what I can say about certain matters because of the existence of court orders and ongoing court proceedings. I hope in the future to be able to revisit these matters when I am not so restricted.

I could not have written this book without the support of my family and friends. I am indebted to my parents, Alistair and Mary, and to my sister Alison, her husband Eoghain, and my nephews Jamie and Ronan for their unstinting support through some very challenging times. Throughout those years I also had the steadfast support of Fraser Thompson, my former chief of staff, his wife Sarah and loyal members of my staff team.

My feminist and lesbian activism have brought many wonderful women into my life. Without them I could not have sustained that activism in the face of the antagonism that came from both within and outwith the SNP. Foremost among those women are my current partner, Dr Sue Regan, and my former partner, Dr Victoria Whitworth. I would also like to thank Kate Harris, Bev Jackson and Eileen Gallagher, whom I met through LGB Alliance, and to pay tribute to Eileen's late partner, the wonderful Anne McManus. Thanks are also due to Rhona Hotchkiss and her partner Linda Semple who read early manuscripts of this book and offered invaluable advice. I also want to pay tribute to Lynne Anderson and Caroline McAllister, formerly of the SNP Women's pledge group; Marion Calder, Susan Smith and Trina Budge of For Women Scotland; Lucy Hunter Blackburn, Lisa Mackenzie and Kath Murray of Murray, Blackburn MacKenzie; Julie Bindel and Kathleen Stock at the Lesbian Project; Allison Bailey; Lucy Masoud; Shereen Benjamin; Jo Phoenix; Maya Forstater, Helen Joyce, Fiona MacArena and all at Sex Matters.

There are many other women who have supported me who are too numerous to mention, but I would like to acknowledge here J.K. Rowling, Martina Navratilova, Karen Ingala Smith, Rosie Duffield, Karen Davidson, Caroline Spry and Elizabeth Woodcraft, Catriona and Vivienne MacDonald, Kim Burns, Elaine Miller, Denise Findlay and all those women who came out to support me during the General Election campaign of 2024.

I have also been blessed with some good friends and political allies in the independence movement including Joan McAlpine, Tasmina Ahmed Sheikh, Patricia Gibson, Kenneth Gibson, Carol Monaghan, Marion Fellows, Neil Hanvey, Kenny McAskill, Douglas Chapman, Angus Brendan MacNeil, Alex Neil, Fergus Ewing, Annabelle Ewing, Eilidh Whiteford, Geoff Aberdein, Jim Sillars, Michelle Thomson, Eva Comrie and Ash Regan. Anne Harvey, who ran the SNP's whips' office at Westminster, was a rock for me in difficult times, just as she was for Alex Salmond, and exemplifies all that was good about the SNP when they were a nobler party. I also want to thank everyone who has supported my election campaigns over the years. Three out of four wins in nine years ain't bad. It is invidious to single anyone out, but I particularly want to mention Lisa Clark and Andrew Ewan, who organised my ground campaign in 2024 when the SNP election machine had collapsed.

Colleagues in the Faculty of Advocates have also been a huge support to me in difficult times.

I want to thank my publishers, Icon Books, in particular Connor Stait and Nick Hayward, for believing in me and having the courage to publish this book when others did not. I also want to thank my agent, Caroline Hardman of Hardman Swainson, and David McKie of Levy & McRae for their invaluable guidance.

I also want to thank my generous friends Antony Harrison and William Collier, who lent me their beautiful home in Tighnabruaich, Argyll to work on the manuscript as the final deadline threatened.

I have drawn on many sources to write this book. One of them was the blog Wings over Scotland, run by Stuart Campbell. As he is something of a controversial figure, I wish to make it clear that do not agree with him on everything he says nor with the manner in which he sometimes choses to express himself. However, there is no doubt that he has been demonised by people within the SNP for his forensic truth telling and his exposure of many troubling matters long before conventional media became at all interested in them. There is a reason why data shows that his is the website most read by Scottish government employees.

Finally I want to acknowledge my dear late friends to whom this book is dedicated: Professor Nina Hallowell, the most wise, funny and kind friend anyone could wish for; and Alex Salmond, a political giant who believed in loyalty to his friends and comrades – and a dream that shall never die.

INDEX

MAJOR TOPIC AND EVENTS

SIGNIFICANT PEOPLE